The Progressives

The American History Series

The Progressives

Activism and Reform in American Society, 1893–1917

Karen Pastorello

WILEY Blackwell

Registered Office
John Wiley & Sons Ltd, The Atrium, Southern Gate, Chichester, West Sussex, PO19 8SQ, UK

Editorial Offices
350 Main Street, Malden, MA 02148-5020, USA
9600 Garsington Road, Oxford, OX4 2DQ, UK
The Atrium, Southern Gate, Chichester, West Sussex, PO19 8SQ, UK

For details of our global editorial offices, for customer services, and for information about how to apply for permission to reuse the copyright material in this book please see our website at www.wiley.com/wiley-blackwell.

Library of Congress Cataloging-in-Publication Data

Pastorello, Karen, 1956–
 The progressives : activism and reform in American society, 1893–1917 / Karen Pastorello.
  pages cm
 Includes bibliographical references and index.
 ISBN 978-1-118-65120-9 (cloth) – ISBN 978-1-118-65107-0 (pbk.)   1. Progressivism (United States politics)–History.   2. United States–History–1865–1921.   3. United States–Politics and government–1865–1933.   4. United States–Social conditions–1865–1918.   I. Title.
 E661.P3354 2014
 973.8–dc23

                                                      2013028280

A catalogue record for this book is available from the British Library.

Cover image: Row of tenements, 260 to 268 Elizabeth Street, New York, 1912. Photo by Lewis Hine / Library of Congress Prints and Photographs Division
Cover design by Simon Levy

Set in 10/13 pt Meridian by Toppan Best-set Premedia Limited
Printed in Malaysia by Ho Printing (M) Sdn Bhd

1   2014

Contents

Contents

Contents

Acknowledgments

It is with heartfelt gratitude that I recognize the many individuals who have contributed to this work. First and foremost, I would like to extend my sincere appreciation to Andrew Davidson for generously working with me as the consummate editor that he is from the beginning to the end. He helped me to refine my approach and then encouraged me to render the sharpest analysis possible. The other half of Andrew's team, Linda Gaio, kindly stepped in during the final stages using her expertise to streamline the complex permissions process. Nothing short of a profound thank you to both of you will do. Georgina Coleby and Lindsay Bourgeois from Wiley-Blackwell have helped guide me through the publishing process at every turn, answering every question no matter how small.

Thanks also go out to the many who have given their time to read through the preliminary pages and offer their insights. Randi Storch inspired me to consider this project. Richard Greenwald and Annelise Orleck provided valuable comments at a crucial stage. Paige Cameron carefully directed her talents toward broadening the appeal for the younger generations of students. I am thankful for the gracious and efficient assistance of archivist Patrizia Sione at Cornell University's Kheel Center for Labor-Management Documentation. Lucy Yang is a marvel in the world of Interlibrary Loans, and when it comes to articles and images,

Acknowledgments

Margaret Anderson possesses the kind of tracking skills that never cease to amaze me.

Other colleagues at Tompkins Cortland Community College have come through once again. Bruce Need deserves special thanks for his scrupulous editorial skills while in the midst of a busy semester. Jeanne Cameron is an abiding source of support and inspiration. Bev Carey and Lolly Carpenter are always willing to assist with any task that I may have.

Numerous friends and relatives continue to indulge my forays into centuries past. They include Paula Crawford, Nancy Di Liberto, Barbara Kobritz, Kathy McDonough, Berchie Rafferty, Brett Troyan, Judy Van Buskirk, and Nancy DaFoe, whose generosity of spirit and laughter sustains me. My husband, Jim, gives me the space that I need and inquires far less than he is entitled to concerning the status of my efforts. My children, David, Dominique, Chris, and Jamie have grown into young adults as this project came to fruition. I have watched as each of you in your own way has demonstrated your own commitment to social justice. And to the smallest member of our household, Mercedes, you are the one whom I dedicate this book to in the hope that the beacon of Progressivism will light your path as you dance on.

Introduction

Anyone reading the news in the winter of 1890 might easily have missed a short *New York Times* article announcing the upcoming World's Columbian Exposition, scheduled to open in Chicago in 1893 to celebrate the anniversary of Columbus's "discovery" of America. Nonetheless, the article boldly predicted that the Exposition would be "a grand success, at least as a display of American genius." When it opened three years later, the Exposition, or Chicago World's Fair as it became more commonly known, surpassed expectations. Twenty-seven million "excursionists" attended the ten-month event, which returned more than one million dollars in profits to its investors. In his *Book of the Fair* (1893), historian Hubert Bancroft pronounced, "The Fair has been to the world a revelation, to Americans an inspiration. It has shown, as no written or spoken works could show, the power and progress of a nation where all are free to strive for the highest rewards that energy and talent can win." In addition to touting American ingenuity, the Fair marked Chicago's future as a metropolis and foreshadowed the rise of the Progressive Era.

The Progressives: Activism and Reform in American Society, 1893–1917, First Edition.
Karen Pastorello.
© 2014 John Wiley & Sons, Inc. Published 2014 by John Wiley & Sons, Inc.

By 1890, the population of Chicago had surpassed one million, as newcomers flocked to the city to take advantage of job opportunities in its many factories; forty percent of the city's population was foreign-born. Chicago became a major transportation hub connecting the East to the West. Union Stock Yards, with its vast network of rail lines, housed meat packers like Swift and Armour, employing more people than any other industry. The men's garment industry was the city's second largest employer, with McCormick Reaper Works, Illinois Steel Company, Crane Elevator Company, and Montgomery Ward's retail mail-order business also ranked among companies that employed large numbers of workers.

The fact that Chicago prevailed over New York, Washington, and St. Louis in the Congressional contest to host the World's Fair seemed fitting. Chicago had literally been enhanced for the purpose of hosting the event. City promoters had held an election in 1889 to bolster the size of the city so that it could compete on a more equal level with its archrival, New York. The election resulted in the immediate incorporation of 125 square miles and 225,000 people. Virtually overnight, Chicago became the country's second largest city.

Quick to recognize the sudden demand for new housing created by the Fair, industrialist George Pullman seized the opportunity by erecting Market Square in Pullman, Illinois, fourteen miles south of Chicago. Pullman, who made his fortune manufacturing luxury sleeping and dining railroad cars, built apartments to house fairgoers and ran trains directly into the fairgrounds. Chicago's dramatic growth, coupled with the promise of banker Lyman Gage to raise several million dollars in seed money in a twenty-four-hour period, spelled victory for the city intent on displacing New York as the epicenter of the nation.

From the Fair's opening day on May 1, 1893, patrons marveled at the fourteen neoclassical "great" buildings situated on more than 600 acres. The fairgrounds, seven miles south of the Loop, were designed by renowned landscape architects Frederick Law Olmsted and Daniel H. Burnham and constructed by over 40,000 workers, featured grand vistas and exquisite landscaping in an attempt to present the ideal city. Cultural displays and artistic exhibits featured countless technological innovations, including over 90,000 incandescent lamps. The reflected light bouncing off the gleaming white facades of the buildings intensified the glow of what became known as the "White City."

Fairgoers bore witness to a scientific and technological revolution. Massive industrial growth also meant that business interests were more visible than ever before. Americans and visitors from abroad gawked in wonder at the new items manufacturers unveiled at the Fair. It was there that a young Henry Ford glimpsed his first industrial engine. Perhaps the most impressive new technology, electricity, ran everything from the Ferris wheel to massive fountains and merited its own building, the Electricity Building, where visitors were introduced to telephones, phonographs, typewriters, electric lamps, sewing machines, laundry machines, and irons. Consumer products such as dishwashers, doorbells, carpet sweepers, dental drills, picture postcards, carbonated soda, Cream of Wheat, Shredded Wheat, Juicy Fruit gum, and zippers made their debuts. Customers stood in long lines to purchase everything from electric appliances to gadgets, or to taste hamburgers and hot dogs, or to sip Pabst Beer for the first time. The inescapable message that equated the purchase of commodities with the enjoyment of life struck a definitive chord in American consciousness.

In a sense, the Fair symbolized the country's evolution from an agrarian land of rugged, highly independent farmers and westward settlers to a modern, more urban one characterized by an industrial culture of workers controlled by management responding to a national, even international marketplace. Frederick Jackson Turner, then a young professor at the University of Wisconsin, delivered the keynote address at a special convention of the American Historical Association held to mark the Fair's commencement. In his magisterial paper, "The Significance of the Frontier in American History," Turner informed his audience that the nation's western frontier had closed in 1890 – the seemingly endless supply of land had run out. According to Turner, the great many Americans and immigrants who had ventured west to start a new life had defined the democratic and innovative nature of the nation's character. This romanticized version of the Western settlement experience would settle in the nation's historical consciousness for nearly the next hundred years.

As the economy shifted from a traditional, agriculturally based one to a modern industrial system, Chicagoans, like other Americans, grappled with the effects of urbanization. The country began to pull free from its deep agrarian roots and to redefine itself as an urban nation with an urban conscience. City peripheries expanded outward in concentric circles as they grew into commercial and cultural centers. The changing nature of urban life became a popular subject for writers like Theodore Dreiser, who, at the age of twenty-one, moved from his small Indiana hometown to Chicago and experienced firsthand much of the material that made its way into his work. Dreiser's *Sister Carrie* became the first of many "urban novels" to reveal the darker side of city life, one depicting the sense of alienation and frustration unwelcome newcomers often experienced. Naïve newcomers often found themselves hardened by the harsh realities of big-city living.

Cities assumed new meaning as centers of production and consumption that served urban residents as well as those in outlying areas. Private enterprise placed a firm hold on the urban industrial economy and fostered the growth of powerful corporations. Business interests brought vitality to the marketplace, but at the same time, their seemingly unending pursuit of ever-rising profits gave rise to a demand from the American people for some type of economic regulation. Labor reacted to the grip of corporate control over the workplace by attempting to organize unions to fight for workers' basic rights, including a fair wage, reasonable hours in the workday, and safe conditions.

Following the well-worn paths of those who permanently migrated to the United States, people traveled from across the globe to attend the Fair. Nineteen foreign nations participated in the event. While select foreign governments established their headquarters in the dignified White City, non-white nations were relegated to the outlying section of the Fair, an area set aside for entertainment and amusement known as the Midway

Plaisance. Ethnological exhibits replete with artifacts lined the "Midway" depicting daily life in African and Asian cultures. Visitors marveled at the recreated African Village and Streets of Cairo.

Subtle changes that many observed for the first time at the Fair were also gradually integrating into American life. Activist Chicago women established a formidable presence in the Women's Building at the Fair. The vibrant women's political network, which had its roots in various Chicago women's clubs and then expanded into the city's premier settlement house, Hull House, continued its work at the Fair. Two women in particular, art collector and philanthropist Bertha Palmer and clubwoman and reformer Ellen Henrotin, took center stage. Palmer was appointed president of the Board of Lady Managers, which was in charge of overseeing the Women's Building exhibits and programs. Henrotin served as the Board's vice president. Both women were committed to women's equality. Dedicated to the idea that women could become empowered through becoming economically self-sufficient, Henrotin assigned over 30 chairwomen to the various Women's Congresses at the Fair. At these Congresses, women could speak on labor, education, suffrage, the arts, medicine, household economics, and religion.

Through her work at the Fair, Henrotin catapulted to fame and leadership in a number of other national organizations, including the Women's Trade Union League and the General Federation of Women's Clubs. Their experience at the Fair showed women how far they had come but also revealed how far they still had to go. Women realized that if they were to effect meaningful social change, their political empowerment was necessary. To accomplish that goal, they began enlisting male politicians and the support of male voters who sympathized with the cause of women's suffrage.

Similarly, the embattled presence of African Americans at the Fair foreshadowed their painful experiences in a Jim Crow South. A dispute erupted between civil rights activist Ida B. Wells, who wanted fellow blacks to boycott the Fair because they had been excluded from its planning and execution, and the black educator

Booker T. Washington, who encouraged their attendance at the high-profile event. Wells was particularly perturbed by the special "Negro Day" on August 25, which promoters encouraged blacks to attend by offering them free watermelon. In a way, the Fair foreshadowed the racist "separate but equal" doctrine that would soon become the law of the land with the Supreme Court's decision in the seminal case of *Plessy vs. Ferguson* (1896). With the sole exception of the Women's Building, the vision for the future projected at the Fair revolved around a white male-dominated world.

Indeed, the Fair straddled a watershed between eras. It bore witness to the end of the Gilded Age and forecast the hard economic times to come. Workers at Andrew Carnegie's steel mill in Pennsylvania endured a major setback in 1892, in the Homestead Strike, when Carnegie's manager, Henry Clay Frick, broke the Amalgamated Association of Iron and Steel Workers Union. Violent labor strikes in New Orleans among dockworkers, among Buffalo railroad switch operators, in Tennessee among coal miners, and in Idaho among copper miners evidenced massive worker discontent. Then came the Depression of 1893, the worst economic downturn before the Great Depression. Unemployment rates climbed into the double digits as an army of jobless men led by Jacob Coxey marched to Washington to protest the federal government's indifference to the growing crisis.

In Chicago, a smallpox epidemic erupted during the last days of the Fair, ravaging the Jewish and Italian West Side by the following spring. Residents of the city also endured the tragic assassination of Mayor Carter Harrison by a disgruntled job seeker and the actions of an arsonist who set fire to the Fair's abandoned buildings. Host to labor unrest, trade unions, political bosses, settlement houses, radical politicians, and a new graduate school of social work, Chicago in many ways represented the high points and the low points of what was to become known as the Progressive Era.

Chicago's radicalism had first surfaced with the infamous Haymarket Square Bombing in 1886, an incident resulting in the conviction of seven accused anarchists on scant evidence. Less than a decade later, in 1894, the city would erupt in chaos when 5,000 workers at Pullman Palace Car Company were fired when they struck against a wage cut. A court injunction declared the strike illegal and federal troops marched in to crush the workers' efforts. The leader of the American Railway Union, Eugene Debs, served a six-month jail term and converted to socialism as a result. In short order, Chicago seemed to have become the radical epicenter of the nation. Progressivism, like Populism before it, would radiate from the heartland.

Progressivism can be defined as the multifaceted effort of reformers to first identify and then to remedy the problems inherent in an industrializing and increasingly urban society. As times grew tougher in the wake of the Depression of 1893, reformers expanded their efforts beyond individual cities to states and then regions to try to formulate a more holistic, national approach. In the process, their work became more proactive and systematized. Influenced by the ongoing efforts of Christian charity workers and pragmatic philosophies at home, Progressive reformers also looked to Europe for direction. They also began to rely on the knowledge of experts – particularly social scientists – who emphasized the usefulness of the scientific method in solving societal problems. The new graduate program in sociology at the University of Chicago, for instance, helped train a new cadre of reformers known as social workers. These concerned professionals ventured into tenements and sweatshops where they observed and interviewed people (Figure I.1). After compiling and analyzing their data, they shared their findings in contemporary publications.

As the twentieth century commenced, a larger percentage of urban residents than ever before were immigrants who had come to the United States, primarily from Southern and Eastern Europe. By 1920, more than half of all Americans lived in industrializing urban areas. Poor working conditions and low wages plagued many city dwellers, as did the lack of housing and adequate medical care and the prevalence of child labor, prostitution, alcoholism, racism, malnutrition, disease, illiteracy, disenfranchisement, and other ills associated with poverty. In time,

Figure I.1   Laundry hung outside row of tenements, 260–268 Elizabeth St., New York, 1912. Library of Congress, Prints & Photographs Division, National Child Labor Committee Collection (LC-DIG-nclc-04208).

Progressives learned how to voice and effectively address the conditions of factory workers newly emigrated from Europe or newly relocated from family farms to cities.

Most Progressives concurred on the issues at hand but were less cohesive when it came to determining the best solutions. Many agreed that a high level of reform, sometimes in the form of governmental regulation, was necessary to improve the quality of life for those most adversely affected by industrialization. The staunchest Progressive reformers insisted that the state should step in to play a more active role in solving social, economic, and political problems. They sought to supplement private charities with public social services, settlement houses, urban reforms, and public health and labor legislation. Progressives led the call for a more streamlined and efficient activist government that involved itself in American life. The majority of reformers were not interested in advancing their own agency; instead, they were genuinely concerned with betterment for all.

In 1982, historian Daniel Rodgers asserted in his seminal essay, "In Search of Progressivism," that to begin to assess Progressivism accurately, one must first understand what was happening at the end of the nineteenth century. Rodgers's piece implies that historians studying the era would benefit by employing the tools and methods of social history to gain insight into how all Americans, no matter how ordinary, tried to make sense out of the chaotic world around them.

Until about forty years ago, most historians tended to present a somewhat romanticized, monolithic interpretation of the nation's past through their studies that concentrated on the political and intellectual elite, in most cases powerful men and momentous events. Enlightened by the Civil Rights movement, historians in the 1960s and 1970s began to focus more astutely on the experiences and actions of ordinary Americans. These practitioners of what became known as social history began to seek some relationship between everyday life, the values and behaviors of ordinary people, and the larger mechanisms of change that evolved over a long period of time. Social historians sifted through the details of individuals' lives to determine how those living at the time understood the meaning of their lives.

This emphasis on ordinary Americans meant that previously unrecognized or marginalized groups attracted the attention of historians who respectfully recognized cultural differences while attempting to understand the power of diversity. Women, Native Americans, African Americans, Asians, Hispanics, and industrial workers became subjects of historical inquiry. Historians like Thomas Bender considered them actors who shaped the meaning of "public culture."

Social historians have become adept at gathering and interpreting quantitative data to answer questions about demographic and mobility patterns and community composition. The trends that they have revealed, taken in conjunction with the analysis of formal institutions of social control such as schools, churches, and political structures, answer questions about how individuals resist or succumb to social control. Historians of the Progressive Era have probed the nature and strength of traditional culture and explored the texture of daily life through diaries and unique sources of imagery like parade banners and strike slogans and songs. They have examined demographic transitions using reports of charity institutions and immigrant presses. They have used records of home ownership by race and ethnicity to demonstrate patterns of social and even occupational mobility. While social historians have successfully linked many major historical events to the experiences of ordinary people, it does not mean that they have overcome all the challenges that this type of work presents. Fragmentation is a big problem, and the lack of synthesis is another.

Most striking was the plight of the poor urban population, most of whom were recent immigrants. In the decades following the Civil War, those seeking moral reform and charitable relief for individuals began to demand social and economic justice for the masses. As the nineteenth century drew to a close, Americans stood poised on the brink of modernity with the Progressives combating the ills associated with industrial life.

While the Progressive Era arguably marks the most transfiguring time in American history, it remains one of the most elusive periods for historical inquiry. The fundamental question of how to define progressivism continues to perplex scholars to this day. Students of the era quickly come to realize that progressivism is not a cohesive, unified movement but, instead, the sum of a variety of reform efforts.

Since the concept of progressivism remains fluid, it also is challenging to date definitively the era. It lays, as historian Melvyn Dubofsky informs us, "in the center of a historical continuum that runs from the Civil War to the establishment of mass bureaucratic order in the wake of WWII." Dating the Progressive Era from 1893 to 1917, as I have chosen to do in this volume, helps sharpen one's analysis of the period. The three phenomena that shape the era – industrialization, urbanization, and immigration – are evident by the early 1890s. More specifically, 1893 marks the beginning of a major depression; the opening of the

World's Columbian Exposition; the ascendency of Populism or agrarian discontent and a related third-party movement in the national political arena; the completion of the immigration induction center Ellis Island; the inauguration of Democrat Grover Cleveland as President; and the rise of the first national labor union, the American Federation of Labor (AFL). The April 1917 entry of the United States into World War I stalled and, some have argued, brought the Progressive thrust to an abrupt end.

This book poses several questions. Who, exactly, were these Progressive reformers? What were their origins, causes, and goals? When were they most active? How did they establish their agency? And, most important, what in their accomplishments leaves a legacy for twenty-first-century Americans?

Even a brief consideration of the period's historiography (the history of written history) enables students to view the Progressive Era through a multitude of lenses. Drawing on the work of diverse scholars, I will attempt to both balance competing perspectives and capture the essence of the era, providing insight into the Progressive years for today's students. The "Bibliographical Essay" at the end of the book highlights the topics covered in the book. These sections will enable serious students to learn more about the debates surrounding progressivism, as well as guide them to good sources for further study.

Not all historians are comfortable with the idea of transformational moments, which, as they point out, may seem neater and more definitive in hindsight than they were at the time. But others, myself included, are inclined to picture the American narrative as a series of ups and downs, periods of mounting internal strife crystallized by momentous events. Students will be introduced to the many people and groups who worked toward bettering society for the poor, urban, mostly immigrant workers. Learning something about the individuals involved in the Progressive Movement, some might be encouraged to imagine what their own lives might have been like if they had lived in the Progressives' rapidly changing world.

Progressive Era reformers did not refer to themselves as *Progressives*. Writers popularized the term during the 1910

Congressional elections when they applied the label to candidates who by 1910 began to advocate basic political, social, and economic reforms. Progressives ranged from those who revered the efficiency of large corporations but disliked corporate trusts to those who praised "the people" and sought a white, educated electorate who spoke the language of social order and moral uplift. Progressives did share some common characteristics. All of them had faith in social science and government to solve problems, to help improve the lives of the less fortunate.

Before the movement ran its course, Progressives and their followers came to include religious leaders, businessmen, professionals, civic leaders, settlement women, suffragists, African Americans, civil rights advocates, union members, nativists, immigrants, workers, farmers, and politicians. Assigning exclusive membership to "special interest groups" is complicated. Some categories overlap, so that some people may have belonged to more than one or even two such groups. In addition, as historian Richard McCormick points out, a focus on special interest groups often fails to account for the unorganized public. A more pertinent question when trying to identify who the Progressives were might be to ask, what effective coalitions did they form? Regardless, despite the lack of a unified, formal movement, the phenomenon that is progressivism provides a useful framework for the study of American history in the late nineteenth and early twentieth centuries.

By the dawn of the twentieth century, for the majority of Progressives, as for the majority of Americans, government seemed the most likely source through which to accomplish sweeping social, economic, and political change. Understanding our contemporary circumstances necessitates tracing the evolution and expansiveness of social, economic, and political institutions and policies from the turn of the twentieth century forward. Most important are the directives the Progressives left us for contemplating the way we live now.

1

Setting the Stage
The Birth of the Progressive Impulse, 1893–1900

By 1890, sixty-three million people lived in the United States, the majority of them making their homes in small towns and rural areas, living life much as they had before the Civil War tore the nation apart. Farming, especially prevalent in the Midwest and South, outranked all other occupations. In the North, however, once the war ended, the trend toward industrialization that had begun before the war resumed and gained momentum. In the three decades following the conflict, industrial output in the United States tripled. Approximately five million Americans – or thirteen percent of the population – worked in one of the more than 350,000 industrial firms located mainly in the Northeastern cities. By 1920, census records officially classified the United States as an urban nation for the first time in its history.

On the Farm

For many Americans, life on the farm symbolized a peaceful yet productive way of life. By the turn of the century, crop

The Progressives: Activism and Reform in American Society, 1893–1917, First Edition.
Karen Pastorello.
© 2014 John Wiley & Sons, Inc. Published 2014 by John Wiley & Sons, Inc.

production had soared. American farmers were producing more than twice as much cotton, corn, and wheat than they had in 1870. Surpluses and profitable crop prices improved the farmers' standard of living. "In the country," wrote Harvard University president Charles W. Eliot, "it is quite possible that a permanent [farm] family should have a permanent dwelling." While those who wrote about farming tended to highlight its positive aspects, in reality it was a demanding and risky business, one fraught with tensions.

Romantically perceived as a self-reliant people of plenty, American farmers were not immune from fluctuations in the economy. Expenses for supplies and animals continued to rise throughout the nineteenth century. Large and small farmers who wanted to increase or merely insure their output mechanized. While the use of farm machinery appeared to relieve farmers of some of the backbreaking physical labor, the purchase of new and replacement equipment put farmers constantly in need of cash and credit. As mechanization took hold, any profits from farming were spent on farm equipment, which took priority over household improvements.

In addition to the pressure to maintain status and power by mechanizing, farmers also had to compete with increasing com- mercialization. The 1910 federal census confirmed that family farms continued to dominate agricultural production, but the seeds of agribusiness had already been sown. In New Jersey and Maryland, commercial farmers employed seasonal migrant labor to pick beans, peas, tomatoes, blueberries, and cranberries. Increasingly, seasonal farm hands were unrelated, even foreign. Some migrant farm workers traveled from harvest to harvest their entire lives, living in shacks or tents without any benefits or ever owning land. The children of these nomadic workers suf- fered, too. Their parents' transiency meant that the young usually lacked both a stable home life and a proper education.

As industrial farms began to hire more employees, they introduced mass production and new management techniques to American agriculture. These more highly commercial farms raised vast quantities of agricultural products and sold them in distant markets. Commercial farms relied on rail transportation supported by low freight rates, and the rise of these large-scale enterprises reflected the changes taking place in the larger American society.

No longer could ordinary Americans expect to move west to take advantage of the allegedly free and open space. In 1890, the United States Census Bureau had announced the disappearance of a contiguous frontier line. In his speech to a gathering of historians at the Chicago World's Fair in May of 1893, thirty-three-year-old University of Wisconsin professor Frederick Jackson Turner expounded on the significance of the frontier in American history: "The existence of an area of free land, its continuous recession, and the advance of American settlement westward explain American development." While Turner's characterization of the West as the most democratic region of the nation came to dominate the American mindset for the next half century, it did not accurately portray what the Western experience meant for the majority of Americans, especially Native Americans, many of whom were forced onto reservations in the West during the Trail of Tears in the 1830s and who would not even be granted U.S. citizenship until 1924. By 1900, many of the roughly 250,000 Native Americans were farmers. A small number of Indians farmed their own land in the same way as did whites, but most Indians tried as best they could to continue communal land use practices on tribal reservations. Displaced from their ancestral lands and marginalized by mainstream society, Native Americans suffered in silence.

White farmers in the Northeast generally inherited family land that had passed down through several generations. Farm families at the time were typically nucleic, consisting of a husband, a wife, and their children. Small family farmers tried to use local labor whenever they needed extra help. Regardless of the kind of farming in which the family was involved, the long production process required the cooperation of each family member. Farmers coped with challenges by maintaining strong bonds within their families and communities. Kinship ties facilitated the exchange of labor, machinery, and financial assistance. No matter how geographically isolated their land was, farmers and their families were rarely alone.

Despite the rapid pace of change around them, the work routines of farm families changed little over time. To the casual observer, it seemed like men made the decisions when it came to deciding what type of crops to grow or when to purchase equipment, while women kept the family going on a daily basis. However, Nancy Gray Osterud's study of farm women in New York's Nanticoke Valley, *Bonds of Community* (1991), revealed that by virtue of the degree of cooperation required to run a successful farm, men and women crossed over the boundaries of gender roles to assist each other more than historians initially realized. In other words, farm wives participated in decision making at all levels.

Women's days were hard and long, but their work was not considered as important as their husband's, primarily because women's efforts were not always associated directly with income-producing labor. What was being grown or raised dictated the kind of work demanded from women. For example, since dairy farming, and more specifically, the chores associated with maintaining large herds of cows and milking them, was so intense, women as well as children had to work on the farm. Growing corn, on the other hand, required less care latter in the season, once the plants reached a certain height. Farm women's domestic labor almost always entailed preparing food, washing clothes, and spring cleaning, essential but arduous tasks, especially in light of the fact that these chores required hauling wood and water into the home.

Life on the farm meant that the whole family, including the children, maintained the same daily schedule, waking before dawn to do early morning chores in the home or barnyard. Before heading off to the fields, the family, often joined by hired hands, ate a hearty breakfast of meat, eggs, potatoes, and porridge in cold weather or cereal in warmer weather. Coffee was the adult beverage, while the children drank milk. Farmers took a lunch break at around noon and then returned to the fields to resume their work until supper time. Most farm children attended school during the day. They left for school after breakfast but had to walk or ride the long distance to town to get there. Country schools ran from 8:00 a.m. to 4:00 p.m. and tended to be small, one-room schoolhouses with instruction focused on recitation. Almost every "pupil" used William Holmes McGuffey's *McGuffey's Eclectic Readers*, which was heavy on morality and conformity, and idealized and extolled the virtues of seemingly uncomplicated rural and village life. Evening time after dinner was generally a quiet one, with children doing schoolwork, men reading a local newspaper or perhaps *Harper's* or *Atlantic Monthly* magazine, and women sewing or mending by the light of kerosene lamps. On weekends, community suppers and church socials were popular pastimes. Annual county and state fairs where members of farm families displayed their agricultural wares and handicrafts and competed for blue ribbons provided welcome diversions from the routines of rural life.

Turn-of-the-century farmers and their families grew most of what they needed or bartered among themselves, trading surplus food for manufactured products such as tools, medicine, and liquor. They also purchased from general stores where owners tried to avoid clutter by stocking groceries on one side of the store and dry goods such as tobacco, patent medicine, thread, thimbles, candy, and shaving implements and other toiletries on the other. Gloves, stocking caps, milk pails, and cooking pots hung from the ceiling. Store keepers sold kerosene and whiskey in the back of the store. Rural merchants sold new products by demonstrating them, installing wall clocks and telephones in their stores to prove their usefulness. Fall markets in the town centers in rural areas featured the surplus products of farm wives and daughters, homemade foodstuffs and crafts such as applesauce and sauerkraut, feathers for pillows, as well as brooms, soap, baskets, and potted plants.

In general, some farmers accepted and others resisted what historian Hal S. Barron's *Mixed Harvest* (1997) refers to as the second great transformation – the move from rural to modern life. The first phase of this transformation entailed the migration of former farmers to the cities, where, once settled, they sought factory jobs. But even farmers who stayed behind on their farms were affected by modernization. Many became active consumers who ordered desired merchandise from mail-order catalogs rather than purchasing supplies and finished goods at the local general store. Despite their contributions toward meeting consumer demands, farmers saw their overall status in society decline. They formed farmers' organizations known as granges to strengthen social connections and to promote communitarian practices and, later, more formal farmers' alliances to facilitate cooperative buying and advocate on their own behalf in the open market. Eventually, those who spent their lives working the land sought a voice in politics through such alliances.

Those farmers who chose to migrate to the cities became factory workers alongside European agricultural workers who had crossed the Atlantic Ocean in search of employment or a new life. Regardless of their origins, new factory workers found promise in the possibility of steady pay and regular hours. Whether native- or foreign-born, former farmers exchanged the seasonal rhythms that had guided their work lives for the constant grind of industrial gears. Large industries like iron and steel manufacturing set the pace of their workdays. Nonetheless, former rural residents viewed Sundays off and freedom from the elements as tangible benefits of urban industrial life. As the rate of migration from farm to factory escalated, the number of Americans making their living from the land dropped dramatically. In 1870, farmers constituted approximately one-half of the American workforce. By 1920, farmers comprised only about one-quarter of it.

City Life

As newcomers flocked to urban areas, they created a huge new demand for housing, one that landlords large and small tried to meet. Many urban homeowners rented out extra rooms and provided meals for extra income. Others opened boardinghouses to capitalize on the flood of newcomers to their respective cities.

Lodging houses in which a worker could rent a furnished room without meals for a week or a month sprang up. So-called flop-houses, on the other hand, were typically run-down accommodations in which one could only rent a bit of space. Housing at all levels was in such demand that in extremely overcrowded slums, men rented beds where they could sleep for a nickel a shift, a different man "flopping" down on the same dirty bed shortly after the prior one rose. Eventually, two Protestant charitable organizations that tried to help urban working people, the Young Men's Christian Association (YMCA) and Young Women's Christian Association (YWCA) provided support by offering rooms for reasonable prices for single adults who moved to cities. Immigrants who came to the city as family units often found homes in tenements, where they shared sanitary facilities with other tenant families and cooked on a single burner. Apartment houses with private facilities, a suite of rooms on a single floor, electric lighting and appliances, and elevators were built for the most affluent families or single men.

Despite the trend toward multiple-unit residences, from 1870 to about 1910, many city dwellers lived in single family homes. Most working-class families lived in unpretentious "laborer's cottages." These houses were simply furnished, one-story dwellings with a parlor, a kitchen, and two bedrooms. Middle- and upper-class families preferred houses featuring ornate Victorian architecture. Those who could afford them had houses with formal parlors, separate dining rooms, and elaborate lawns and gardens. Front porches adorned almost every house regardless of the family's means. Electricity, running water, and telephone service became available to city residents by the late nineteenth century. Central heating was virtually nonexistent, and, because of their reliance on potbellied stoves, most Americans awoke to cold mornings (Figure 1.1).

While some optimistically viewed cities as the greatest hope for a democratic life, cities also seemed to breed conditions that alarmed middle-class Americans. Some worried about the many powerful interests that had muscled their way into local politics. Transportation and utility companies, public works contractors,

Figure 1.1 Poor women and children gathering coal from the coal yards in Chicago in the early 1900s. Chicago Daily News negatives collection, Chicago History Museum (DN0000522).

liquor dealers, and purveyors of assorted vices exerted their influence over the urban bosses who controlled the city's politics. At the same time, the large numbers of workers all in the same industry in cities such as New York, Chicago, and numerous others saw the rise of organized labor. As a result, cities experienced multiple, sometimes violent, labor conflicts and worker strikes. Finally, the arrival of so many people from different parts of the nation and the world in American cities gave rise to sharp racial tensions, as were evidenced in the first decade of the new century by deadly race riots that broke out in New York City, Atlanta, Georgia, and Springfield, Illinois. Further complicating urban problems, pollution and crime increased proportionally with urban density.

Urban residents wrestled with crowded and cramped conditions at home, but the world outside their doors hardly offered them much respite. Smoke and soot, both by-products of industrial production, greatly affected urban air quality. Air pollution first surfaced in heavily industrialized cities like Pittsburgh and Chicago but later became a problem in other population centers such as Philadelphia and New York with the shift from the use of anthracite to cheaper, but dirtier, bituminous coal. Public health reformers were shocked by the disease-breeding conditions prevalent in virtually every neighborhood. Garbage such as food waste, wood and coal ash, and horse manure littered the streets. Outdoor privies bordered almost every thoroughfare, and inadequate drainage systems failed to carry away the sewage effectively. The constant noise from streetcars, factories, vendors, and the hustle of life on the streets only added to the unpleasantness of the urban environment.

In addition to the challenging physical conditions dwellers of increasingly crowded cities faced, some people also began to worry about the potential moral harm to urban residents. In late-nineteenth-century New York, the Bowery, an impoverished neighborhood on the Lower East Side, became synonymous with tenement slums. Viewed as a netherworld by many, the area was dominated by brothels, cheap saloons, gambling halls, and rooming houses that rented by the night. Large numbers of homeless persons roamed the streets. These downtrodden urban slums were considered dens of iniquity. The notorious Levee, a vice district in Chicago, housed "sporting clubs" of all kinds that attracted vulnerable newcomers. Twenty-Second Street in the Levee hosted entertainments ranging from the most extravagant brothels to small unadorned houses of prostitution located in boardinghouses and in the backrooms of saloons. Some enterprises provided male prostitutes for interested clients.

The Levee district's unscrupulous trade was so flagrant that Mayor Carter Harrison II appointed a commission in 1910 to investigate vice conditions throughout the city. The following year, the commission released its report entitled *The Social Evil in Chicago*, which prompted a flurry of reforms, including the closing of the Levee's most famous brothel, the Everleigh Club. Soon afterward, the U.S. State's Attorney launched an attack on the Levee that quieted the once-thriving landscape of concentrated prostitution. As a result of anti-prostitution campaigns led by Protestant reform groups, officials around the country shut down red-light districts, which were usually located near the hearts of cities in hotels, railroad stations, rooming houses, and other nighttime leisure venues. With local government now monitoring public morals, urban police forces could concentrate on fighting crime. Police and fire departments, along with sanitation services, became part of a cadre of standard urban services in Progressive Era American cities.

Despite the downside of city living, it did offer some opportunities for immigrant residents in particular. In his early study of workers in ethnic communities, *Steelworkers in America* (1960), David Brody observed that various ethnic groups creatively carved out social networks that supported their own with churches, fraternal organizations, mutual aid societies, businesses, and religious schools. The literate among them read ethnic-language papers. Most first-generation immigrants spoke their native languages whenever they could.

Diverse immigrant groups clashed with each other and also with native-born reformers who tried to "Americanize" them. While the first generations of immigrants were reluctant to relinquish their native ways, nearly everyone seemed to take part in urban holiday revelry, especially on Christmas and decidedly American celebrations such as Labor Day and the (often rowdy) Fourth of July. Groups gathered in lodges and churches to link the celebration of American independence with their own notions of freedom, play, and ethnic pride. In 1894, President Grover Cleveland signed a federal law declaring Labor Day a national holiday. It became the only official worker holiday between the Fourth of July and Christmas.

To casual observers who avoided the poorest sections, American cities appeared to be vibrant centers of working-class culture. There were over 200,000 drinking establishments in the United States by 1897. In Chicago, saloons outnumbered grocery stores, meat markets, and dry goods stores combined. By 1915, Chicago housed one saloon for every 335 people, and New York had one saloon for every 515 people. Many saloons catered to particular ethnic or trade-based groups. After long hours on the job, working men centered their social lives around exclusively male domains, including bars, fraternal lodges, and sporting events. Middle-class men preferred to drink at private clubs or in hotels, while working-class men flocked to neighborhood saloons. At the time, saloons provided a variety of services for their customers, from drinking and reading newspapers to keeping valuables in a safe or storing luggage in the basement. With their swinging doors and welcoming owners, they served as centers for local gossip, served food, and provided stages for local politicians. Saloon patrons concerned with their own public image could impress others by buying rounds of drinks for the house.

Turn-of-the-century women and children located their leisure activities in public spaces within close proximity of their homes. They were inclined to use the streets, their front stoops, and local parks for recreation and socializing. Most young children of immigrants attended public schools during the day. Many of these immigrant children would, however, leave school before eighth grade to go to work to help support their families. It was not unusual to see young children playing unattended on the streets while both their parents worked.

Settlement houses, neighborhood centers geared toward improvement, were springing up in immigrant ghettos where so-called settlement workers sought to create a sense of community by bridging the gap between classes and races. Workers tried to help Americanize recent arrivals, alleviate sources of distress, and improve living and working conditions. Many settlement workers had experienced the city and its problems firsthand. Others had read about urban injustices in newspapers and magazines. Most settlement house workers took their religion seriously, with religious sentiment playing an important factor in settlement and reform work.

Hard Times: The Depression of 1893

Caught up in the rush of modernity, Americans watched as towns swelled to cities. One by-product of rapid population growth meant ever-expanding markets. Extractives like coal and oil became increasingly important as raw materials in the production process and as fuel for industrial machinery, farm equipment, and electrical equipment, even as more efficient forms of energy such as electricity increasingly powered industry and commerce. Massive industrial expansion and diversification saw the production of American products create a new independence from European imports.

Technology further stimulated industrial development. Innovative Americans, ranging from backyard inventors to college-educated engineers, developed new machines and created new and more efficient production processes. These inventions facilitated the growth of major industries including steel, oil refining, farm machinery, locomotives, canned food, machine tools, cigarettes, cameras, rubber, and automobiles. Railroad expansion opened new areas to agriculture and linked formerly isolated regions to broader national and international markets. This unprecedented growth, however, was soon interrupted by the fourth and final economic "crisis" of the nineteenth century.

On May 3, 1893, just two days after the World's Columbian Exposition (the Chicago World's Fair) opened in Chicago, the stock market collapsed, intensifying an economic downslide that had started in February. The Philadelphia and Reading Railroads fell to the crisis, followed by the country's leading manufacturer of rope and twine, the National Cordage Company. Amid rumors of stock fraud and other corrupt practices, other railroads, including the Erie; Northern Pacific; Union Pacific; and the Acheson, Topeka, and Santa Fe, failed. Approximately 500 banks and 16,000 businesses, including one-third of all railroads, went bankrupt. By November, economists began to call attention to the unemployed in the nation's three largest cities: approximately 100,000 people in Chicago; 85,000 in New York; and 50,000 in

Philadelphia. Unemployment figures well above ten percent would continue to plague the nation for the next several years.

Urban laborers were not alone in their plight. Farmers' situations grew increasingly precarious. By 1890, approximately thirty percent of farmers had mortgages and were in debt. In 1893, crop prices plummeted along with the economy. Many Americans lost their farms to foreclosures and tax sales. Business owners felt the pinch too. Some manufacturers blamed federal monetary policies that caused inflation and high tariffs on imports for their woes. Others faulted the lavish spending of the Cleveland's administration for their troubles. A few even pointed to the diversion of millions of dollars to the World's Fair to explain the reason for the economic downturn.

The Depression of 1893 marked the starkest economic crisis confronted by Americans to date. When it struck, a greater number of Americans were earning wages than ever before in the nation's history. They used their wages to purchase goods with cash. More Americans were now susceptible to economic forces completely beyond their control.

As the depression deepened, workers around the country suffered. Tens of thousands lost their jobs. The unemployed relied heavily on the kindness of family and friends. Local sources of relief like public assistance and charities offered only marginal aid. Not all Americans were willing to help others. Followers of Social Darwinism believed charitable acts interfered with the natural course of selection – weeding out the weak or unfit. In their minds, hard economic times heightened the competitive environment in which only the "fittest" would survive – the rest would perish. A countervailing, yet increasing popular school of Protestant thought known as the Social Gospel, which sought to attend to social ills by promoting a civic consciousness, supported not only benevolent acts by individuals and voluntary agencies but government action to both alleviate the plight of the unfortunate and prevent future crises.

Just when many had given up hope, almost inexplicably, in late 1897, the economy began to surge. Sales at the New York Stock Exchange skyrocketed, wheat exports soared, and railroads turned profits. With credit becoming widely available once again, factories began to rehire, and new firms sprang up. With the help of investment bankers, the businesses that survived the depression consolidated, helping to create more powerful amalgamated corporations. As the economic climate prospered, unemployed Americans went back to work.

Businesses: Small to Large

From the debut of his first novel, *Ragged Dick* (1867), Horatio Alger established a new genre of fiction that heroicized young street urchins living in poverty in large, urban centers teeming with industry. With uncommon courage and moral fortitude, Alger's young protagonists struggled against adversity to achieve wealth and acclaim. The hero in *Ragged Dick*, as in other "city stories," started out as an ambitious shoeshine boy who, with hard work and a little luck, rose from poverty to a respectable middle-class position as a postal clerk. Intended as success manuals for boys, Alger's stories became bestsellers. By the time he died in 1899, Alger had written approximately 100 novels set in New York City. Alger's contemporary, William Dean Howells, capitalized on another version of the self-made-man theme with *The Rise of Silas Lapham* (1895). Born into a poor farm family, the entrepreneurial Silas Lapham becomes a millionaire from his success in the paint business. Howells's novel was one of the first to focus on the rise of an individual businessman. Both Alger and Howells popularized the "dime store" novel motif of rags to riches that soon pervaded American culture.

Small businesses evolve

In *A History of Small Business in America* (2003), historian Mansel Blackford contends that small businesses were the mainstay of the American economy throughout the Civil War era. Virtually all of the corporate giants started out as small businesses and many small businesses remained sole proprietorships. Until the

1880s, the business of America was small business. As the mete-oric growth of large influential enterprises such as railroads, manufacturing corporations, and banks came to dominate a new economic order in the land, businesses had to adjust their basic structures to meet growing demands: some of them had to fight merely to stay in business, while a few of them grew very large.

The retail trade provides a good example of the evolution from small business to large business. Irish immigrant Alexander Turney Stewart pioneered the idea of the department store in the mid-nineteenth century. Stewart started as a linen seller in New York City but quickly diversified to supply customers along the Erie Canal with the merchandise they needed to settle in the hinterlands. In the 1860s, using money inherited from his grand-father, he opened a store on Broadway in New York and catered to urban shoppers by expanding his dry goods inventory to include ready-to-wear clothing and a variety of nonperishable goods. He appealed to women by offering clothing imported from Europe displayed on models at fashion shows. He also started a mail-order business.

Stewart's ingenuity set the model for future department stores. Retailers followed his lead and began to buy goods directly from the factory. They departmentalized their merchan-dise. Starting in Philadelphia in an abandoned railroad depot, John Wanamaker built branch stores in other cities, paving the way for the rise of chain stores including Filene's in Boston, Marshall Field's in Chicago, and Macy's in New York. Wana-maker realized that the more time shoppers spent in his store, the more they would buy. Seeking to transform the shopping experience, Wanamaker introduced store advertising and elec-tric lights and installed an elevator and restaurant in his store. To attract more affluent shoppers, he pioneered the concept of the money-back guarantee and the price tag. Wanamaker catered to the immigrant market before other large store owners. He drew on practices reminiscent of European marketplaces by placing cheaper merchandise in basement bargain bins, hiring sales clerks versed in immigrant tongues, and letting customers haggle for their purchases.

Rowland Macy was the fourth of six children born into a Massachusetts Quaker family. After opening four unsuccessful dry goods stores in Massachusetts, Macy moved to New York City to open a store in 1858. He added "fancy" consumer lines to dry goods, including clothing and toiletries. Macy eventually sold silverware, china, flowers, books, stationery, and household appliances. The red star that Macy had tattooed on his hand while he was working on a whaling ship as a teenager in his native Nantucket became the store's trademark. He eventually expanded his store and moved it to the main shopping district in Manhattan, taking only cash until the 1950s.

The expanded size and increased variety gave rise to what Wanamaker called "the New Kind of Store." These department stores resembled architecturally designed bazaars. They were lit with skylights and chandeliers, adorned with displays in plate-glass windows, and contained restaurants, a postal service, ladies' lounges, restrooms, gardens, and libraries. By the early twentieth century, these "consumer palaces" became the first choice for urban shoppers. Three- and four-story department stores in city centers became the symbol of urban mass markets.

Other merchants capitalized on the concept of chain stores. The Great Atlantic and Pacific Tea Company (later renamed A & P) became one of the first chain grocery stores. It opened in 1869, the same year as the transcontinental railroad. The Great Atlantic & Pacific Tea Company arose from the partnership between George Huntington Hartford and George Francis Gilman. Using Gilman's connections as a grocer and son of a wealthy ship owner, Hartford purchased coffee and tea from clipper ships on the docks of New York City. By eliminating middlemen, the partners were able to sell their wares at "cargo prices." The partners soon expanded across the country, using promotions and giveaways of crockery and lithographs at new store openings to attract customers. By 1900, there were over 200 A & P stores nationwide. The company's success was largely due to its innovative strategy of offering savings and incentives to the consumer. The store kept its management costs low and did not extend credit to customers. Its "club plan" offered an additional one-third discount for customers who formed clubs to make bulk mail-order purchases. By 1886, hundreds of such clubs had been formed. The company pioneered the idea of private labels and house brands; Great American Tea introduced its own inexpensive tea and coffee blends, including the popular "Eight O'Clock" blend.

Frank Winfield Woolworth started his Woolworth's store as a "five-and-dime" drug and variety store in 1881 in Lancaster, Pennsylvania, where shoppers could buy inexpensive items like crochet hooks, watch keys, and baby goods on impulse. Woolworth, who had worked as a dry goods clerk, had tried several times before in his native northern New York to open novelty stores but failed. His vision of selling specialty and novelty items for under a dime proved so successful that he opened a store in England. Within a few years, Woolworth became a millionaire, controlling more than 600 stores. In 1910, Woolworth commissioned a 792-foot Gothic-style skyscraper on Broadway in New York City to serve as his company headquarters.

In rural areas, mail-order catalogs – first Montgomery Ward's and later Sears and Roebuck – made buying vastly more convenient. Montgomery Ward made use of his affiliation with the Grange movement's supply house to offer mail-order supplies. Richard Sears was a railroad agent who got into the mail-order business in 1886. No longer having to trek to the nearest city to shop, even rural families could order finished goods from clothes to farm equipment from the pages of a catalog. Despite resistance by grocers and local merchants, virtually every rural family owned a Sears catalog, known colloquially as the "Farmer's Bible." They were so popular that schools often used them for math and geography lessons. By 1910, an estimated ten million Americans shopped by mail, buying products sight unseen with satisfaction guaranteed. Astute urban advertisers catered to an ever-growing immigrant market. Advertisers used postcards, newspaper advertisements, business cards, and free calendars to deliver their messages and to pique curiosity.

Fear of competition generated a great deal of tension between large and small businesses. Some shopkeepers tried unsuccessfully to lobby for the passage of laws restricting the growth of department stores. Others like the entrepreneur William Wrigley, Jr., who initially were hard hit by competition from large stores, profited from the latter's innovations.

William Wrigley, at the age of thirteen, had proven himself a phenomenal salesman, one noted for his unfailing politeness peddling soap for his father's company in Philadelphia. After marrying Ada Foote in 1885, Wrigley decided to try his luck in Chicago, where he sold his own brand of scouring soap and baking powder to merchants. Part of his sales strategy was to include a free product with each sale. He tried umbrellas, cookbooks, and toiletries. Then, at some point, he included a free pack of Zeno chewing gum with each sale. When customers began to demand more gum, Wrigley decided to develop his own brand of chewing gum. After starting his own chewing gum company in 1891, by 1893, the Wrigley Chewing Gum Company introduced Juicy Fruit and Spearmint gum. Despite an economic downturn in 1907, he sustained his company with a $250,000 loan. Wrigley continued to concoct creative advertising schemes, and in 1915, he gathered addresses from all the published telephone books in the country and began a wildly successful marketing campaign sending a free package of gum to every household in the country. His profits in chewing gum allowed him to invest in the Chicago Cubs, and eventually he bought Catalina Island off the California coast.

A Confederate veteran who earned his medical degree at nineteen, Atlanta pharmacist and chemist John Pemberton developed an ingenious marketing scheme for his nerve stimulant and headache remedy, which had originally been based on a French recipe. He reformulated Pemberton's French Wine Coca, by substituting sugar for wine after Fulton County passed a prohibition law in 1886. Pemberton advertised his coca syrup by recommending that it be mixed with carbonated water to create a "delicious, exhilarating, refreshing, and invigorating" soda-fountain beverage but also as the ideal "temperance drink." Renaming his nonalcoholic drink Coca-Cola, he put his son, Charles, in charge of marketing it so that he could turn his attention back to the production of French Wine Coca when Atlanta repealed the prohibition law in 1887. Pemberton sold the company in 1888, the year he died, and the new owner, Asa Candler, propelled the company to international success.

At the end of the century, Chicago attorney Adolphus Green decided to capitalize on recent advances in mechanization, railroad transport of products, and ready-to-eat foods. He founded the American Biscuit and Manufacturing Company which, through mergers, became the National Biscuit Company (later Nabisco) in New York. In the meantime, workers at the company used shortening to create Uneeda Biscuits, "a flakier cracker" soon to become the company's premier product. Green's law partner, Frank Peters, experimented with packaging. His moisture-proof cardboard box with sealed wax paper liners both kept the crackers dry and protected them from breakage. The company's owners agreed to assure their freshness by delivering the individual boxes of soda crackers directly to grocers who prior to this had sold loose crackers out of massive wooden barrels.

Nabisco launched the first million-dollar advertising campaign to promote sales of what quickly became a recognizable national brand. The crackers sold for five cents a box. The boxes with the little boy in a yellow slicker carrying a box of Uneeda Biscuits were one of the most successful advertising campaigns in history. His image permeated American culture when it appeared on toys and in cartoons and photographs. The use of the cardboard boxes gave a tremendous boost to the box industry. Food had been sold in cans since the 1880s, but Uneeda changed the way many foods and other items were packaged. This was the first advertising campaign to feature packaged, ready-to-eat food. Other food companies like Quaker Oats, which first debuted its product at the 1893 World's Fair in Chicago, would follow, packaging its cereal in a carton and advertising its trademark Quaker nationwide. The National Biscuit Company became a leader in food quality and the push for sanitation, and it advocated for legislation at the national level. The company was instrumental in lobbying to pass what became the Pure Food and Drug Act in 1906.

Processed foods in sanitary sealed cans, boxes, or bottles labeled with brand names, made easily recognizable across the country through advertising campaigns, transformed how Americans ate. While flour had been a processed food since the 1880s, its premixture with other ingredients as premade "mixes" began when St. Joseph, Missouri, newspaper editor Chris L. Rutt and his friend Charles G. Underwood decided to market pancake mix using surplus flour from a mill that they had purchased in 1888. They faced a glutted flour market and needed a way to use the excess flour from their mill. Drawing on the popularity of minstrel songs and vaudeville shows, Aunt Jemima Pancake Mix, named after a popular song, "Old Aunt Jemima," was introduced at the Chicago World's Fair in 1893, paving the way for packaged mixes and puddings.

In Pittsburgh, the son of German immigrant parents, Henry John Heinz revolutionized the processing of food traditionally "put up" or "canned" at home. Heinz began his career by growing vegetables in his mother's garden at a very young age. As a teenager, he established a list of faithful customers who appreciated the young man's polite sales approach. After marrying at the age of twenty-five, Heinz peddled bottled horseradish and celery sauce, which proved unsuccessful, but he restarted his efforts with the help of relatives by bottling ketchup in 1876. A combination of commercial farming, new canning methods, and advertising campaigns made him the largest food processor in the country by 1900. Along with a few other successful food entrepreneurs, Heinz worked toward the passage of the Pure Food and Drug Act.

Philip Armour was born on a farm in Upstate New York and spent time in the goldfields of California and worked at a packing plant in Milwaukee before renting a hog-packing plant with his brothers in Chicago in 1872. They purchased a plant in 1874. They used what Henry Ford referred to as a "disassembly line" that used all parts of the animal. Armour's methods proved profitable but resulted in massive pollution and unsanitary practices. He considered himself a philanthropist, yet his largely immigrant workforce lived and worked in squalid conditions, much like those depicted in Upton Sinclair's now classic novel *The Jungle* (1906). Armour also detested labor unions and broke two strikes, one in 1886 and the second in 1894.

By 1915, due largely to health reformers' efforts, cereal produced by brothers John and William Kellogg and C. W. Post replaced the hearty but calorie-laden American breakfast. John Kellogg moved to Battle Creek, Michigan, with his Seventh Day Adventist family and at an early age began his work experience in his father's broom factory and later in a number of print shops. He eventually earned his medical degree from Bellevue Medical College (now part of New York University) in 1875. With his solid medical background, Kellogg became the medical superintendent of the Adventists' Western Health Reform Institute in Battle Creek and immediately began to reform it to "a place where people learn to stay well." He began to test the "Battle Creek idea" regarding the effect of diet, exercise, correct posture, fresh air, and adequate rest on the health and fitness of individuals. His successful program had roots in the Adventist principles of vegetarianism and temperance. John and his brother experimented with processing wheat meal into a food for sanitarium patients and stumbled upon the idea for toasting the dry flakes. William Kellogg kept experimenting by adding sugar and eventually toasting corn. After a falling out with John over this addition, in 1906 Will opened Battle Creek Toasted Corn Flake Company. Kellogg's Cornflakes became extremely popular with Americans looking for a quick, convenient breakfast.

Charles William Post was also considered a pioneer in the packaged food industry. After attending what is today the University of Illinois, Post became a manufacturer of agricultural machinery. In 1891, inspired by a visit to the Battle Creek Sanitarium when seeking a cure for work-related stress, Post founded the Postum Cereal Company. In 1898, Grape Nuts made its debut as a cure for appendicitis, consumption, malaria, and loose teeth.

Across the country small- and medium-sized businesses continued to compete alongside large enterprises. Some smaller manufacturing firms managed to survive by making specialized products. For example, in Philadelphia, basic cloth production was taken over by large mills, so smaller textile mills turned almost exclusively to producing high-quality cloth. Many other small businesses such as restaurants, laundries, saloons, newspapers, and companies that produced clothing, jewelry, lumber, leather, and furniture, continued to fare well and were not immediately threatened by competition from large businesses. Most small businesses remained single-owner proprietorships or partnerships.

While many single-owner proprietorships, partnerships, and family-owned businesses operated uninterrupted, a number of small businesses did fail in the face of corporate growth. Corporations could establish sales and distribution networks that broke merchants' reliance on small distributors. A prime example of success gained through the use of these modern marketing techniques is the Singer Sewing Machine Company. Isaac Singer did not invent the sewing machine, but his firm dominated the industry due to Singer's use of door-to-door marketing. Singer offered an installment plan to working-class families so that they could make a series of affordable payments on their purchases. Singer salesmen hawked their products in urban neighborhoods as well as trekked into the countryside to appeal to remote rural residents. Sales to farmers' wives accounted for much of the Singer Company's early success. Singer would also be among the first to market his products by advertising internationally. Office machine and farm equipment manufacturers learned from Singer's innovative techniques that effectively outmaneuvered the competition and captured the market.

Big business

Historian Glenn Porter, in *The Rise of Big Business* (1992), asserts that in the aftermath of the Civil War, "the nation remade itself to accommodate the requirements of the modern corporation." While some might disagree with Porter's assessment, all would agree that big business played a major part in transforming the United States from an agrarian society to an urban, industrial nation. Beginning in the 1880s, the completion of national railroad and telegraph networks and the development of energy technologies, including coal and oil, opened the door for the ascendency of huge corporations.

As the first corporations, railroads developed complex accounting procedures and business practices. To create a system of synchronized nationwide schedules, railroads adopted four standard time zones. By 1899, six railroad lines controlled ninety-five percent of all the railroad tracks in the United States. Through consolidation by combination, they had grown past the point of a big business into a trust. Railroads and telegraph companies were marked by a separation of power between a board of directors who set policy and professional managers who developed production plans with goals for manufacture and marketing. The board of directors controlled the capital – money and materials – and established the policies that guided the firm. Bankers often sat on boards and influenced corporate direction by loaning them money and thereafter placing restrictions on them. Separate ownership and control is perhaps the most striking feature of big business.

Some business owners modeled themselves after banker and investor Andrew Mellon, who bought up enormous blocs of securities to gain control of both the Gulf Oil Company and the Aluminum Company of America (ALCOA). Professional managers synchronized the corporate workplace and supervised the workforce. With sanitized precision reflected in what the business world came to consider proper attire, blue serge suits with tie and white-collar shirt, the managers summarized progress in organizational charts.

Certain businesses, like John D. Rockefeller's Standard Oil, initially grew through "horizontal integration," the control of most or all of the supply of a single commodity or product, in his case kerosene, which, among other things, powered all the gas lamps in the nations. Rockefeller, who hailed from Richford, New York, learned the value of saving money from his mother, a disciplined and religious farm wife. Rockefeller's father provided little guidance for his son, the elder Rockefeller frequently away from home, on the road hawking a "cure" for cancer that he sold for as much as twenty-five dollars a treatment. As a farm boy doing chores for local farmers and raising turkeys for his mother, the young Rockefeller had saved fifty dollars, which his mother persuaded him to lend to a local farmer. When the farmer paid him back after a year with seven percent interest, Rockefeller learned a valuable lesson – he would let his money work for him rather than becoming a servant working for money.

After the family moved to Cleveland, Rockefeller attended a business college for a short time and at the age of sixteen secured his first job as an assistant bookkeeper for a produce shipping firm. He impressed his employers with his diligence and ability to broker complex transportation deals. Eventually, Rockefeller opened his own grain shipping firm at the age of twenty with a neighbor. Soon thereafter, Rockefeller saw opportunity in the new oil-refining industry and became involved in the processing and shipping in the nascent industry. He quickly became quite successful and bought out all of his competitors, coming to control all of the kerosene production in the nation. If Americans needed kerosene, after 1863, when Rockefeller consolidated his horizontal control of the kerosene market, their only choice was to buy it from a Rockefeller-owned company. Rockefeller went on to monopolize the entire American oil industry.

Other industries that produced food, chemicals, machinery, oil, and metals emerged in capital- and energy-intensive areas. Northeastern industries in particular were amenable to high-volume standardized production. These industries tended to integrate "vertically," meaning that they tried (and in many instances succeeded) to control all the aspects of the production and sale of a product, from the supply of raw materials to the manufacture, sales, and distribution of the final product. Some factory owners went as far as coordinating their own tanker fleets to sell their products internationally.

A number of businesses such as railroads, steamships, urban traction (electric streetcars and cable cars), communications (including telephone and telegraph companies), electric lighting, chemicals, petroleum, coal, and the insurance industry began to reach beyond national borders in the 1890s. Coca-Cola and the United Fruit Company are early examples of American companies that started to market their products and invest millions of dollars in

Canada and Mexico to cushion their profits during the Depression of 1893. Companies that constructed one or more foreign plants by the early twentieth century included DuPont, Ford Motor Company, General Electric, and Gillette. By 1917, due largely to U.S. involvement in industry as part of the World War I effort, giant manufacturing firms were concentrated primarily in areas of metals, food processing, transportation equipment, machine making, oil refining, and chemical products.

Mergers and monopolies

On the eve of the Depression of 1893, the United States produced more timber and steel, refined more oil, packed more canned meat, and extracted more gold, silver, coal, and iron than all of its competitors. There were several reasons for this brisk economic growth. First of all, corporations needed a stable and orderly environment in which to flourish. With the exception of isolated labor strikes, the economic climate of the United States met this need. Additionally, the legal structure in the U.S. accommodated the early growth of big business, for there were not yet any regulations in place that checked the growth of businesses. In cases of labor unrest, governmental authorities sided with the employers. Lastly, as business historian Alfred Chandler contends, American businesses thrived because of homegrown resources. But business leaders were also willing to borrow capital and ideas from abroad. Charles Alfred Pillsbury went to Europe and brought the industrial steel dough roller back to his mill in Minneapolis, making his flour popular internationally, and soon-to-be steel magnate Andrew Carnegie imported Henry Bessemer's steel process, the first inexpensive industrial process that allowed the mass production of steel from molten pig iron, from England. Business leaders networked. They exchanged patents, attended expositions and fairs that displayed new products, and read trade and technical journals.

The "merger movement," which began around 1895 and lasted about a decade, accounted for a significant portion of unfettered corporate growth. In their quest for market control, companies bought out competitors and went from big to bigger. When U.S. Steel merged with 158 companies into one organization in 1901, American business began exchanging the entrepreneurial model, one man running the show for a corporate model, with control in the hands of a board of directors.

Labor

Accounts of Progressive politicians and reformers who tamed robber barons, cleaned up cities, purified politics, and paved the way for social welfare fill the pages of early books on Progressive history. Throughout most of the last century, however, students interested in studying workers' lives during the Progressive Era were hard pressed for sources. Labor history did not emerge as a formal field of study until the 1970s. Moreover, when scholars finally did begin to write about workers and their experiences, they focused primarily on native-born men in the organized trades. African American, Mexican American, and women workers received only scant attention. Labor historians quickly realized that most workers – white or otherwise – were simply too busy working long hours to compose memoirs of their lives. Minority workers, many of them illiterate, were relegated to history's most obscure shadows.

While investigative journalists of the era, known at the time of their rise as "muckrakers," cast the first light on workers' experiences, it is only in recent decades that scholarly studies have included workers as actors in what labor historian Melvyn Dubofsky in *Industrialism and the American Worker, 1865–1920* (1996) calls "the drama of reform." The whims of employers and the fluctuation of the open marketplace came to dictate workers' lives. Workers suffered throughout the Depression of 1893, during which the national rate of unemployment spiked in 1894 and remained high for the next three years. In the first year of the depression, the AFL. the nation's largest labor organization, estimated that the number of unemployed workers exceeded three million, and AFL leaders encouraged mass demonstrations of the jobless. The hard times forced AFL President Samuel Gompers to suspend his belief in voluntarism, which held that workers should not rely on the government for support on the shop floor but should strive to be self-sufficient. During the summer of 1893, Gompers asked the city of New York to provide direct cash relief for its unemployed workers. By the end of the year, the AFL demanded that the federal government issue $500 million in paper money to fund public works programs. The calls went unheeded.

Some, like Ohio businessman Jacob S. Coxey, went even further. In the spring of 1894, Coxey, the owner of a successful silica sand company, amassed an "industrial army" of unemployed men to march on Washington, D.C., to demand "employment for every man able and willing to work." The job-creation scheme that Coxey proposed relied on the federal funding of public works to provide jobs for the jobless. Onlookers cheered Coxey and his men as they marched through industrial towns on their way to Washington. Coxey's followers (who numbered fewer than 500 by the time they walked into the Capital) were met by about 1,500 U.S. Army troops. Neither President Grover Cleveland nor Congress responded to Coxey's demands. Instead, police arrested Coxey for trespassing, and the marchers disbanded. Although the government failed to respond in the manner Coxey had hoped, his demonstration did force the government and the public to take notice of the situation. A young observer at the time, sociologist Thorstein Veblen saw significance not in the size of the effort but in the demand for relief dispensed by the federal government. Veblen agreed that the government had a basic responsibility for its citizens' welfare, a radical notion at the time. After serving twenty days in jail, Coxey returned to Ohio, where, as the economy picked up, his support dwindled.

Coincidently, the depression began to lift in 1896, just as prospectors discovered gold in Alaska's Klondike River. The depth and duration of the economic downturn had, however, left workers "bewildered" by the changes that they experienced in the modern workplace. In addition, the simultaneous advent and adaption of technology meant that the sheer pace of life intensified. Synchronized clocks, first introduced at the Fair, were adopted by factories, schools, and even churches. Once back on the job, low wages, long hours, and unsafe workplace conditions topped the workers' list of concerns. Workers lacked even basic safety nets like unemployment insurance if they lost their jobs or workers' compensation if they were hurt or permanently disabled at work. In the closing years of the nineteenth century, working men and women embarked on a long road to improve their situation.

The workplace in transition

Between 1880 and 1900, the ranks of gainfully employed workers in the United States rose by 12 million. The number of workers employed in agricultural pursuits declined, while the number of workers in the garment and tobacco industries doubled. In addition to the increase in the sheer numbers of workers pushing through the factory gates, the rhythm of work changed drastically. For workers who left family farms to venture into the factories or who traveled to the United States onboard a steamship, the slow natural pace of rural life under the sun quickly gave way to the roar of machinery under the glare of artificial lighting. Rather than looking at the sun to keep time, workers had to punch a time clock. In a strange place, surrounded by unfamiliar faces, many workers were directed to learn to perform a sole, monotonous task, one that they performed repeatedly from the time they "clocked in" until the time they "clocked out."

Tensions in the workplace revolved around the workers' desire to control their labor and the managers' efforts to control the workforce. Bosses had little patience for "greenhorns" – newly arrived immigrants who did not understand the expectations of the modern workplace. They were especially irked by the newcomers' diverse ethnic and religious practices. Foremen pushed immigrants to Americanize: learn English, speak it on the job, and strive for efficiency. Likewise, those workers who moved into cities from the country felt alienated.

By the end of the nineteenth century, "sweatshops" employed larger numbers of workers than ever before. Manufacturers provided the raw materials, designed the clothes, and marketed the final product, but manufacturers handed over the actual assembling of the ready-to-wear garments to contractors. The contractors would rent a workspace in a tenement, equip it with sewing machines, and hire approximately ten to twenty workers, usually female immigrants. Each worker performed a specific job. Manufacturers paid contractors a set price for each garment produced, so workers were in turn paid a "piece rate" based on how many finished garments the shop turned out. In the interest of making the highest profits possible, contractors "sweated" their employees by forcing them to work long hours at low wages (Figure 1.2).

New York City quickly came to dominate garment production. Manufacturers in New York benefitted from advances in

Figure 1.2 Lewis Hine photograph of sweatshop workers just finishing their week's work at 87 Ridge Street, New York City, 1908. Library of Congress, Prints & Photographs Division, National Child Labor Committee Collection (LC-DIG-nclc-04456).

transportation, the introduction of commercial-grade machinery, and the specialization of labor. The 1904 opening of the subway system gave workers, even poor ones, a way to commute to their jobs. In turn, the garment industry modernized, moving uptown and consolidating its workforce in larger factories that housed more and faster sewing and cutting machines. Rather than stitching together the whole garment, sewing-machine operators specialized in sleeves, lapels, pockets, buttonholes, and cuffs. In Chicago, a center for the production of men's clothing, manufacturers competed in the open market by producing higher grades of garments using finer material and quality workmanship. Hart, Schaffner and Marx, one Chicago firm, also pioneered a national advertising campaign to promote the image of ready-to-wear garments.

The struggle to organize

In 1877, the same year that Reconstruction ended, the United States experienced its first truly national strike when railroad workers rose up to protest continuous wage cuts in Martinsburg, West Virginia. The strike spread from the railroads to the factories and mills and across the country from Baltimore, Maryland, to San Francisco, California. The use of federal troops by President Hayes against the workers provided the impetus for a more powerful working-class movement that tipped power in favor of the industrialists: their businesses continued to grow; they made alliances with government, and technological advancements that could do the work of one or more persons undercut workers' power. Workers suffered major defeats at the hands of business owners, and labor issues would continue to fester during the coming Progressive Era.

At various times throughout the late nineteenth century, workers acted collectively to try to improve their situations. One of them, the 1886 Haymarket Riot in Chicago's Haymarket Square, proved a dismal failure for labor. It began as a work stoppage on the part of McCormick Reaper workers to protest workplace conditions and secure an eight-hour day. The Noble and Holy Order of the Knights of Labor (KOL), a predecessor to the AFL, promoted "one big union" an inclusive workers' association to which all workers, regardless of skill, could belong, organized a rally in support of the workers' cause. The rally on May 1, 1886, ended peacefully, but two days later, there was a clash prompting police to fire into the crowd, fatally wounding four workers. The next day, a second smaller crowd organized by anarchists and radicals to protest the shootings at the hands of the Chicago police assembled in Haymarket Square. At one point, someone tossed a bomb into a group of policemen, killing eight of them. Police responded by firing wildly into the crowd, killing eight and wounding about 100. A number of the anarchists and radicals were rounded up and indicted for conspiracy. Although to this day no one is sure who threw the bomb, all eight of those charged were convicted. One committed suicide, four were hung, and the remaining four were pardoned in 1893 by Illinois Governor John Peter Altgeld. The Haymarket Affair or Haymarket Massacre, as it came to be known, caused the public to label all members of labor unions and their organizers, even those of the rather innocuous KOL, the largest organization in the country at the time, as radicals or anarchists. Indeed, Haymarket dealt a severe blow to organized labor's reputation, which was further damaged over the next decade with the nationally covered Homestead Steel Strike in 1892 and the Pullman Palace Car Strike in 1894.

In June 1892, steel magnate Andrew Carnegie left the country for an extended vacation in his native Scotland, leaving his manager, Henry Clay Frick, in charge of his twelve-mill Homestead steelworks near Pittsburgh, Pennsylvania. Carnegie aimed to employ a compliant and inexpensive labor force numbering almost 4,000 workers. Frick directed his energy toward breaking up the Amalgamated Association of Iron, Steel, and Tin Workers, a union of about 700 skilled craftsmen trying to organize under the auspices of the AFL. Later that same month, Frick built a barricade to lock the union workers out and called in replacement workers, whom strikers derisively call scabs. He also employed 300 armed guards from the Pinkerton Detective Agency. A battle between the locked-out union workers and the Pinkertons ensued on July 5, killing about a dozen men on both sides and injuring many more. Although the Pinkertons eventually retreated, the conflict dragged on for six months and workers in other Carnegie mills in Pennsylvania struck in sympathy. Finally, at the Carnegie Company's persuasion, the state militia was called in by the governor of Pennsylvania to end the strike. Even though the workers failed to gain any of their demands, they learned a hard lesson about the overwhelming power of capital and were now wary of businessmen's newfound influence on the government at the state level. The bold and brave call for industrial unionism in the steel industry gave rise to a more grandiose idea of industrial unionism throughout the country. For a few weeks, newspaper coverage of the violence at Homestead did much to turn public opinion to the side of labor. However, within a few weeks after the strike ended, Alexander Berkman, an anarchist who had no known connections to the union, tried to assassinate Henry Frick in his New York City office. Although Berkman shot Frick twice and almost killed him, Frick recovered and the general public renounced the labor movement.

Two years later, in the midst of the depression, workers initiated a strike in Pullman, Illinois, where George Pullman, the manufacturer of passenger rail cars that featured sleeping berths, had built a model company town. Under the Pullman system, workers at his Palace Car Company, lived in company-owned housing, attended company-sponsored churches, and sent their children to Pullman-operated schools. Rents in Pullman were approximately twenty-five percent higher than in neighboring Chicago. When Pullman cut wages by as much as forty percent but did not reduce rent or utility rates, a committee of workers tried to discuss the matter with him, but rather than engaging in discussions, he fired three of the workers. The workers appealed to Eugene Debs of the American Railway Union (ARU) for help. Debs's union issued a passionate call for a nationwide boycott against all railroads that used Pullman cars on their lines.

The boycott, along with sympathy strikes involving a quarter of a million workers in a total of twenty-six states, halted the nation's railroad traffic by midsummer. In the meantime, the General Managers' Association, composed of twenty-six Chicago-area railroads, ordered the dismissal of any worker who refused to report to work. The probusiness Cleveland administration allowed mail cars to be attached to the trains so that strikers who halted most of the U.S. mail traffic were charged under a federal injunction that barred interference with mail delivery. Attorney General Richard Olney, who served on the boards of several railroads, obtained a sweeping injunction against the strikers in the federal court system. Federal troops and state militia were called out in six states. Violent clashes between the troops and strikers resulted in the death of at least fifteen workers. In an unlikely move, AFL president Samuel Gompers urged the workers belonging to AFL affiliates to return to work. Debs and his ARU associates landed in jail.

Within five years, the ARU dissolved. For his part, Debs emerged from the clash as a hero among working-class Americans, joined the Socialist Party, and went on to run for the presidency four times. In the three labor conflicts at the end of the century, the employers, with the aid of the authorities, defeated the workers' efforts. The condition of working people would not begin to improve until the government began to step in on the side of the employees instead of the employers.

The Noble and Holy Order of the KOL rose from ashes of the nation's first labor federation, the National Labor Union, by the late 1860s to become the largest labor organization in the country by the 1870s. Founded in secrecy in 1869 by nine Philadelphia tailors and led by Uriah Stephens, the KOL defied characterization and openly supported the concept of industrial unionism. Welcoming almost all workers regardless of occupation, gender, and presumably race meant that the 1880s membership of the KOL was estimated at nearly one million members. Under President Terrance Powderly, the Knights barred Chinese workers, and their constitution excluded all such "parasites" as gamblers, lawyers, bankers, stockbrokers, and liquor dealers. The Knights' goals included abolition of child labor, wage equality for women, integration of black workers, and the institution of a graduated federal income tax. Their Knights' most profound legacy would lie in their call for the eight-hour workday.

Within a decade, the Knights quickly fell out of favor, largely because labor's reputation had been damaged as a result of the labor conflicts. In addition to the Knights helping to organize an abortive strike against Jay Gould's southwestern railroads, they led the general strike on Labor Day, May 1, 1886, which ended in the violent and disastrous Haymarket affair. Blamed for the violence, the Knights disbanded.

As the Knights succumbed to public pressure, the AFL, led by cigar maker Samuel Gompers, emerged. This new organization appealed exclusively to skilled white men who were willing to work for large corporations. The workforce changed over time so that "skilled" workers generally came to mean those who were skilled in types of work associated with the factory workplace. As the Depression of 1893 ended, the demand for collective action by workers intensified and membership increased in both traditional and radical labor unions. The AFL numbered 447,000 members in 1897 then doubled in size to boast almost 868,000 members by 1900.

Working women

By 1890, one in four women in the nation's largest urban areas worked for wages. Historians of American women agree with Alice Kessler-Harris's assertion in *Women Have Always Worked* (1981) that poor minority women have always worked, regardless of marital status. The majority of working women did not, as was commonly assumed, work for "pin money" – extra money to be spent on life's luxuries – but out of economic necessity. Many worked as machine operators in textile plants and commercial laundries, as retail clerks in department stores, and as kitchen or counter help in restaurants. Male employment tended to be concentrated in the "hard industries" like railroads, construction, metal working, and mining.

Toward the end of the nineteenth century, clerical work became one of the most rapidly growing areas of employment for women. Before 1870, the typical business office was small and staffed exclusively by men, but by 1900, one-third of all office workers were mostly young, native-born, white women. Since typewriters were a fairly new invention and had no historical tie to either sex, women took advantage of the opportunity to learn to operate the machines in high school, business schools, or even in classes at the local YWCA. The money in clerical work was good, and since male office clerks were expected to work their way up to become executives, women filled the constant and growing need for clerical workers in the industrial bureaucracies and as civil servants for the government. In addition to typewriters, women learned to operate Dictaphones, mimeograph machines, and adding machines. A white shirtwaist (blouse) worn with a black skirt was considered practical office wear for female clerks. Hair worn in an "updo" completed the look. Artist Charles Dana Gibson immortalized this style in his illustrations that featured the "Gibson Girl" (Figure 1.3).

Women's workforce participation varied by ethnic and racial group. For example, unmarried Polish women in Buffalo, New York typically took jobs in factories or in private homes as domestic servants, while their counterparts from southern Italy tended to become agricultural workers or took in "homework," paid industrial labor performed at home. Female homework allowed women to remain at home where they could work, supervise their children, and perform the household chores that their husbands expected of them. Women homeworkers often gathered in a single sunlit apartment in which they could keep each other company while performing the monotonous handwork. One of the best-known photographers of the era, Lewis Hine, photographed entire families working around the kitchen table assembling artificial flowers, shelling nuts, or doing the finish sewing on garments.

Until 1900, when household technology began to displace them, more women worked as "private household workers" than in any other occupational category. About one-third of all working

Figure 1.3 Drawing from 1903 by artist Charles Dana Gibson entitled "The Weaker Sex" shows four young "Gibson Girls" observing a diminutive man through a magnifying glass. One woman is about to poke him with a hat pin. Library of Congress, Prints & Photographs Division (LC-DIG-ppmsc-05887).

women largely earned their living as domestic servants. In this category, white native-born women were replaced by Irish immigrants and later by African American women from the South. In Philadelphia by the late nineteenth century, ninety percent of all African American women who worked outside the home did so as domestic servants.

In addition to race and ethnicity, marital status tended to determine women's workplace participation. Many Progressive Era Americans felt that married women employed outside the home had overstepped their domestic boundaries. Virginia Yans-McLaughlin's study of Italian women in Buffalo, *Family and Community: Italian Immigrants in Buffalo, 1880–1930* (1982), revealed that the married women almost always helped supplement the family's income doing work deemed acceptable by their husbands either by taking in boarders or by doing seasonal work in canning factories.

By the early 1900s, the Victorian attitude that married women belonged at home gradually began to recede, as an increasing proportion of wives joined the workforce. In 1890, fewer than five percent of married women worked for wages, but by 1920, that percentage had doubled. The historical reality is that working women have always endured lower wages and fewer opportunities than men. Skilled male workers founded unions to demand higher wages and a shorter workday, but those unions took little interest in organizing or recruiting female members.

African American workers

Since the 1970s, historians have chronicled the Great Migration – the mass migration of African Americans from the South to industrial cities in the North and West that began in the pre-World War I years. With their routes predetermined by the railroads, for decades, millions of poor blacks came up out of the poverty-stricken sharecropping South to places like Philadelphia, New York, Chicago, Detroit, and even as far west as San Francisco. At the turn of the twentieth century, ninety percent of all blacks lived in the South. By 1920, one-half of all American blacks lived in northern or midwestern cities.

Once in the North, blacks did not necessarily escape prejudice and discrimination, yet the new arrivals did manage to free themselves from the ever-present threats of lynching and the convict-lease system that haunted them in the Jim Crow South. New scholarship contained in Isabel Wilkerson's *Warmth of Other Suns: The Epic Story of America's Great Migration* (2010) reveals that southern blacks who risked migration were not as illiterate or destitute as many scholars once believed. Surprisingly, the migrants generally experienced higher employment rates and more stable families than northern-born blacks. While the relocated African American men found only a few menial jobs open to them, African American women had an easier time finding domestic work and eventually factory jobs in the North. Life in the North also presented more educational opportunities for black children. Historians have speculated that because African American workers were for the most part absent from the industrial arena until after World War I, white Progressive reformers – men and women – paid little attention to them regardless of their sex. Some middle-class black women did become active Progressive reformers and founded their own race-specific organizations to end segregation and lynching. They too, however, seemed to ignore the plight of black wage workers.

Immigrant workers

Between 1880 and 1920, more than twenty million immigrants entered the United States. By 1900, immigrants comprised at least one-third of the population of Chicago, New York, and Boston. Newcomers from Scandinavia and Central Europe filtered west in search of farmland, while masses of unskilled European peasants, mostly from Southern and Eastern Europe, filled the factories, sweatshops, warehouses, docks, and freight yards of American cities. In small cities, different ethnic groups crowded together into a single neighborhood close to factories or railyards where immigrant men, often along with their children, found employment.

In larger cities, specific immigrant populations – Poles, Italians, Russian Jews – clustered near one another in their own neighborhoods where they managed to maintain at least some aspects of their native-born life and culture. Local merchants spoke the native language, stocked food items that immigrant customers wanted, and extended credit to families. Peddlers hawked meats and produce from their pushcarts that appealed to the tastes of specific immigrant populations, particularly Jews and Italians densely packed in tenement neighborhoods. They sold goods and services ranging from clothes and brushes to dentistry. Here also, traditional religious practices could be reestablished. Ethnic fraternal orders including the Sons of Italy, Polish Falcons, and (Irish) Order of Hibernians provided health benefits and burial insurance in addition to camaraderie. Immigrants constantly relied on networks of friends and family to find jobs and housing.

While the earlier wave of immigrants from Northern and Western Europe, who began to arrive in the 1830s, had generally been welcomed by white native-born Americans, Southern and Eastern European immigrants were not. The latter often became targets of anti-immigrant sentiment, especially as particular ethnic groups developed monopolies over particular trades or services in the urban economy. Italians dominated construction jobs in excavating and tunneling; Eastern European Jews comprised the majority of the labor force in the garment industry; Poles and Central Europeans filled the steel mills and meatpacking plants; and Irish immigrants held longshoremen jobs on the East Coast. One xenophobic group that blamed the Depression of 1893 on competition from immigrant labor founded the American Protective Association, a primarily anti-Catholic organization, in 1894. Social workers and other Progressive reformers recognized the need to protect the vulnerable new workers at home, at work, and out in the streets.

A New Era Dawns

Although those who would become known in the future as the Progressives spent the majority of their time reacting to the ills they perceived around them, the nature of their responses has enabled historians to regard the era named in their honor as one characterized by optimism. By the early twentieth century, modernization had crept into virtually every aspect of American life. Nowhere could this be better seen than in the world of leisure. By the early 1900s, new forms of entertainment attracted millions of working-class people who spent their hard-earned money on commercial leisure. For the first time in history, workers could devote part of their days to patronize dance halls, nickelodeons, and other forms of entertainment. Boxing, baseball, and other sports grew from games, played by children and young adults, to tremendously popular big businesses.

Before movie houses were built, single-reel movies were projected in storefronts (vacant stores converted to temporary theaters) across the country by the end of the nineteenth century, but the idea of developing movies as a separate form of entertainment grew out of the penny arcade or amusement parlor. The kinetoscope, or moving-picture "peep" show, proved more popular with arcade goers than slot machines, fortune-telling machines, automatic scales, muscle-testing devices, or even phonographs in largely male commercial entertainment districts. Edwin S. Porter's film *The Great Train Robbery* became a huge hit from the time it previewed in 1903. John P. Harris and Harry Davis opened the first theater designed for the purpose of showing motion pictures in McKeesport, Pennsylvania, in 1905, using the seats from a closed opera house. Movies theaters, called nickelodeons, after the nickel admission price patrons were charged, were extremely popular in working-class tenement neighborhoods where immigrant mothers sent their children on Saturdays to watch silent movies all afternoon. One study estimated that in 1910, approximate one-quarter of New York City's residents attended movie theaters. Although "nickel madness" swept through urban areas in the early 1900s, the middle and upper classes at first did not patronize the movies out of concern for their respectability. Instead reformers tried to have theater owners' licenses revoked.

Vaudeville theater, descended from the minstrel shows and saloon burlesque of the prior century, became one of the most popular forms of American entertainment of the early 1900s. Tied to a central booking agency, the vaudeville circuit boasted over 2,000 theaters throughout United States and Canada. Highly paid performers used railroads to travel between the cities in which they played and booked acts over the telephone and telegraph lines. Performances consisted of nine acts that were played twice a day. The acts capitalized on sex appeal and humorous ethnic skits, with writers often referencing local and cultural values in cities and towns in their scripts. Ragtime, the so-called folk music of the American city, accompanied the popular productions. Ragtime melodies were well suited for brass bands and energetic dances. The songs also provided lively and raucous lyrics suited to musical comedies on stage. In cities with large Jewish populations, Yiddish theater attracted large audiences.

In general, young immigrant workers were excited by the prospects of modern life in turn-of-the-century America. They began to patronize amusements aimed specifically at the younger working class. With their boardwalks filled with games and shows to the rides that were spectacular to the senses, amusement parks eventually began to cater to the middle class and became so popular that by 1919, there were more than 1,500 amusement parks in the United States. The parks offered a secure public meeting place that afforded young people a chance to escape for a few hours or a day the lack of privacy in the tenements. Young women and men previously allowed away from home only in large groups or accompanied by chaperones now began to date without supervision. The casual atmosphere at the parks freed adult minds from the stress of daily life and allowed imaginations to wander.

Many working-class Americans visited museums, libraries, and music halls on their days off. One of Andrew Carnegie's most tangible philanthropic efforts supported the building of free public libraries. With literacy rates on the upswing, more Americans than ever before could read and write. By 1900, approximately ninety-five percent of native-born whites, about ninety percent of immigrants, and almost half of all African Americans were literate. Carnegie wanted to provide access to education and opened more than 1,900 libraries across the country. A famous editorial cartoon of the day posits Andrew Carnegie as a Siamese twin with one-half of him building libraries and the other half cutting the wages of his workers (Figure 1.4).

Other behaviors began to change as well. Mass production not only employed tremendous numbers of workers but made consumer products such as canned milk and food, packaged meats, soap, cigarettes, cereals, and matches readily available for workers to purchase. Ready-made clothes, appliances, and radios rounded out the list. Henry Ford prided himself on the fact that his workers

FORTY-MILLIONAIRE CARNEGIE IN HIS GREAT DOUBLE ROLE.
AS THE TIGHT-FISTED EMPLOYER HE REDUCES WAGES THAT HE MAY PLAY PHILANTHROPIST AND GIVE AWAY LIBRARIES, ETC.

Figure 1.4 Cartoon of Andrew Carnegie representing the conflicting roles played by the wealthiest American capitalists, 1892. *Source*: "Forty-Millionaire Carnegie in his Great Double Role," *The Saturday Globe*, July 9, 1892.

could afford to buy the cars that they produced. Marketing became a science. Advertising professionals began to appeal to all types of consumers, including those of the working class, even the Americanizing children of immigrants.

In the closing decade of the nineteenth century, the country had learned a hard lesson. Ordinary Americans learned that a national slump in the economy translated into personal financial vulnerability. The mass protests, social and political radicalism, labor strikes, and violence that marred the final years of the century seemed, however, to be quickly forgotten in the dawn of the new century. Supported by an increasing number of Americans, a new generation of hopeful reformers emerged who would fundamentally change the relationship between the American people and the government. These were the Progressives. The idea of direct government action that previously had been associated with modern, industrial societies in Europe contributed to the intellectual foundation for the broad-based movement that in the United States would come to be called Progressivism.

It would not be until the 1930s, however, when in the grips of the Great Depression, that the federal government under President Franklin Delano Roosevelt (FDR) finally adopted policies that assumed some of the responsibility for working peoples' welfare inside and outside of the workplace. Several fundamental questions, then, beg answers. What changes had occurred between the 1890s and the 1930s to create the modern welfare state? And how much credit did the Progressives deserve for having created it? But before we can answer these questions, we need to answer the most pressing question of all: who were the Progressives?

2

Saving Society
Who Were the Progressives?

For years, historians have discussed and even debated who the Progressives were. Glenda Gilmore's *Who Were the Progressives?* (2002) presents one of the most recent attempts to arrive at an understanding of this diverse group of reformers. Gilmore and others who came before her recognize that in the simplest sense, whether they were settlement workers, professionals, business-men, workers, politicians, or members of clubs or other special interest groups, Progressives were mostly middle-class women and men seeking to better a society they perceived as suffering from the pitfalls of industrialization.

Writing about the California Progressives in the early 1960s, George Mowry observed that Progressivism coincided with a prosperous economic climate in which the notions of progress and modernity challenged the social order. Since the tactics and goals of the Progressives differed, it becomes necessary to identify the different Progressive groups and the causes with which they identified. In general, however, and regardless to which group or category they belonged, Progressives were products of their time, and, their relatively prosperous circumstances bred optimism,

The Progressives: Activism and Reform in American Society, 1893–1917, First Edition.
Karen Pastorello.
© 2014 John Wiley & Sons, Inc. Published 2014 by John Wiley & Sons, Inc.

fostering a spirit of hope that characterized the era. The Progressives may have approached problems differently, but most of them emerged as energetic activists who saw real possibility for improvement in the future.

The Muckrakers

Crusading writers and reporters comprised the most profound and influential calls for reform. By the turn of the century, several of the most talented reformers began to use the still-new technology of photography to document living and working conditions. In 1890, Jacob Riis, a Danish-born police reporter turned social reformer, published the widely popular book *How the Other Half Lives* to detail the impoverished situations of tenement dwellers for middle- and upper-class readers because, as Riis explained, "one half of the world does not know how the other half lives." The vivid ghetto scenes that Riis captured immediately came to the attention of Theodore Roosevelt, then serving on the Civil Service Commission in Washington. Shortly after the book's publication, Roosevelt dashed off a note to Riis: "I have read your book and I have come to help." Within five years, that offer to help became reality when Roosevelt found himself back in his native New York serving as Police Commissioner and working closely with Riis. Through their work together, Roosevelt grew to consider Riis "the most useful citizen in America" (Figure 2.1).

For a historical moment, investigative journalists and photographers, otherwise known as muckrakers, seemed to personify Progressivism in its early stage. Hoping that their exposés would effect social change, in addition to probing greed and corruption in businesses and government, the muckrakers investigated many issues related to life in urban areas, including child labor, inhumane prison conditions, systems of justice, prostitution, women's inequality, the drug trade, the tax system, the insurance industry, exploitation of natural resources, and beef, oil, and tobacco trusts. Muckrakers' shocking photographs and scathing accounts in books, as well as in newspapers and magazines

Figure 2.1 Portrait of Jacob Riis, author of *How the Other Half Lives* (1900). Library of Congress, Prints & Photographs Division (LC-USZ62-47078).

informed middle- and upper-class readers who otherwise had little knowledge of the problems associated with industrialization. Ultimately, these journalists and photographers, men as well as women, wielded an enormous amount of influence on policy makers and legislators.

It was none other than Theodore Roosevelt who inadvertently coined the term *muckraker* during a 1906 speech at the dedication of a new congressional office building when he likened this new breed of journalists to the pilgrim in Puritan writer John Bunyan's seventeenth-century classic *Pilgrim's Progress*. Roosevelt observed that there were some journalists who raked the muck from earth always looking down, therefore rejecting a celestial crown. Roosevelt agreed that muckrakers helped to advance Progressive causes, but he also believed that they sometimes went too far with their caustic assessments on and pessimistic views of American society.

Advances in typing and printing technology at this time enabled mass distribution of inexpensive newspapers and magazines, the very vehicles in which muckrakers presented their findings. The communications empires created by newspapermen including Horace Greeley of the *New York Herald Tribune*, Joseph Pulitzer of the *New York World*, and magnate William Randolph Hearst changed the worldviews of literate Americans. The communications leaders oversaw and financed investigations that probed the injustices of life in the new urban society. In New York, Pulitzer's *World* and Hearst's *Tribune* competed for articles detailing the Spanish American War in 1898. The sensationalism contained in these papers and their imitators led to the nickname the "Yellow Press" after the popular Yellow Kid color comic strip. This sentiment easily transferred to the domestic arena.

In Boston in 1892, Irish immigrant Samuel S. McClure founded one of the first magazines especially intended to provide a forum for the muckrakers' exposés. By October 1902, the sales of his *McClure's* magazine soared following the publication of Lincoln Steffen's account of political bossism in "Tweed Days in St. Louis," a reference to Democrat William Tweed's control of local politics in New York City. Many considered the article the first muckraking piece in the nation. Other periodicals, including *Munsey's*, *Cosmopolitan*, *Everybody's*, *Pearson's*, *Success*, and even *Ladies' Home Journal* scrambled to publish tantalizing reports of their own. *McClure's* published compelling pieces written by some of the most well-known muckrakers, including Ida Tarbell's exposé of Standard Oil, Lincoln Steffen's *Shame of the Cities*, and Ray S. Baker's series attacking the railroad trusts.

Lincoln Steffens was born in California in 1866 and moved to New York, where he worked as a police and financial news reporter for the one of the city's leading dailies, the *New York Evening Post*, from 1892 to 1897. He learned his way around Wall Street and the slums of the Lower East Side and became a good friend of Police Commissioner Theodore Roosevelt in the process.

In 1901, Steffens joined the prestigious *McClure's* magazine as managing editor. In one of his most memorable exposés, "Shame of the Cities," which *McClure's* published in 1904 as a serialized piece, with readers anxiously awaiting the next monthly installment, Steffens laid out the results of his tour of St. Louis, Minneapolis, Pittsburgh, Chicago, Philadelphia, and New York. In this purportedly firsthand account, he described the rampant and systematic political corruption and inequality that characterized city life. According to Steffens, political parties raised money to dispense to the urban masses – in the form of gifts, bribes, and favors – in exchange for their votes to keep "machine" candidates in office. Much of Steffens's account actually was based on information he had summarized from local papers. In this piece, he did, however, create enduring stereotypes of ruthless favor-dispensing city bosses and the overzealous reformers who tried to oppose them. Moreover, Steffens's vivid descriptions of urban life highlighted the stark challenges facing urban residents and attempted to prod those who sought reform into action. As Chicago, for example, made its meteoric rise to the nation's second largest city, muckrakers exposed its unseemly underworld. In Steffens's estimation, Chicago was "first in violence, deepest in dirt; loud, lawless, unlovely, ill-smelling, new; an overgrown gawk of a village, the teeming touch among cities. Criminally it was wide open; commercially it was brazen; and socially it was thoughtless and raw."

Exposés of political corruption went beyond the local level to reach the halls of the U.S. Senate. David Graham Phillips's 1906 series of articles in *Cosmopolitan* on the "Treason of the Senate" placed the Upper House at the center of a major drive by Progressive Era reformers to weaken the influence of large corporations and other major financial interests on government policy making. Direct popular election of senators fit perfectly within this call to bring government closer to the people. After St. Louis district attorney Joseph Folk was elected governor of Missouri in 1904, he joined Detroit mayor Hazen Pingree and Wisconsin governor Robert LaFollette to sponsor a Constitutional amendment calling for the popular election of U.S. senators rather than by state

legislators. Although the proposed amendment met with resistance from a powerful bloc of Southern senators, it finally passed
in 1913.

While Steffens and Phillips directed their energies toward
revealing political corruption, other muckrakers sought to uncover
other ills plaguing American life. Following his graduation from
what is now Michigan State University and after a brief stint at
the University of Michigan law school, Ray Stannard Baker began
his career in 1892 as a journalist with the twice daily newspaper
The Chicago News Record. There he covered both the march of
Coxey's "Army" and the establishment of a workers' strike fund
by Alderman Hopkins to keep the strikers and their families from
starving during the long Pullman strike. By the time he joined
McClure's staff in 1898, Baker possessed a sense of empathy for
the nation's industrial workers, particularly unemployed ones.
He spent a great deal of his time at the magazine detailing the
corruption of railroad companies. Within a decade, he wrote
an influential book investigating lynching as a prelude to other
journalistic studies of the condition of African Americans. Baker's
Following the Color Line (1908), which spared neither the residents
of the North nor the South when it came to racial prejudice,
caught the attention of reformers across the nation.

Ida Tarbell, one of the few female muckrakers, grew up near
the oil fields of northwestern Pennsylvania, where her father had
a prosperous business manufacturing oil holding tanks and eventually became a refiner. Things were going nicely for her family
before the implementation of the South Improvement scheme,
a collaborative effort led by John D. Rockefeller and railroad
interests to eliminate all competition in the oil industry that
devastated all of the small oil-related businesses in the region.
The adolescent Tarbell watched as her father's business and those
of her neighbors went into decline. Despite her families' hardships, Tarbell went on to graduate from Allegany College and
taught school for a few years. She then traveled to Europe
to gather material to write a biography of Madame Roland, a
leader of the French Revolution. When she returned to the
United States, Tarbell was hired by *McClure's*. After researching

Rockefeller's background for more than two years, the forty-five-year-old Tarbell single-handedly exposed his unethical business practices in a series of articles published in *McClure's*, beginning in December 1902 and eventually in book form as *The History of the Standard Oil Trust* (1904). Tarbell's work was so widely read and influential that Rockefeller hired a publicity agent to repair his damaged reputation (Figure 2.2).

While working for the Chicago Bureau of Charities, radical journalist Algie Martin Simons was among the first to chronicle the plight of workers who packed diseased meat for public sale in articles first published in the *Journal of American Sociology* and then in *Packingtown* (1899). Moved by such probing studies, and desiring to provoke reform, an obscure twenty-eight-year-old

Figure 2.2 Ida Minerva Tarbell at the turn of the century, about the time she began to expose the corrupt practices of John D. Rockefeller's Standard Oil. Library of Congress, Prints & Photographs Division (LC-USZ62-53912).

writer named Upton Sinclair elaborated on the inhumane conditions that largely immigrant workers faced in Chicago's stockyards, and the depredations suffered by their families, in book form, the now-classic novel *The Jungle* (1905). Sinclair's alcoholic father moved the family from Baltimore to Brooklyn when he was ten. Although his parents lived in a series of cheap apartments and struggled financially, the young Sinclair spent time with his affluent grandparents and developed his Socialist beliefs in reaction to their lifestyle. He later explained that witnessing the extremes between his parents' and his grandparents' lifestyles led him to socialism. Academically gifted, Sinclair entered New York's City College at the age of fourteen. By the following year, Sinclair had published a boys' story and earned the money that would put him through college. After graduating at the age of seventeen, he went on to graduate school. While Sinclair was doing graduate work at Columbia University in 1904, the editor of *Appeal to Reason*, a popular Socialist weekly, convinced him to write a novel about wage slavery. Sinclair spent almost two months in Chicago's Packingtown during a bitter stockyard strike, where he chronicled the plight of the workers. Even though Sinclair's primary intent in writing the novel was to elicit sympathy for poor industrial workers, *The Jungle* is remembered more for its graphic descriptions of the unsanitary, even revolting, practices and standards of industrial food processing. Nevertheless, Sinclair earned a reputation as a social crusader, and his book resulted in government intervention into the meatpacking industry.

Muckraking reached its zenith around 1906, when the journalists' articles successfully convinced government reformers to initiate a number of antitrust suits. Ida Tarbell's work resulted in the Department of Justice hauling the Standard Oil Trust into federal court in 1911. Ray S. Baker's reports increased the regulatory actions against the railroads and resulted in the passage of the Hepburn Act, which enabled the Interstate Commerce Commission to regulate railroad rates. Muckraking crusades by Simons, Sinclair, and a multitude of others led to the establishment of the United States Department of Agriculture and the passage of the Pure Food and Drug Act, while David Graham Phillips's series on political corruption and greed in the Senate in Hearst's *Cosmopolitan* helped lead to the Seventeenth Amendment establishing the direct election of senators. In 1910, however, as muckraking magazines saturated the readers' market and the government began to take over some of their investigative functions, their appeal waned. By 1912, only a few muckrakers still challenged corruption and even fewer offered practical solutions.

From Religious Roots to Secular Salvation

In addition to the muckrakers' exposés, religious zeal contributed to the rise of Progressivism. The economic hardships that began during the depression in 1893 intensified deep-seated tensions that accompanied the rise of industrial urbanism in the late nineteenth century. Some of the controversy was closely linked to religion. Especially troubling were the perceived disparities between the nation's fundamental political and moral traditions and the stark realities of big-city life. Principal custodians of these traditions, the native-born, Protestant, old-stock Americans, most of them members of the middle and upper reaches of society (especially business and professional families), distrusted the massive increase in immigrant populations in the nation's largest cities.

Hailing primarily from Southern and Eastern Europe, including the countries of Italy, Poland, Russia, and the Austrian-Hungarian Empire, many of the recent immigrants were Catholics or Jews. Catholic churches, with their parochial schools, orphanages, weekly newspapers, hospitals, and cemeteries, anchored many of the new or growing immigrant communities. Some old-stock Americans feared that the primary allegiance of the urban Catholics was to their churches and the Pope in Rome rather than to their newly adopted city and the President of the United States. In addition, a substantial number of Jews chose to make their homes in northeastern and midwestern cities at the time. German-Jews had tended to immigrate to the United States earlier than most other European Jews, and in the aftermath of the Civil War, many of the former had established successful businesses as merchants, publishers, or factory owners. Those Jews who came later, migrating mainly from Central and Eastern Europe, were generally less prosperous and often worked in unskilled positions after coming to America. The German-Jews who owned Chicago's largest clothing factory, Hart, Schaffner and Marx, hired large numbers of Eastern European Jews after they began to arrive in the 1890s. Admirers of the rural past, many of whom were white, middle-class Protestants, felt threatened by the escalating power of the Catholic Church, the influence of Jewish tradition, and the potential erosion of the traditional Protestant authority.

Fundamentalists

Whether recent arrivals or native-born Americans, many turned to religion to confront the myriad of problems facing them. Born in Iowa in 1862 and orphaned by the age of twelve, Ashley "Billy" Sunday embarked on a remarkable religious career by the time he was in his early thirties. The former baseball player turned revivalist captivated crowds with his passionate turn-of-the-century fundamentalist sermons. Sunday's ultraorganized crusades and zany antics propelled him from a Midwest gospel ministry to national fame by 1908. Headquartered in Chicago, Sunday amassed an impressive organization complete with agents, musicians, and their personal masseurs. As Sunday and company toured towns and cities across the nation, an army of ushers collected millions of dollars in donations from sinners and curious spectators alike, while a massive souvenir stand stood at the back of the temporary wooden tabernacles. Sunday and his team staged over 500 revivals before he died in 1935, having reached an estimated 100 million people. He became so popular with middle-class Americans that a few newspaper commentators encouraged him to run for president on the Republican ticket in the 1920s. Billy Sunday tried to remedy the problems inherent in American society by saving souls. According to his simple message, sin, not society, was the problem, and the individual, not the state, was the solution.

Christian fundamentalists like Sunday believed that each person was responsible for his or her own salvation. In 1910, a group of Christian theologians published a twelve-volume series of essays entitled *The Fundamentals* to try to persuade readers to get back to the basics of conservative Christianity. The essays emphasized the necessity of a conversion experience. Thanks to a grant from brothers Milton and Lyman Stewart of Union Oil Company, adherents distributed three million copies of work, mostly to churches. Religious fundamentalism's traditional and seemingly solid emphasis on Bible basics made it irresistible to many Americans trying to grapple with the transition to modernity.

Progressives, however, adamantly disagreed with Sunday and the Fundamentalists who placed the blame for sin on the individual rather than on society. Instead, the reformers felt that it was their responsibility to protect the unfortunate from the ravages of unmitigated capitalism. It was society that needed to be saved – and it was up to them to save it – if there was to be any hope for the individual.

The Social Gospelers

Inspired by the theology of Ohio's Congregationalist Reverend William Gladden, the Social Gospel, a broad program of reform that merged the sacred and the secular, emerged in the late nineteenth century in response to the profound problems associated with industrialization. His sermons held out the possibility of social change necessary in a sinful urban industrial society by following Christian doctrine. For example, he encouraged parishioners to consider the labor situation in the industrial centers of the day. Gladden believed that employers should treat their workers less as parts of the industrial machine and more as members of a larger Christian family – the notion of a "Social Gospel." He was probably the first religious official to support the unionization of workers.

Although both of them were inspired by religious movements, the Fundamentalists and the Social Gospelers attempted
to counter corruption and greed through distinctly different
approaches. While the Fundamentalists felt that individuals
should take responsibility for their own actions, Christian Progressives following the Social Gospel assumed the moral responsibility for the urban poor and responded by performing active
charity work.

If Gladden was the theologian of the Social Gospel, other
Protestant clergymen like Walter Rauschenbusch were its practitioners. Rauschenbusch, a Baptist minister and leading propo-
nent of Christian social action, started a ministry in Rochester,
New York, later moving to New York City to work directly with
the impoverished in the Hell's Kitchen neighborhood. Appalled
by the low wages and deplorable living conditions of those whom
he served, Rauschenbusch rejected the idea that poverty was the
product of sinful behavior on the part of the individual, such as
drinking or gambling, and instead insisted that devout Christians
adopt Jesus's concern for the poor by working in concert toward
the alleviation of poverty. Wherever Rauschenbusch went, he
tended to the sick and the poor, the working class, and the elderly.
He, like many other Progressives, hoped to improve society by
stepping into communities to enact change, in his words to offer
"friendship and hope to men of all races and creeds." Followers
of the Social Gospel combated employers' exploitation of workers
and abuses such as the use of child labor and encouraged the
construction of better working-class housing. Some of adherents
of the Social Gospel went on to found the Salvation Army, which
aimed specifically at helping the homeless and the needy.

Intellectual inspiration

While the origins of benevolent work often stemmed from religious belief, the foundation for later Progressive reform activism
included an intellectual approach that embraced the power of
new ideas. Urban settlement-house leaders allied closely with the
leading philosophers of the day, particularly William James, John

67

Dewey, and George Herbert Mead. James, a Harvard University philosophy professor and his student Mead, advanced the uniquely American theory of pragmatism, which emphasized applied knowledge rather than abstract concepts. Pragmatists stressed the importance of using practical action to press for societal reform. According to James and his followers, the value of any reform could be determined by it effects, the changes it actually effected. Empirical research could help determine how a society really functioned, both before and after the application of a particular reform, and the new social sciences – sociology, anthropology, political science, and economics – furnished the methods necessary to measure the level of success. John Dewey, who had connections to both the University of Chicago and Columbia University, saw public schools as potential agents for social change. After studying the work of the local settlement houses, both James and Dewey encouraged their students to reject the popular Social Darwinist notion that individuals in a competitive society should be left on their own to sink or swim according to their merits and capabilities.

In short, the philosophers agreed with the reformers – the poor were victims of their environment and needed help to negotiate the perils of urban industrial life. The job of reformers, then, was to create positive changes to solve the problems of a democratic society. Following the lead of their European counterparts, American reformers eventually sought the assistance of the government to right the wrongs of American life through the drafting and enactment of new legislation and social policies, and, in the process of applying knowledge to empower a growing class of poor workers and their families, created the welfare state that we know today.

From Charity Cases to Social Work

Just as icy spring rains began to melt the record snows of 1893, a homeless eighteen-year-old woman, weak with hunger, collapsed on a street in downtown Rochester. National suffrage leader and Rochester resident Susan B. Anthony would later recall at the founding of the Rochester Women's Educational and Industrial Union in 1893, "There being no other place for her to go," patrolmen carried the unconscious woman to their station to revive. Although similar incidents had escaped public notice, this one was different. When Anthony, Rochester's most distinguished woman citizen, learned that the destitute young woman awoke in a jail cell, she was incensed. At that moment, Anthony stoically pledged to safeguard the welfare of the city's poor women. Within a matter of days, she traveled to neighboring Buffalo to meet with Harriet Townsend, president of the Buffalo Women's Educational and Industrial Union, to seek advice about how Buffalo residents dealt with similar circumstances. Despite Rochester's long-standing tradition of political activism and benevolent sentiments, the homeless woman's case exposed a raw reality: existing charity organizations fell short of remedying the situations of the neediest citizens, who more often than not were its women.

No one group worked more diligently toward saving underprivileged urban dwellers than did social workers. As a group, social workers were the driving force behind many crucial changes during the Progressive Era. The evolution of social work as a profession can be traced to the formal organization of charity workers.

By the end of the nineteenth century, so-called charity workers in cities across the country included upper- and middle-class women and men, missionaries, and ministers who concentrated on helping the indigent poor, often the victims of the greed of others. The charity workers established missionary societies, orphanages, and homes for women. They also coordinated campaigns to try to improve public sanitation and to eliminate prostitution, alcohol consumption, and gambling. Some charity workers distinguished between the deserving and undeserving poor, but, in any case, by the early 1870s, many of the charity workers took it upon themselves to act as "friendly visitors" to the homes of the poor and soon realized that abject poverty was rarely the fault of a moral or character flaw but instead the result of not being able to find decent-paying, steady work. Therefore, charity workers resolved that poverty could only be eradicated by planned intervention, rather than solely by financial relief alone. Benevolent volunteers established countless independent and church-affiliated charities. In 1877, Buffalo became the first city to organize its agencies under the auspices of a single agency, the Charity Organization Society. Over the next twenty years, virtually every American city hosted some form of a centralized charity organization.

Cleveland's charity structure typified that of other cities. By March 1881, benevolent workers in that city founded the Charity Organization Society to coordinate service delivery and prevent recipients from becoming "sadly pauperized in spirit." The society's workers acted as advocates for the poor, calling for a day nursery to care for the children of working mothers, and the maintenance of a job registry. To address the wide array of urban philanthropy, a central system of record keeping was instituted so that the names of those who received relief could be systematically recorded to discourage recipients from receiving relief from more than one agency. Workers tried to register the names of all those who received aid from any source and called for cooperation among charities by urging agencies to send beggars and others in need to the society. Certificates of relief were awarded to persons deemed "needy and worthy." Annual society memberships of five dollars or life memberships of $100 supported the society's work.

Women Progressives

Club women

In many cities, women who had initially organized clubs to discuss literature and to study art ultimately turned their attention to social activism. One such organization, the Women's Christian Temperance Union (WCTU), provided the reform model for many other "clubwomen" to follow. The WCTU went beyond its initial crusade to ban alcohol to fulfill its comprehensive "do everything" motto. WCTU leaders like Frances Willard encouraged members to seek gender equality for American women.

Frances Willard was born in 1839 in Churchville, New York, to strict Methodist parents who took her to Illinois as a child. At the age of sixteen, the intellectually curious Willard grew frustrated by the constraints placed on "proper" women and girls in Victorian America, including tight corsets and long skirts and the lack of sound educational opportunities offered to them. Following her education at a Methodist college, the unconventional Willard broke her engagement to a deceptive suitor and entered the teaching profession. After working her way up to a position as an administrator at a local college, at which her former fiancé became president, she resigned. Unhappy and at a low point financially, Willard aligned herself with the women's movement and was elected vice president of the Association for the Advancement of Women, an organization that sought to improve women's education and to facilitate their entry in the professions. After participating in a temperance demonstration in 1874, Willard became the corresponding secretary for the Chicago chapter of the newly formed WCTU. Willard had been involved in the temperance movement as a young adult in Evanston, Illinois, taking the abstinence pledge in 1856.

In 1877, Willard became involved with Dwight L. Moody's evangelical crusades. Although Willard and Moody both preached evangelical temperance, they disagreed on women's place in society. Moody sought to save souls by holding separate meetings for men and women, a practice with which Willard took issue. Moody also disapproved of Willard's connections with women outside of evangelical circles. The two were unable to resolve their differences, and by 1879, Willard had broken with Moody.

At the 1879 national convention of the WCTU, Willard was elected president. She advocated for the support of prison reform, public kindergartens, day care for the children of working mothers, and facilities to aid dependent and neglected children. She also encouraged support for industrial job training for young women as well as for organized labor in their fight for the eight-hour (maximum) workday. Willard worked to abolish prostitution and the spread of venereal disease. In 1893, just as her health began to deteriorate, the WCTU passed an anti-lynching resolution.

Willard and the WCTU laid the foundation for some of the twentieth century's most important reform agendas and women's central place in the struggle toward these reforms. By the late 1800s, the WCTU grew to become the largest and most important women's organization in the nation, one that along the way embraced a wide range of social legislation, including advocating for mandatory health and safety measures in the workplace and woman's suffrage.

As the WCTU and many other women's clubs affiliated with a national umbrella organization, the General Federation of Women's Clubs (GFWC), after its founding in 1890, so-called club women largely devoted their efforts to reform work. Progressive Era historian Maureen Flanagan has detailed the crucial place of Chicago women in shaping urban political reform in *Seeing with Their Hearts* (2002). By the early 1900s, the GFWC headquartered in Washington D.C., included more than 500 women's clubs, making it the largest grassroots women's organization in the Progressive Era.

For all its good intent, the GFWC was a racially exclusive organization, one that failed to accept black or Jewish women or to fight for their rights. Shut out of the white, middle-class women's clubs, influential African American women of the day such as Harriet Tubman and Ida Wells-Barnett led the struggle against lynching and segregation under the auspices of their own organization, the National Association of Colored Women (NACW), founded in 1896. Poor and working-class blacks sometimes accused middle-class black clubwomen who wanted to address society's ills as well as uplift their race of possessing a somewhat elitist attitude. Jewish women, too, founded their own organization, the National Council of Jewish Women, to attain rights for women and children, to assist Jewish immigrants, and to advocate for social welfare.

72

Settlement workers advocate to social justice

At the same time that women's clubs were forming coalitions and adopting new agendas for reform, a new breed of reformers that included charity workers, clergymen, settlement workers, and ultimately professional social workers also came to view the social environment rather than individual circumstances as a starting point for reform. Private and public charities continued to serve selective populations, but support for more comprehensive, publicly funded social programs was growing. Social workers, in particular, employed a secular scientific approach to curb society's ills. Since social workers saw the poor as victims of their circumstances, the key to alleviating their plight, they reasoned, lay in improving their neighborhoods and workplaces. This commitment to social justice – the notion that everyone deserves equal economic, political, and social rights – gave rise to settlement houses. What amounted to a transition from nineteenth-century charity work to twentieth-century social welfare work gave rise to the development of professional social work.

Building on the strong tradition of women's activism in Chicago, a young woman named Jane Addams combined the idealism of the Social Gospelers and the realism of pragmatist philosophers to become a major force in initiating the Progressive movement. (Laura) Jane Addams was born to John Huy Addams and Sarah Weber Addams on September 6, 1860, in Cedarville, Illinois. Her father, a prosperous miller, went on to serve sixteen years in the state senate, served as a Union officer in the Civil War, and became a friend of Abraham Lincoln. After Addams's mother died when Jane was only two years old, she became extremely close to her father. Although he supported the idea of higher education for his daughter, when Jane proposed attending Smith College in the East, John Addams refused to send her there because he wanted her to stay closer to home. In 1877, Jane enrolled at nearby Rockford Female Seminary (now Rockford College in Rockford, Illinois), graduating as the valedictorian in 1881. While a student at Rockford, Addams rejected the soul-saving Christian evangelicalism sweeping the Midwest at the time, instead envisioning a secular version of a more cooperative democracy that demanded civic action and social rights.

Within weeks after she graduated, Addams had to endure the sudden death of her father while the two were on vacation together. In 1882, Jane had surgery to correct a congenital spinal defect. From 1883 to 1885, accompanied by her stepmother, Addams toured Europe and visited London's poor neighborhoods. In 1887, Addams returned to Europe with her college friend, Ellen Gates Starr. During their trip, the two companions visited Toynbee Hall, a settlement house founded in 1884 in the slums of London's East End to eradicate poverty among the poor Jewish and Irish dwellers. By the time Addams and Starr arrived, Toynbee Hall had attracted a number of notable social activists. What Addams saw at Toynbee Hall gave her life direction.

By the late nineteenth century, in England, the wealthy and the poor rarely interacted with each other. In fact, a mutual distrust had developed between the two groups. So, in order to reestablish contact with the needy and to learn firsthand about their problems, affluent reformers took up residence in settlement houses located in the hearts of poor and troubled neighborhoods, and in so doing literally "settled" among the poor.

Settlement residents worked toward solving social problems by creating a climate of "mutual understanding." Settlement workers at Toynbee Hall were often ministers or "university men" – recent graduates from Oxford University who provided a daily round of cultural, recreational, and social activities for the poor in settlement neighborhoods. The settlement house provided a base, so that some settlement workers also went out into the neighborhood and into homes of poor urban residents. Observing the work being done at Toynbee Hall, Jane Addams reflected upon the failure of more prosperous Americans to deal with the problems of immigration, industrialization, urbanization, and poverty in general.

Fresh from her European tour, when she returned to the United States, Addams used her inheritance to purchase the dilapidated mansion of Charles Hull and settled on Halsted Street in Chicago's Nineteenth Ward. The working-class neighborhood around Hull House was teeming with poor recently arrived immigrants. With the 1889 founding of Hull House, and imbued with her clear vision of stewardship, Addams helped to forward the settlement-house movement in the United States and soon established herself as the country's leading social reformer.

Although Hull House quickly became the most influential settlement house in the United States, it was not the first. In 1886, Stanton Coit, who visited Toynbee Hall a few years before Addams, founded Neighborhood Guild (later known as University Settlement) on New York's Lower East Side, hoping to regenerate the neighborhood. To avoid religious barriers, Coit and other early settlement leaders emphasized the secular nature of settlements. They felt that promoting the idea of neighborliness by living with and providing activities for poor urban residents would prove to be an effective way to help them. Although its founding received little publicity, Neighborhood Guild was followed by the College Settlement in New York, which was established by a group of Eastern women college graduates in 1889 only a week before Hull House opened. The more prominent settlement houses included Robert A. Woods's South End House in Boston (1892); Emily Greene Balch's Denison Settlement, also in Boston (1892); Lillian Wald's Henry Street Settlement in New York (1893); Graham Taylor's Chicago Commons (1894); and John Lovejoy Elliott's Hudson Guild, also in New York (1895). By the late 1890s, Hull House reigned as the nation's premiere settlement house, providing the model for the over 400 American settlement houses established in cities of all sizes across the United States by 1920.

When Addams opened the doors of Hull House on the Near West Side, the neighborhood housed nine churches and 250 saloons. Corrupt ward bosses controlled the city's politics, and it was the bosses and their cronies who dispensed city services to the various neighborhoods in return for their loyalty. Chicago was overcrowded, filthy, and crime ridden. Sixty percent of the city's residents were immigrants, the majority of whom lived in abject poverty. In Chicago, as in all the other cities across the country, the word "immigrant" carried the stigma of inferiority.

Addams, assisted by Starr, set to work trying to bridge the divide between rich and poor by attempting to expose the residents of impoverished neighbors to literature and art. The newly minted American settlement workers quickly realized, however, that classes in Shakespeare and exhibits of reproductions of European masterpieces meant little to hungry persons who could not feed their families. The settlement workers soon engineered an alternative approach, one that veered away from trying to bring culture to their neighbors and moved toward effectively serving the immediate needs of the entire community.

Settlement women nurtured their communities by stepping into the fore of what historian Paula Baker called "domestic politics," into the political realms where no government regulatory agency yet existed. Progressive women's concerns for their families did not end at their own doorsteps. These "municipal housekeepers" carried their domestic concerns onto their city streets as they vied for pure water, safe milk, and improved sanitary and sewage conditions. Hull House residents and workers affiliated with the settlement adopted pragmatic methods of reform to effect policy changes. They stepped out of their homes into the public arena at the local level to assert their rights as citizens and demand that the city government provide education, recreation, transportation, protection, and a morally safe and clean environment. Over the last few decades, historians have convincingly demonstrated the vital role that women reformers played as political actors during the Progressive Era.

Whether closing houses of ill repute or campaigning for hygiene, the reformers' motives were questioned by their critics, many of them white male politicians and clergy, who accused them of attempting to assert their middle-class values in poor neighborhoods. Teaching manners and promoting "clean minds, clean lungs, and clean skins" for immigrant children might have been totally acceptable to reformers, but immigrant parents had a hard time with what they perceived as an uninvited intrusion into their private homes and personal lives. The question, then, of whether settlement houses were democratic institutions or institutions that fostered social control persisted throughout the era. Through their leadership, reformers did indeed try to impose morals and values in certain instances, but they also provided democratic models replete with a multitude of community resources and, not incidentally, did manage to bring culture to immigrants.

Reformers' neighborhood work did not always go smoothly. Some neighborhood residents viewed reformers as college-educated interlopers who segregated themselves from the local population by living in settlement houses rather than in tenements. They lived among but not with the urban poor. Consequently, the reformers did not always accurately gauge the needs of those whom they served. For example, tearing down tenements to build playgrounds eliminated substandard yet affordable housing. When reformers proposed the construction of new housing, the higher rents that inevitably resulted proved problematic as well.

While social workers regarded settlement houses as innovative entities that helped immigrants adjust to life in the United States, others criticized the settlement workers for their efforts to Americanize immigrants. The 1893 Annual Report of New York City's Educational Alliance posited that in their efforts to "spread distinctly American ideas on government, polity and civil life," a number of reformers encouraged settlement clientele to shed traditions and allegiances and to recast themselves. Some critics even frowned on the extraordinarily popular English classes, seeing them as placing pressure on the immigrants for complete assimilation. Henry Street Settlement founder Lillian Wald opposed the literacy test and other qualifications for U.S. citizenship. Wald eventually distanced herself from the Americanization movement and chose instead to work for immigrant rights by lobbying against the xenophobic "100 percent American" campaigns and the immigration restriction later associated with World War I.

Italian immigrants were especially suspicious of settlement-based reformers. Italian men resented the efforts of settlement

77

workers to entice their wives away from their homes to attend settlement lessons and other activities. Even more offensive were the reformers' efforts to encourage immigrant parents to send their children to public schools. Many immigrant parents relied on the wages of their older children in order to make ends meet. At first, when Italians did allow their younger children to attend school, they preferred parochial schools. By 1900, however, perhaps due in part to settlement work, even these parents increasingly began to send their children to public schools.

Settlement houses subtly dissipated ethnic rivalries. Immigrants, who had previously established ethnic-specific mutual aid societies and churches to help them adjust, could all come together to engage in collaborative activities at the settlements. They provided a sense of social unity in diverse neighborhoods, bridged class differences, and encouraged people of different homelands to dream the same American Dream.

The moralistic overtones of reformers challenged neighborhood values and often met with a mixed response. Their attempts to close dance halls and gambling dens, for example, naturally angered those who ran and profited from them. Reformers wanted to exert their control over leisure spaces for what they thought were good reasons. They even questioned the respectability of the modern amusement park, which was born in Coney Island, New York. By the turn of the century, Coney boasted three amusement parks: Steeplechase with its mechanical rides aimed at attracting working-class youth, and later, Luna Park and Dreamland, both inspired by the Midway and the grounds at the 1893 Chicago World's Fair and designed to attract middle-class patrons. In a twenty-four-square-block area, one could find hundreds of amusements: restaurants, saloons, sandwich counters, sideshows, concerts, vaudeville acts, mechanical rides, pavilions, and bathhouses. The area surrounding the parks was also known for its cheap hotels, brothels, and girlie shows. Coney's reputation for immorality, vulgarity, vice, crime, and public disorders stimulated reform efforts to clean up the area. Fearing a drop in their profits, the businessmen who ran the park as well as those who owned the nearby businesses met reformers' efforts with resistance. Patrons of such establishments also resented the reformers' intrusion into their private lives. Local businessmen and showmen who wanted to satisfy both the reformers and the working-class demand for leisure fenced in rides and games to exclude undesirables.

Nevertheless, historian Allen Davis's 1967 contention in *Spearheads for Reform* that settlements were "spearheads for reform," remains accurate over fifty years later. Despite the controversy that often surrounded them, the reformers' efforts without question led to more effective regulations including tenement laws, school reforms, public playgrounds, mothers' pensions, and the creation of public playgrounds and parks. Most important of all, by the late nineteenth century, settlements and their leaders offered a base for reform and activism. At the vanguard of continuing reform activity, the Hull House community allowed women to advance their collective power and to develop reform strategies by enhancing ties to other women's organizations and cooperating with the men in their organizations.

Settlements enthusiastically responded to the urban demands in a way that limited government could not. To encourage the spread of reform, settlement leaders held conferences, published reports and journals, organized city-wide federations, and eventually founded the National Federation of Settlements (NFS) in 1911 in an effort to promote and improve settlements throughout the United States and Canada. For the first few years, the NFS met jointly with the National Conference of Charities and Corrections (NCCC), the organization that it grew out of initially. NFS leaders, however, decided to disassociate from the NCCC because they wanted to be sure that settlements were not cast merely as charity organizations but as empowering neighborhood residents to improve their own conditions. By the time the United States entered World War I, there were approximately 400 settlement houses in the United States; the majority of them were located in the industrial centers in the Northeast, but several were located in southern cities. Some of them relied on church support, while others like Hull House subsisted largely on the donations of wealthy local patrons. Due to recently enacted political reforms that addressed their concerns, Progressives began to engage in political action to provoke the government to carry out broad social reforms.

Women comprised the majority of settlement residents. By 1914, nine-tenths of settlement women were college educated. Some of these women viewed their colleagues at the settlement houses as a surrogate family. Some women achieved leadership positions in the settlement houses, including Addams at her Hull House in Chicago and Lillian Wald at her Henry Street Settlement in New York City, and they participated equally with men in the staffing and administration of others. Male settlement workers, most often graduates of Protestant theological seminaries, ran Chicago Commons and Boston's South End House. Female-run settlements tended to resemble homes, while those run by males had a club-like atmosphere. Both settlement women and men went on to become leaders in the agencies such as public health clinics and social service departments that grew out of settlement work.

Professionalization in the Progressive Era

Reformers who belonged to the new middle class that emerged during the Progressive Era tended to be responsible for what historian Stephen Diner in *A Very Different Age* calls "the modern bureaucratic culture of contemporary America." The rise of professionalization in the Progressive Era created competition for economic rewards, social status, and autonomy, producing gains for some and losses for others.

The growth of the professions during the Progressive Era reshaped class and social structures, and altered the way problems were solved and the way services were delivered. Aside from ministers, the best educated and most successful practitioners of law and medicine and a number of other professions enhanced their prestige and economic rewards by restricting professional membership and upgrading professional standards. The

Progressives' vision depended on their ability to apply specialized skills to social problems.

Social workers

While not all settlement workers had formal training in social work, they were considered the first social workers because of the nature of the work that they performed. Settlement workers reached out to newly settled immigrants and supported specific reforms such as government-provided mothers' pensions, health and maternity care, better working conditions in factories, home economics and industrial education, citizenship and English classes, city sanitation, sexual hygiene campaigns, housing codes, and labor organizing. As the settlement movement became more politically active, the goals of the reformers expanded from seeking a mutual understanding with those they served to a quest for their full rights to U.S. citizenship and social justice.

In this setting, more formal organizations with stricter membership requirements began to emerge. In 1908, seventeen settlement leaders including Jane Addams and Graham Taylor took the first steps to create a social welfare organization devoted to the promotion and improvement of the settlement movement across the United States. Only those settlements without a religious affiliation could belong to the NFS the leaders founded in 1911. Now social workers joined other members of a new middle class that historian Robert Weibe in *Search for Order* believed wanted to remake the world by seeking scientific solutions to social, economic, and political problems.

By 1898, the New York Charity Organization opened the first school for social workers, the New York Summer School for Applied Philanthropy, which conducted classes replete with six full weeks of field work. Several other urban agencies created casework training programs for their employees. Graham Taylor, Social Gospel minister, professor of sociology, and founder of the Chicago Commons settlement house, combined social work education with actual social work by initiating a research program

to determine the causes of inadequate housing, juvenile delin-
quency, and truancy. Taylor, along with Mary McDowell
at the University of Chicago and Jane Addams at Hull House,
established a School of Social Service Administration in 1903. In
1908, after securing a grant from the Russell Sage Foundation,
the school became the Chicago School of Civics and Philanthropy. Hull House residents Julia Lathrop, Sophonisba Breckin-
ridge, and Edith Abbott transformed the vocational program at
the Chicago School of Civics and Philanthropy into a graduate
program in social welfare policy that in 1920 became the School
of Social Service Administration housed at the University of
Chicago.

Students at the new school used Chicago as a vast urban
laboratory to study the effects of poverty and the relationships
between environment, family structure, and local politics on an
individual's social and economic opportunities. Faculty members
like Charles Henderson from the University of Chicago's sociology department collaborated with settlement workers who led
social investigations using the latest social science methodology.
These investigations would become the hallmark of Progressive
reformers.

In addition to improving life for countless urban residents,
settlement houses enabled women to move into careers as professional social workers during an era when employment opportunities for college-educated women were all but completely
limited to teaching, nursing, and librarianship. In the early 1890s,
Mary Richmond, director of the Baltimore Charity Organization
and author of the classic text in the field of social casework, *Social
Diagnosis* (1917), developed training programs for social workers.
Richmond only had a high school education, but her early work
as a charity worker coupled with her love of learning allowed
her to advance to become an authority in her field.

In 1910, college-educated women constituted about half of all
social workers, and by 1920, women comprised sixty-two percent
of the profession. Regardless of their marital status, these career
women enjoyed relative freedom from the constraints of their
husbands or families. Since opportunities for women's profes-

sional work remained scarce and women still could not vote or influence public policy, they poured their energies into their work and quickly came to dominate the settlement movement.

The medical field

The medical field experienced the most profound changes during the Progressive Era. In the late nineteenth century, the germ theory of disease, including the science of bacteriology developed by British surgeon Joseph Lister, revolutionized the practice of medicine with advances in microbiology and immunology. Now experts in the field began to focus on conquering specific diseases with vaccines, serums, and other bacteriological products. Between 1894 and 1910, the bacteriological laboratory became the locus of public health work. During this time, researchers developed tests for the diagnosis for devastating diseases that had plagued people for thousands of years, including tuberculosis, syphilis, and typhoid fever. Anti-toxins were created to treat diphtheria and to retard or prevent the transmission of malaria and yellow fever. As these advancements ushered in a new sense of hope, administrators began the work of transforming hospitals from terminal institutions of last resort for the care of charity patients to modern centers for medical treatment and resources for medical education (Figure 2.3).

American reformers had successfully eliminated the proliferation of patent medicines, often concocted and sold by traveling hucksters and others with no formal medical training, by the late nineteenth century, but doctors still were not required to hold medical degrees. The doctors' special interest group, the American Medical Association (AMA), had existed since the 1840s, but it only became a nationally active organization after 1902, when it established a set of rules for doctors who practiced medicine. The new rules insisted that doctors belong to the AMA, which required both an undergraduate degree from an accredited institution and a completed medical degree. Only after the publication of the Flexner Report in 1910 (a study commissioned and funded by one of Andrew Carnegie's philanthropic arms) did the

Figure 2.3 A group of tubercular children with their nurses outside Sea Breeze Junior Hospital, New York City, 1911. Library of Congress, Prints & Photographs Division (LC-USZ62-109719).

AMA reorganize at the state and national levels and call for systematic licensing and standards and the closing of substandard medical schools. Thereafter, the number of doctors who belonged to the AMA increased dramatically. Yet the campaigns to upgrade the medical profession made it even more difficult for women and African Americans who aspired to become doctors.

In this atmosphere, socially conscious doctors and public health officials began to professionalize the field of public health. Progressive physicians collaborated with local public health officers and voluntary organizations to lead campaigns that worked toward the eradication of tuberculosis, dysentery, and cholera in large cities in the North and parasites like hookworm in the rural South. Tuberculosis, also known as the "white plague" or consumption, was the country's number one fatal disease prior to 1915. In New York State in 1907, the mortality rate from the disease was 152 per every 100,000 residents. Tuberculosis victims typically were hospitalized in general wards of hospitals or in charity hospitals where they spread their disease to other patients. But once the state undertook a preventive anti-tuberculosis campaign, which included taxing citizens in each county to provide funds for the erection and maintenance of separate institutions for tuberculosis victims, the mortality rate was cut in half. New York State also created the first Public Health Council at the state level to coordinate and deliver services.

Tireless advocate for the poor, Lillian Wald of Henry Street Settlement in New York, trained corps of visiting nurses who were often seen toting their large leather black bags crossing from tenement to tenement over the rooftops to visit the impoverished immigrants in their homes. Progressives involved in health-care reform pushed for clean water and safe milk for infants and volunteered their time in school health clinics. They also lent their support for sexual hygiene campaigns that attempted to educate the public about venereal diseases and for the placement of nurses in public schools.

Public-health advocate, birth control activist, Margaret Sanger, risked imprisonment in her call for open education on and the distribution of birth control information. Sanger grew up in an Irish-Catholic family in Corning, New York. As a young girl, she watched as her mother died a premature death at the age of forty from tuberculosis. Sanger believed that her mother's frequent pregnancies (she endured eighteen pregnancies and had eleven live births) had contributed to her contraction of the disease and death. To escape the same fate, Sanger, with the help of her sisters, enrolled in nursing school. By 1912, Sanger was married, living in New York City, and writing a column on sex education for the Socialist magazine the *New York Call*. Within two years, Sanger had coined the term "birth control" and began to publish her own newspaper, *The Woman Rebel*, to cautiously encourage contraception. In August of 1914, however, the Postmaster General of the United States indicted her for violating the Comstock Laws (a series of draconian postal laws passed in the 1870s at the urging of devout Christian and anti-obscenity crusader Anthony Comstock), that deemed the distribution of birth control information obscene. Sanger's husband, William, from whom she would separate in 1914, continued to distribute birth control pamphlets and was jailed for thirty days. Jumping bail, Sanger fled to England, and, when she returned in October 1915, to face the charges at a trial she hoped would garner positive attention to her cause, her only daughter five-year-old Peggy died suddenly. Public sympathy resulted in the dismissal of the case. In 1916, with the profits she earned on a speaking tour, the support of wealthy donors, and with the help of her sister Ethel and a friend, Sanger opened the country's first birth control clinic in the Brownsville neighborhood of Brooklyn. The clinic provided contraceptives (diaphragms and condoms) and birth control advice to poor immigrant women. Within ten days, the police raided the clinic, arrested the women, and confiscated the birth control materials. Undaunted, Margaret Sanger founded the American Birth Control League in 1921 (renamed Planned Parenthood in 1942) and continued her fight to make birth control accessible to American women.

In 1922, Sanger married James Noah H. Slee, a successful oil man who contributed funds toward Sanger's efforts. By 1926, Sanger opened the first legal birth control clinic in the United States. In 1917, she befriended Katharine McCormick, wife to the heir to the International Harvester fortune who was committed to the birth control movement but, since she did not have control of the family fortune, was not able to offer financial support to Sanger's controversial cause. McCormick had made the conscious decision not to have children after her young husband, Stanley, was diagnosed with schizophrenia in 1906. After Stanley died in 1947, McCormick, by then in her 70s, had full access to the fortune and, on the advice of Sanger, contributed it to research that by the 1960s resulted in the development of a safe and effective oral contraceptive. At the time of Sanger's death in 1966, approximately twelve million American women were on "the Pill." By the time Katharine McCormick died at the age of ninety-two in 1967, despite the fact that she had been the sole funder of oral contraceptive research, her contribution to the Pill has not been recognized in history texts.

Generally, the progress made by the organized public health movement contributed to improved social and economic conditions for many Americans. Better laws, health education, hospitals, and public health nursing helped to lessen the morbidity and mortality rates of tuberculosis, diphtheria, syphilis, and other communicable diseases. Complementing the better practices were new medical discoveries, improved nutrition and even free school lunches in some public schools.

The field of psychiatry also underwent significant changes. New practices meant that patients formerly relegated to state insane asylums now began to be treated in state psychiatric hospitals dedicated to the mentally ill. This relatively new branch of medicine struggled to understand the social and psychological causes of mental illness. Improvements directed toward more sympathetic treatment of "the insane" included training courses for hospital attendants and provisions for aftercare. According to one Connecticut social worker, "a chief aim of the work is to revolutionize the attitude of the public toward mental diseases." At the same time, however, many of the leading Progressives subscribed to the practice of eugenics, which supported the idea of applying social engineering to reproduction. They went as far as to advocate for the compulsory sterilization of the mentally deficient.

Settlement workers also began to try to provide special education for mentally deficient and physically handicapped children. Workers involved in an early project at Henry Street Settlement convinced the New York City Board of Education to allow Elizabeth Farrell, a neighborhood teacher interested in working with special needs students, to teach them in an ungraded classroom. By 1908, the Board recognized the importance of her work, buying special equipment for her and granting the establishment of a separate department, the precursor of special education departments in public schools across the country.

In 1906, the American Association of Labor Legislation (AALL), a group of lawyers, economists, and other reformers, led the campaign for compulsory health insurance. In 1912, they created a committee on social welfare, which held its first national conference in 1913. Despite its broad interests, the committee decided to concentrate on health insurance, drafting a model bill in 1915, which limited coverage to the working class and all others that earned less than $1,200 a year, including dependents. The services of physicians, nurses, and hospitals were included, as was sick pay, maternity benefits, and a death benefit of fifty dollars to pay for funeral expenses. Costs were to be shared between workers, employers, and the state. Many doctors supported a more universal form of public health care, yet others, like the American Federation of Labor President Samuel Gompers, remained opposed to the idea because they frowned on direct government intervention.

The legal profession

Legal training evolved during the Progressive Era. The practice of "reading law" while apprenticed to an attorney shifted to more formal training conducted in law schools. Like the medical profession, lawyers founded a professional association, the American Bar Association, in 1878 as a way of regulating and maintaining control over their profession. Bar Association leaders sought to restrict the number of immigrants, Jews, African Americans, women and working-class men from their ranks. The number of white male lawyers, however, grew so rapidly that lawyers began to complain that the increased competition drove down their incomes. Some proposed increased educational requirements such as law schools and state bar exams, but others argued against these ideas.

The legal profession's educational requirements were slow to change. Even by 1917, not one state required attendance at a law school as a prerequisite for becoming a lawyer, although some kind of schooling was required. A small number of lawyers began to establish specialized firms to deal with the complexities of corporate and business law. Even by the end of the Progressive Era, the idea of specialization was still so new that only about one percent of all attorneys fell into this category.

Engineering

Until the late nineteenth century, engineers spent the majority of their time designing canals and railroads. Like other professionals, they learned much of their profession on the job. As opportunities for engineers multiplied due to industrialization, engineering colleges began to train the new legions of professionals who specialized in civil, electrical, mechanical, and industrial engineering. Engineers who began to identify with management fought the idea of state licensure and enjoyed the monetary and status rewards that they received as managers. In the meantime, a small number of independent engineers employed outside corporations lent their support to regulating the profession through state licensure. Minorities rarely sought entrance into the engineering profession, rendering it almost exclusively a white male-dominated profession.

Academia

Prior to the Civil War, colleges tended to be small denominational institutions staffed by five or six professors, often ministers, who adhered to classical curriculum including languages and philosophy. After the war, with federal help, states established land-grant colleges including Cornell, Johns Hopkins, the University of Chicago, and Stanford. These new institutions of higher learning responded to industrialism by encouraging a scientific approach to agriculture, science, and engineering. Convenient locations and lower tuition meant that more students than ever before could pursue postsecondary degrees. Faculty members at many of the older liberal arts colleges, including Harvard, Yale, and Columbia, concentrated on research and developing new disciplines at the graduate level. The number of undergraduate students attending colleges and universities grew dramatically during the Progressive Era, reaching an all-time high of 598,000 by 1920.

Graduate schools focused on research and the professionalizing of the social sciences. New masters and Ph.D. programs in disciplines such as sociology, political science, history, economics, and statistics emerged, helping to elevate the reputations of certain schools. The first research universities were Johns Hopkins, especially known for medicine and economics, and the University of Wisconsin, for history and labor economics. Graduate schools like the University of Chicago, renowned for its sociology program, provided experts with ideas for social policy and governmental reform. In turn, professors sought public recognition and influence as policy experts in their chosen fields in government and public administration, as well as in charity and reform organizations.

Certification of professional competence as well as social respectability depended on the acquisition of Ph.D. degrees for academicians. This practice paralleled the German style of higher education. Although academicians gained a higher level of professional autonomy than engineers, colleges and universities did not grant them tenure in the pre-World War I years. In 1915, to protect their autonomy, a group of professors founded the American Association of University Professors (AAUP). The AAUP quickly gained control over their disciplines and the majority of activities within their institutions. The members were mostly white Anglo-Saxon Protestants who controlled the attainment of advanced degrees and opposed the entrance of Catholics, Jews, women, and African Americans into the major disciplines. A small number of persons of color did, however, did make headway in professions of sociology, anthropology, and law. Women tended to be limited to positions in all-female colleges in traditional fields like home economics. According to historian Joan Jacobs Blumberg, author of *The Body Project: An Intimate History of American Girls*, by the early twentieth century, these "women played a major role in Progressive Era." Blumberg points to their contributions in the development of welfare state, in the triumph of modern hygiene, scientific medicine, and the application of scientific research in a number of industries and the popularity of important research on child development, family health, and family economies. It is only in recent decades, however, that these women have begun to receive the recognition they deserve.

The female professions: teaching, nursing, and librarianship

While women were not entirely shut out of all professions, those seen as extensions of women's traditional role of service, such as settlement work, were considered the most socially acceptable for them to undertake. By 1880, one out of every three college graduates were women, but despite the increase in college enrollment for women, once they graduated, most women were still forced to choose between family and a career, with little middle ground.

As the number of free public schools in the United States grew between 1870 and 1900, the number of teachers tripled. By 1900, the majority of elementary and high school teachers were poorly paid women, more often than not unmarried ones. Many Americans, male and female, considered teaching a "natural" career fit for women. Young single women from modest rural families trained to be teachers in "normal schools" often connected to high schools; many normal-school graduates took positions in villages and small towns. Gradually, teaching jobs opened to immigrants or the children of immigrants. By 1900, persons of Irish ancestry made up about a quarter of all teachers and black teachers in segregated schools held roughly five percent of all teaching jobs. Although the educational requirements for teachers rose substantially during the Progressive Era, there remained very few opportunities for women to advance in the realm of education. Leadership positions such as principals and supervisors were exclusively for men. Boards of Education could also be very controlling and often refused to allow teachers to join unions or to select textbooks.

Formal nurses' training programs started after the Civil War. The country's first nursing school opened at Bellevue Hospital in New York City in 1873. New York became one of the first states to require that its nurses be licensed. Between 1900 and 1910, the number of nurses in the United States grew sevenfold. Nurses educated at the best schools dominated professional organizations and advocated to upgrade educational requirements and standards for entrance into the profession, with little success. Female nurses routinely had to cope with condescending and overbearing male doctors and hospital administrators.

After teaching and nursing, librarianship constituted the most popular profession for women. Librarians were the lowest paid professional women. University library schools taught librarians in training to organize, classify, and care for books, but the average library worker had few opportunities for independent work in research or archival collections. While women librarians held influential positions in small community libraries, they were virtually never in charge of large collections.

By 1910, women comprised approximately eighty percent of the nation's teachers and librarians and ninety-three percent of its nurses. Yet despite their education and expertise, they secured only modest remuneration and minimal autonomy throughout most of the twentieth century. A group of women's colleges cooperatively established a Bureau of Vocational Information in New York in 1915 to secure employment for female professionals. The Bureau also encouraged professional women to seek careers rather than resign themselves to lives as professional homemakers once they married. The U.S. entry into World War I in 1917 challenged the idea that women lacked the physical stamina or intellectual capabilities to perform in the professional arena. For the first time in U.S. history, women were hired as mail carriers, street car conductors, and in supervisory capacities in the business sector. These changes were, however, only temporary. Once the war ended in 1918 and the soldiers returned from abroad, the men resumed their prior positions in the workforce. Women were expected to resign from the jobs they had held during the war voluntarily or were simply fired, as was the case in Cincinnati when 125 female street car conductors summarily lost their jobs without legal recourse.

New opportunities for women also meant changes in their behavior in the prewar years. "New women" and flappers as they came to be called, typically traveled more freely, spent unchaperoned time in mixed company, shimmied in dance halls, smoked in public, rang up friends on the telephone, and maneuvered themselves into automobiles. Changes in behavior were accompanied by changes in fashion first among working-class women and eventually among middle- and upper-class women. Flappers, apparent by 1913, cast corsets aside, bobbed their hair, revealed their necks, exposed their wrists, hiked their hemlines, and painted their faces with cosmetics. Although these changes in deportment and dress were striking, it was the focus on self-development and the emphasis on independence (and in the case of middle-class women, education) that made the concept of the new woman truly new. The consummate modern woman resisted the confines of male control and took charge of her social, economic, and political life.

Growth and prestige of expert professionals proved to be an important development of the era. Many agreed with historian Robert Weibe's assessment that these new professionals helped to shape the modern bureaucratic culture of contemporary America. By upgrading standards and restricting entry into the professions, this new middle class attempted to keep the working class and racial and ethnic minorities out of the professional domain. Female-dominated professions lay at the bottom of the middle-class hierarchy, while doctors and lawyers ranked at the top. Whatever shared values professionals held, they were not a cohesive group and remained divided by social origin, ideology, and gender but united around the idea of limiting opportunities for women and other minorities.

Businessmen

In direct contrast to the muckrakers' accounts, businessmen often described themselves as moral leaders or stewards of society who, rather than adjusting the law to business, because of the work of the Progressives, had to adjust business practices to the law. One group of corporate liberals, or Progressive big business leaders, believed that collaboration between business, government, and organized labor was an attainable goal. Others, like steel magnate Andrew Carnegie and oil baron John D. Rockefeller, merely touted their philanthropic efforts outside their businesses while running a tight and decidedly anti-union ship. Despite their efforts to promote a positive image, most businessmen fell far behind the pace of reform. And although they sought government assistance, they did not feel comfortable with interventionism or paternalism on the part of government.

Businessmen fortified their economic positions by entering politics at every opportunity. Businesses of various sizes united over the issue of government regulation and in their hostility toward organized labor. Industry-specific employer organizations could be found in the banking, hardware, food and drug, lumber, textiles, canning, tobacco, railroads, meat, and iron and steel companies. Some, like the National Federation of Retail Merchants, founded lobbying organizations to protect their interests in the political arena.

In 1895, a group of small businessmen founded their own special interest group, the National Association of Manufacturers (NAM), to have a voice in government policy. The NAM proved to be one of the most influential probusiness organizations. NAM members wanted to protect the domestic market with high tariffs on imports, but because of a major coal strike in 1902 led by the United Mine Workers, its primary goal turned to combating organized labor. Employers conducted a vigorous open-shop campaign to bar unions from their establishments by using spies, strikebreakers (whom the union workers derisively called "scabs"), and blacklists. They also established the American Anti-Boycott Association to try to combat boycotts of goods of services often called for by unions in conjunction with strikes. Fearing a possible coalition of big business and big labor devised by corporate liberals, NAM members did everything they could to prevent the formation of one. The NAM entered politics in 1902, first as an independent pressure group but by 1906 had allied with the Republican Party to try to drive it from within. In essence, NAM's political policy depended on who the president was. Some members disliked the aggressive political policy of the NAM and some politicians resented what they saw as business intervening in their private sphere.

Leaders from the nation's largest corporations established the National Civic Federation in 1900 in order to form a national consensus on policy issues in drafting legislation. The National Civic Federation fought to discourage worker radicalism. While the NAM saw the federation as a conspiracy between magnates and labor, the magnates generally supported it. Its members advocated peaceful labor–management relations through strategies such as welfare capitalism, in which companies supplanted the traditional forms of family and community by offering paternalistic benefits such as cafeterias, medical clinics, housing, and stock options in an effort to foster a content, stable, and dependable labor force – and as an attractive alternative to joining a labor union. The National Civic Federation helped to shape the Federal Trade Commission and the Clayton Antitrust Act, which they hoped would prevent corporations from conducting illegal activities.

Acting on the suggestion of President William Howard Taft, a Republican who declared the need for a "central organization in touch with associations and chambers of commerce throughout the country and able to keep purely American interests in a closer touch with different phases of commercial affairs," a group of moderately prosperous urbanites founded the Chamber of Commerce in 1912. Headquartered in Washington, it attracted roughly 1,000 business associations that signed on as early members. Many outside the organization viewed the Chamber of Commerce as overly supportive of big business, but as local chapters formed, it depended on medium and small businessmen outside major cities for its size and character.

As a special interest group, businessmen had a mixed record of Progressive reform. One question that historians have repeatedly asked, "were businessmen Progressives?" is still open to interpretation. Businessmen joined professionals in resenting certain practices of city government, namely, corruption, fraud, and the breakdown of city services during the Depression of 1893. Some businessmen wanted to elect their own slate of third-party candidates, but most businessmen in the East and Midwest simply allied with the Republican Party. In the South, businessmen operated within the confines of what was still a racist and highly conservative Democratic Party.

Certain historians have recognized that several businessmen numbered among Progressive leaders. Lacking a grand social vision and concentrating solely on business reform, businessmen, according to Richard Hofstadter in *Age of Reform* (1955), represented "the hard side of Progressivism." Strictly concerned with profits, above all else they sought stability and increased prosperity, so they benefitted from government intervention in business when those activities, such as trust busting, kept their competitors in check. Since businessmen organized within their associations to achieve their goals and would soon turn to politics for more direct influence, historian Walter Licht suggested that businessmen may have had a greater impact on a nation's politics than on business. Recent scholarship supports this assertion by indicating that certain corporate executives did indeed participate in Progressive reform efforts for very different reasons than other Progressives. They accepted an increased governmental presence in economy because it often enhanced their profits. Scholars realize that business–government relations still need to be examined more closely. One question that remains is how influential the government was in the decision making of business leaders.

Labor Unions and Radical Movements

Historians studying workers' political power during the Progressive Era traditionally focused on organized labor and its support of political parties rather than on unorganized or individual workers' activities. While it is true that workers had a long history of political activity, including union lobbying efforts and working through independent and third-party campaigns in the 1880s, the majority of those efforts collapsed in the 1890s because workers failed to maintain a strong or even a cohesive voting bloc. Finally, the emergence of a "new labor history" in the late 1960s encouraged a deeper examination of working-class politics. This historical reexamination has enabled Melvyn Dubofsky to pointedly observe that as nineteenth century drew to a close, big business was successful in instituting a bureaucratic-technological society while workers remained "caught between the island communities [the small towns that comprised rural America] and personalism of a dying order and the emergence of a modern industrial society." Dubofsky contends that the early twentieth century appeared less chaotic than the nineteenth in terms of labor strife, despite several major episodes of unrest in the mining industry.

Workers' associations like the Knights of Labor tried education of the workers to further their goals while the American Federation of Labor utilized boycotts and strikes as methods of activism and protest with varying degrees of success. Workers received limited help from the government at the state level in the North with factory inspection acts and protective hour legislation. In the latter years of the nineteenth century, the settlement houses realized the importance of establishing close working relationships with the labor movement and began to invite the organizers of fledgling labor unions to use their quarters for meetings. Still, by 1900, only about seven percent of all workers belonged to labor unions.

Despite the success of conventional labor unions, radicalism continued to thrive. By the early 1900s, the number of Americans who believed that the capitalistic system was fundamentally flawed was growing fast. Socialists, who based their beliefs on the writings of the German philosopher Karl Marx, asked why a few factory owners grew incredibly wealthy on the sweat and blood of their workforce. Socialists suggested that all industries should divide the profits among the workers who produced the goods. Even more radical than the Socialists were the members of the Industrial Workers of the World (IWW, whose members were known loosely as "Wobblies"), who believed that compromise with owners would not work and instead encouraged members to fight for justice against their employers.

The most radical of all were the anarchists, who believed that pursuit of workers' control under capitalism was futile. Emma Goldman, nicknamed "Red Emma," defined anarchism in her autobiography as "the philosophy of a new social order based on liberty by man-made law; the theory that all forms of government rest on violence, and are therefore wrong and harmful, as well as unnecessary." Social and labor reformer, anarchist revolutionary, feminist, agitator for free love, free speech, and birth control, Goldman devoted her life to changing the social order through the abolition of capitalism.

During her Russian childhood, her Jewish family fled to Germany to escape the anti-Semitic violence of the *pogroms*. At the age of sixteen in 1885, Goldman immigrated to the United States and settled with her older sister in Rochester, New York, where she worked in the garment industry and was married for a brief time. Frustrated by her near-starvation wages and by the discord in her marriage, Goldman was further radicalized by the events of the Haymarket Riot and the conviction of the alleged perpetrators. She left Rochester for New York City's anarchist community in 1889. By 1892, Goldman became involved with fellow anarchist Alexander Berkman, who attempted to assassinate Andrew Carnegie's steel plant manager Henry Frick for the murder of strikers during the Homestead Strike. Berkman was jailed for his part in the failed plot, which only wounded Frick. Within a year, Goldman, too, was imprisoned for violating laws that prohibited anarchist speech. Goldman's revolutionary activities came to an abrupt end when she was jailed and deported to Russia on treason charges for protesting conscription during World War I. She lived into her seventh decade and eventually made her way back to Canada, trying but failing for twenty-one years to cross into the United States. Radicals found support as the exploitation of workers spread along with industrial growth, but their enemies were legion.

Other Special Interest Groups

Politicians and early reform

Detroit Republican Hazen Pingree, the nation's first social reform mayor, helped the city's unemployed with a depression relief program in 1893 and forced the city's cable and streetcar companies, as well as gas, electric, and telephone companies, to reduce their rates. Millionaire Tom Loftin Johnson, who moved to Cleveland in 1899 and began a political career as the city's first Progressive mayor, followed Pingree's example. Johnson's campaign pledge to lower streetcar fares from five to three cents touched off a seven-year war with Cleveland's streetcar moguls. Johnson served four terms as mayor and fought for fair taxation and greater democracy with the use of initiative, referendum, and recall – all devices that allowed voters to have a direct say in legislative and judicial matters. Largely as a result of Johnson's efforts, Lincoln Steffens ranked Cleveland as one of the best-governed cities in the country.

The "immigrant problem"

While many middle-class Americans accused recent newcomers from foreign shores of taking jobs away from native-born Americans, immigrants were also blamed for crowding into certain areas of cities and displacing earlier residents. For example, in Chicago by the 1880s, Russian and Polish Jews along with Italians were beginning to displace long-settled German and Irish families on the Near West Side. Lack of urban space made single-family homes obsolete in many large industrial cities of Northeast and Midwest. After the Civil War, middle-class urban dwellers moved into the many apartment houses that lined city streets. Impressed by the White City at the Chicago Fair, Charlotte Perkins Gilman proposed what she called the "apartment hotel" as the solution to urban congestion. For his workers, George Pullman favored company towns like the one he built in Pullman, Illinois, outside of Chicago, while George Eastman, founder of Eastman Kodak Company in Rochester, New York, saw multiunit housing as the solution for the native-born workers that he employed.

As migrants and immigrants pushed into cities looking for jobs, they often made their homes in the tenements, short for "many tenants." A 1900 exhibit designed by Lawrence Veiller, who had

99

worked with the University Settlement in New York, used socio-logical data to depict the shockingly overcrowded and unsanitary conditions in poor neighborhoods. The exhibit immediately generated support for restrictive tenement legislation. Progressive reformers and members of the Tenement House Commission of 1900 convinced Theodore Roosevelt, then governor of New York, that the tenement environment bred sickness (especially tuber-culosis), death, crime, immorality, alcoholism, and family demor-alization. Governor Roosevelt helped to persuade the state legislature to pass the Tenement House Act of 1901. Although the Act applied only to new tenements, it set a much needed precedent for restrictive housing legislation. The new regulations required that residential buildings have adequate lighting, venti-lation, and fire escapes. The ordinance required a window in every room and effectively replaced air shafts with courtyards in new tenements. It also mandated running water and water closets with indoor toilets in every apartment. By 1910, this leg-islation led to the creation of the National Housing Association, aimed at helping cities set requirements for low-income worker housing.

African Americans

To some reformers bearing witness to lynching and episodes of civil disobedience, local government and morality appeared to be under assault. In 1908, in Springfield, Illinois, Abraham Lincoln's burial ground, a riot erupted when a black prisoner accused of assaulting a white woman was taken out of town for safety purposes and anti-black mob violence ensued. In response to the violence, a group of approximately sixty reformers including W. E. B. Du Bois, Jane Addams, Lillian Wald, and William English Walling founded the National Association for the Advancement of Colored People (NAACP) to put an end to attacks on blacks and demand social and political equality. An offshoot of racism, eugenics advocates who initially supported forced sterilization of the feeble-minded, soon targeted recent immigrant groups and blacks. Between 1907 and 1917, sixteen states authorized institutionalization and even sterilization of certain criminals after studies demonstrated that an exceedingly high proportion of criminals exhibited less than average intelligence.

Several social reformers and even the leaders of labor unions opposed the flood of immigrants because it hampered their efforts to ameliorate poor working conditions and to organize workers. Many like Samuel Gompers, an immigrant himself, supported immigration restriction because he wanted to wean the labor movement away from Socialism. Proponents of immigration restriction intensified discrimination against blacks as they began migrating north by the thousands after 1910 in a phenomenon known to historians as the Great Migration. Politically disenfranchised and always facing the prospect of becoming the victims of lynch mobs or other acts of race-based violence in the Jim Crow South, many of the African Americans who had recently come north experienced the trials of arduous and low-paying jobs (the only ones offered to them), prejudice, and resentment on the part of white employees. Largely in response to this less than warm reception, black leaders allied with white Progressives to found the National Urban League in 1910, an organization pledged to combat overt prejudice and to safeguard the socioeconomic welfare of blacks in Northern cities. Urban League members also hoped to find ways to help blacks capitalize on the opportunities in the North.

Nativists

In 1894, Boston's Immigration Restriction League became the first chapter of the American Association of Immigration Restriction Leagues. Capitalizing on nativist sentiment that blamed immigrants for the hard economic times, league chapters opened in most eastern cities. Members doubted the suitability of Southern and Eastern Europeans for U.S. citizenship and were upset about the high concentration of immigrants in the nation's cities. The increasing prevalence of foreign tongues and customs exacerbated what white nativists perceived as an uncomfortable mix. League members noted that by 1880, three-quarters of Chicago's population were immigrants or the children of immigrants. By 1900, there were four million immigrants and their children living in New York City. League members favored the use of a literacy test for admission to the country, which they hoped would serve as an exclusionary device. Attempts to institute a literacy test as an official part of U.S. policy were blocked by presidential vetoes in 1903 and 1905.

Congress added to the tension between native-born whites and recent arrivals with the creation in 1907 of the Dillingham Commission, designed to investigate the effects on society of the influx of new immigrants coming to American shores. Buoyed by accusations that immigrants lacked a proper work ethic and faulting them for having incited labor violence and radicalism (such as the Haymarket Riot), the Commission proposed what would eventually become a closed-door policy toward immigration.

To counter the increasing anti-immigrant sentiment and to help immigrants navigate the hardships of the immigrant experience, in 1908, Hull House leaders founded the Immigrant Protection League in Chicago. The League assisted newcomers by meeting them at Ellis Island to prevent young girls traveling alone from becoming victims of the white slave traders who tried to lure them into prostitution. Grace Abbott became the agency's first director and guided the agency to such a level of success that in 1919, the state of Illinois assumed the jurisdiction for what became the Illinois Immigration Commission.

About this same time, the Ku Klux Klan (KKK) reemerged, its resurrection encouraged by the popularity of the first mass-marketed film, D. W. Griffith's *Birth of a Nation*, which previewed in movie houses throughout the country in 1915. Based on a novel by Tom Dixon, the film portrayed the KKK as the real heroes of the Reconstruction South, fearless crusaders who glorified white supremacy and bravely defended southern womanhood from black Republican politicians and carpetbaggers from the North. This time, the revitalized Klan did not restrict its violent activities to Southern blacks. Klan members in both the North and the South attacked not only Catholics and Jews but feminists, divorced women, and women whom they perceived as promiscuous.

Farmers and Rural Reform

In the early 1890s, stemming in part from the farmer's cooperative organizations, growing agrarian discontent over abuses by railroad companies and the monetary policies of the federal government, resulted in a "third" political party that hoped to provide real representation for farmers feeling increasingly marginalized in an industrializing society. Farmers found themselves in an increasingly precarious position. The Farmers' Alliance organizations tried to compensate for the declining Grange movement by stepping in to promote cooperative purchasing power, specifically their plan to a create a "subtreasury" system whereby the government would help farmers when crop prices were low by subsidizing the building of crop-storage warehouses or "subtreasuries" at railroad crossroads. Once crop prices rose to acceptable levels, the government would release the stored crops and the farmers would sell them. In the meantime, the government would issue monetary loans to the farmers, whose stored crops would serve as collateral. These nonpartisan organizations eventually sought political remedies for the discontented farmers, who complained not only of high supply prices but also of low crop prices and high railroad rates. In the South and Midwest, banks took advantage of farmers by charging them high interest rates on loans they desperately needed to purchase seeds and supplies.

Throughout the late nineteenth century, the nations' alliances continued to seek the support of sympathetic Democrats but also began to sponsor their own candidates under the banner of what became known as the Populist Party – its official name being the People's Party. Gaining state and local offices as early as 1890, at first the Populists were dismissed by the two major parties as what one Kansas senator dubbed "a sort of turnip crusade." Undeterred, the Populists distrusted monopolies and were open to the idea of government intervention to stimulate economic growth, which the Democratic Party opposed, fearing that a strong federal government would only benefit the already privileged.

At all levels, the Populists promoted anti-monopolism, government action on behalf of farmers and workers, and increased popular control of government. The Populists had a significant following among farmers and workers in what remained of the ranks of the Knights of Labor. They also hoped to include a demand for the eight-hour workday in their platform. At the national level in 1892, the Populists added inflation (as a deliberate part of federal monetary policy) and a graduated income tax to their list of demands. They ran former Iowa Greenbacker James Weaver as their candidate for the White House. Although the Populists were ultimately defeated, they did win a strong showing in the Midwest and the South. Some Populists ended up in the Democratic Party after it incorporated their demands into its own party platform and ran William Jennings Bryan in the 1896 presidential election. Bryan, who had started in the Populist movement, was inspired by the Social Gospel quests for reform legislation, including laws to address child labor and unsafe living and working conditions.

Weakened by the mixed reactions to Coxey's Army march and President Grover Cleveland's reaction to the Pullman Strike in 1896, the divided Democrats seemed more sympathetic than did the Republicans to the Populist cause. The presidential campaign of 1896 focused on economic issues that struck close to home for most voters in the midst of a national depression. Bryan, a young and deeply religious Nebraska lawyer with a gift for eloquent speaking, won the Democrats' nomination on the fifth convention ballot. Bryan's silver crusade, which pushed for an end to the nation's gold standard (with gold underlying the value of the nation's currency), appealed to debt-ridden farmers, Western miners, and many ethnic Democrats. The Republican candidate, Union Army veteran, and former Ohio Governor William McKinley, took a different approach to economic recovery, finding broader support among workers for whom a protective tariff on imports meant more secure factory jobs and the middle class, who saw the end of the gold standard as a threat to their prosperity. McKinley also put a damper on moral reforms such as prohibition, which attracted many immigrants and Catholics to his camp. McKinley's victory over Bryan ushered in a generation of Republican domination at the national political level.

New scholarship by Elizabeth Sanders that treats farmers as workers demonstrates how farmers proved far more politically influential as "agrarians" than as Populists. After Bryan's defeat in the election of 1896, the Populists' demands were addressed by the major parties. Agrarians supported the silver standard: simply put, there is a great deal more silver in the world than gold, so putting the currency on a silver standard would put more currency into circulation, devaluing the dollar, causing inflation, and making it easier for them to pay their mortgages and their other debts and raising the prices of agricultural products. By 1920, farmers comprised twenty-seven percent of the labor force, down from forty-three percent in 1900. Their declining numbers, however, did not stop farmers from joining small businessmen and workers in the struggle for political influence in the Progressive Era. Sanders argues that much of the legislation passed during the Progressive Era can actually be traced back to farmers' demands in the aftermath of the late-nineteenth-century depression.

Students of Progressivism are benefactors of almost a century of historiography concerning the Era. Yet the debate among historians over the question of "Who were the Progressives?" persists. What becomes most apparent is the lack of a single definitive answer. In the closing decades of the twentieth century, historians contributed vital information to the historical record by detailing the political activities and the effectiveness of the working-class and women reformers, two groups who had previously been largely excluded from consideration. In continuing to identify and describe the various individuals and groups who embraced the wider Progressive sentiment of improving life particularly for those in urban industrial centers, we can work toward a more accurate interpretation of who the Progressives might have been, or perhaps still are.

3

"Constructing the World Anew"
Progressive Agency, 1900–1911

Stepping into a New World: The Industrial City

Manufacturing dramatically changed the way Americans lived and worked. Newly modernized shops and factories offered jobs to the millions of migrants and immigrants converging on America's metropolises. Shoe, textile, and clothing manufacturing enterprises were the predominant employers in many Northeastern cities. Thousands of immigrant clothing workers crowded into tenement spaces to work and live in Manhattan. (They did both in some of the tenements.) The production and fabrication of metals spurred the economies of Pittsburgh, Cleveland, Detroit, and Milwaukee. In the March 1914 volume of *Poetry* magazine, writer and poet Carl Sandburg dubbed Chicago the "hog butcher for the world," the city's massive stockyards and meat-processing plants employing more people than any other industry in the city. As manufacturing replaced trade as the foundation of the U.S. economy, the production and distribution of goods directly translated into a prosperity rooted in cities.

The Progressives: Activism and Reform in American Society, 1893–1917, First Edition.
Karen Pastorello.
© 2014 John Wiley & Sons, Inc. Published 2014 by John Wiley & Sons, Inc.

As the rise of industrialization fueled the rapid growth of American cities in the late nineteenth century, the unprecedented population increase included a massive new wave of foreign immigration, which changed the composition of urban America. In 1895, New York City continued to rank as the largest city in the United States – a dominant world center for corporations, financial institutions, and mercantile and manufacturing establishments. By 1920, New York had a population density of 143 persons per acre and contained ten percent of the total U.S. population. Chicago's rail transportation network made it the undisputed capital of the Midwest. The population of this "prairie metropolis" soon surpassed that of a number of other cities, including Philadelphia and St. Louis, to assume its place as the second largest city in the country. With a population that doubled every decade, by 1890, Chicago boasted one million residents.

According to the United States Census, in 1920, for the first time in the nation's history, the number of urban dwellers exceeded rural residents. Older, well-established cities like Philadelphia and Boston experienced steady growth. The rapid expansion of newer population centers like Cincinnati, Cleveland, Kansas City, San Francisco, and Atlanta alarmed some social observers. Urban growth could be partially explained by natural reproduction and the decline of mortality rates thanks to progressive measures concerning hygiene and sanitation. The filtration of drinking water and attention to the proper disposal of sewage drastically reduced death rates from typhoid and cholera.

Improvements in transportation aided in the evolution of urban centers from haphazardly expanding pedestrian cities into bustling hubs designed by municipal engineers who came to be known as urban planners. Between 1850 and 1890, horse-drawn streetcars or jitneys were the most important form of local transportation for metropolitan residents, many of whom rarely traveled more than two miles away from their homes. By the early 1890s, electric streetcars, called trolleys, began to replace jitneys. The light-rail trolleys were faster, cheaper, and less polluting than trains or horses. For the fare of a nickel, a passenger could ride all the way to the end of the line. Despite the noise and unsightly overhead wires on which the trolleys depended, the number of street railways more than quadrupled from 1890 to 1917. During this same time, many forms of mass transportation went from being privately to publicly owned. Municipal owner- ship of utilities, including transit services, meant that patrons could now hold public officials accountable for poor service.

Bicycles became a popular form of recreation and transporta- tion in the late 1890s. While they cost considerably less to main- tain than a horse, bicycles at the time required a costly initial investment. For women in particular, the bicycle offered both exercise and a taste of freedom from the isolation of domesticity. Suffragist Susan B. Anthony explained that what many women came to call "the freedom machine" did "more to emancipate woman than anything else in the world." Women's Christian Temperance Union (WCTU) leader Frances Willard prided herself on learning to ride "this new implement of power" at the age of fifty-three, long skirts and all. Whatever their age or gender, early cyclists had to exercise considerable caution in negotiating their way down dirt roads and through crowded city streets.

The high cost of building new modes of mass transit such as elevated railways and subways could only be justified in cities with very high traffic volumes. The construction of Chicago's elevated railway, known to this day as the "El," began in 1892 and was finally completed in 1908. Boston's subway, built in the hope of relieving congestion in the central business district, became operational in 1897. In New York, the construction of its famous subway system started in 1904 and, with trains traveling at speeds up to forty miles an hour, became the fastest urban mass transit system in the world by the time of its completion several years later.

The central business districts of American cities assumed their classic character after 1900 when financial, commercial, and administrative enterprises began to locate close to streetcar and railway lines. Banks, corporate headquarters, government and professional offices, department stores, and hotels became mainstays of the cities, which also housed cultural and entertain- ment establishments. Heavy industry tended to be located on the perimeter of central business districts. The speed and convenience of travel on mass transit systems that began to spread outward from the central business districts allowed urban residents to move increasingly farther away from work. Then, with the advent of the automobile, affluent New Yorkers began to move outside city limits to suburban areas, as did their counterparts in Philadelphia, Chicago, and Newark.

Towering apartment buildings and corporate skyscrapers began to punctuate the skylines of early-twentieth-century cities, further accommodating the concentration of population and commerce. Technological advances such as structural steel and elevators enabled the modern architecture, making the massive buildings not only possible but functional. The ten-story-high Home Insurance Building, built in 1885 in Chicago, and the fifty-five-story Woolworth Building in New York, built in 1913, were two of many multi-storied office buildings that skimmed the urban horizon. Department stores built elaborate edifices in the city centers where shoppers assisted by sales clerks chose from an ever-increasing variety of consumer goods. Hundreds of thousands of people found work in the stores, offices, and factories of urban America.

In this ever-changing environment, Progressive reformers advanced from exploration and identification of modern problems to activism by the early 1900s. Some groups were more successful than others in making the transition. Those who enacted pragmatic solutions to the problems that plagued an urban, industrial America achieved agency. In other words, in many facets of society, Progressives were vital actors who took matters into their hands to help influence and shape their own modern world.

Settlement Workers Transform the Neighborhoods

Prominent Hull House resident and chief Illinois factory inspector Florence Kelley conceived the first systematic social science investigation to describe the ethnic composition of immigrant communities of an American city in her seminal study, *Hull House Maps and Papers* (1895). In order to help Kelley compile the necessary data, a team of settlement workers canvassed every home and painstakingly identified the origins of every family settled around Hull House. They found eighteen different nationalities clustered in an area that measured less than a square mile. Kelley successfully used this detailed demographic and statistical information to pressure the state legislature into leading campaigns to prohibit clothing manufacturing in tenement houses, regulate child labor, and establish a factory inspector's office at the state level.

Hull House founder Jane Addams, too, evolved into a staunch activist. Her neighborhood advocacy facilitated her appointment by Chicago reform mayor George Swift in 1895 as garbage inspector for the city's Nineteenth Ward, the only paid position that Addams would ever hold. This work, coupled with her prolific writing, went a long way in drawing attention to settlement causes.

It was largely the work of Addams, Kelly, and scores of settlement women in cities across the country that exposed the filthy living situations and exploitive working conditions of the urban poor to the general public. Idealistic yet pragmatic, settlement women set out in the words of Jane Addams to "construct the world anew." They eventually began to demand legislation aimed at alleviating specific problems. At first, settlement workers concentrated their efforts at the local level, their early investigative efforts concentrated on meeting the needs of their low-income communities. As time went on, however, their concerns encompassed state, and eventually, national policies.

For many Americans, the most striking component of social investigations seemed to be the enormous gap in lifestyle between the rich and the poor. By the turn of the century, the urban upper classes enjoyed electricity, natural gas, telephones, central heating, and indoor plumbing – all of which were considered luxuries for working-class families. Tenement dwellers still scraped to get by, fueling their stoves with scraps of coal and wood, lit kerosene

110

lamps, and drew water from fire hydrants. Many suffered from tuberculosis and could not afford to stop working or to take fresh air treatments like the rich in the mountains of North Carolina or Colorado or in arid New Mexico. Since the urban poor lacked basic amenities like indoor plumbing, families on an entire floor were forced to share toilet facilities or even outhouses. Tenement sizes and layouts may have differed, but crowding and the absence of sanitation were common factors.

Public baths present an example of the reformers' practical approach to neighborhood improvement. By the 1890s, reformers had begun to petition municipal governments to provide public baths for poor Americans. Lack of bathing tubs and sometimes even basic plumbing in tenements, the germ theory of disease, and new cleanliness standards all contributed to the popularity of public baths. In 1894, yielding to pressure from reformers, the city of Chicago built the first public bath near Hull House. Other settlement houses throughout the country opened their baths to neighborhood residents. In some cities, public baths were the most patronized feature of settlement houses. This was the case in 1913 when a settlement worker in Rochester, New York, reported that "so many people came for baths that it was impossible to stop to have anything to eat before 9:00. [p.m.]" Another Rochester settlement recorded the taking of almost 4,000 baths in a single year in its limited facilities.

In the late nineteenth century, the only public parks seemed to be located in suburban areas. Reformers wanted to secure local space for city parks and to control or supervise that space based on the latest theories of child and adolescent development. They reasoned that team sports and other activities helped people from different backgrounds bond, reduced gang behavior in adolescents, and otherwise hastened the assimilation of immigrants. What started out as local projects soon had national implications. In 1906, hundreds gathered in Washington, DC, for the founding convention of the Playground Association of America. Jacob Riis, Jane Addams, and Lillian Wald shared the spotlight with emergent play experts. Theodore Roosevelt served as the Association's honorary president. By 1915, cities across the country had hired

744 full-time play directors. What started as a grassroots effort had swelled to a movement of national proportions.

By the early twentieth century, philanthropic foundations reaffirmed the work already underway at many settlement houses by granting financial support for social work research and education. Margaret Olivia Sage established the Russell Sage Foundation in April 1907 with a ten million dollar inheritance from the death of her husband. The foundation strove to improve living conditions in the United States. Within a month of its creation, the foundation funded the six-volume *Pittsburgh Survey* (1910), the first systematic survey to examine the working and living conditions among the working class across an entire large U.S. city. Researchers paid special attention to the poor and elderly, hospital and prison conditions, and the development of social work as a profession. The *Pittsburgh Survey* revealed the costs and consequences of low wages, diseases, industrial accidents, substandard housing, and the absence of scientific urban planning. It recommended early health-care reforms, city planning, consumer credit, labor legislation, nurses' training, and social service programs.

Similar investigations in other cities uncovered much of the same evidence, the backing needed by reformers who wanted to remake the urban environment. New problems that surfaced included industrial air and water pollution. The germ theory linked contagious diseases to the environment and the initial lack of urban sewer systems. By 1910, virtually every city had instituted a sewer system and now turned its attention to the water supply, with metropolitan systems implementing filtration and chlorination. Sanitary engineers recommended street cleaning and the eradication of smoke-filled air that stung the eyes and congested the lungs of urban residents.

Despite the extraordinary industrial growth in the new century, workers constantly struggled to find decent-paying work and affordable housing and to provide food for their families. Steady work with a living wage still seemed a distant dream for most. Good housing seemed scarcer by the year, and food and beverages were often too costly or unsafe.

The safe-milk campaign offers a prime example of the challenges that Progressive Era reformers faced. As public health officials in New York State began to investigate alarmingly high infant mortality rates, they found that sixty percent of the milk that they sampled came from tubercular cows, which posed an immediate threat to babies and small children. Dr. George Goler, appointed to direct public health efforts in Rochester, New York, in 1896, warned city residents that in addition to the possible conveyance of disease due to milk watered with typhoid- or diphtheria-infected water, milk contained unsafe levels of formaldehyde used by milkmen to preserve it. Worse yet, infant deaths doubled during the months of July and August in Rochester. Further studies revealed that milk was shipped in open containers and improperly stored at high temperatures. Goler repeatedly requested a local ordinance that called for a 50° temperature requirement for all milk delivered to Rochester. His request met with resistance from milk dealers, who complained that compliance with the measure would drive the price of milk so high that average citizens would not be able to afford it. Aware of these difficulties, Goler proposed paper containers, a municipal effort to pasteurize cow's milk, and government milk distribution.

In 1897, Rochester became the first city in the country to establish municipal milk depots to sell clean, safe milk at low cost to mothers of small children. Modeled after programs in France, the four city milk depots or stations as they became known were strategically located throughout the city. Nurses who staffed the Baden Street Settlement and Davis Settlement provided free advice and sterilized bottles prefilled with pasteurized milk and sold for a penny or two. As a result, the number of infant deaths showed a steady decline, even if problems with the quality of milk persisted. In 1912, social activist Caroline B. Crane conducted "A Sanitary Survey of Rochester" at the invitation of a Progressive women's organization. Crane reported that some of the milk bottles delivered to homes contained dirt, and that some of them had white chalk dust added to the milk to disguise the dirt. Lillian Wald's milk stations at her Henry Street Settlement eventually evolved into full-scale public health clinics.

Settlement houses continually expanded their housekeeping activities to meet the needs of their communities. Residents responded to the desires of their neighbors by initiating classes in cooking, sewing, and carpentry. Instruction in the English language and citizenship classes for neighborhood residents continued to be popular offerings, as did day care for the children of working parents, kindergartens, libraries, health-care services, recreational programs, summer camps, public baths, community theaters, and meeting rooms for unions and political groups. In short, settlements offered something for everyone.

Women's Political Culture Emerges

As women's activism intensified, they began to become more politically involved. By 1890, the General Federation of Women's Clubs drew a vast network of activist women together. From the mid-1870s forward, the foundation for women's activism was rooted in the women's club movement. Access to higher education and a growing consumer consciousness politicized these women. Although shut out of the formal political arena, women exerted their influence by involving themselves in a broad range of politically oriented activities, from achieving temperance through the WCTU to helping working women become participating members of the exclusive male-dominated trade unions through the efforts of the Women's Trade Union League (WTUL).

Many of the settlement leaders had early ties to the women's club movement. This amalgamation of women and their organizations provided female reformers with a social vehicle for independent political action and a way to circumvent the male dominance of associations and institutions. In the shelter of the settlement community, middle-class and working women allied across class boundaries to achieve their goals outside mainstream politics.

The settlement activists in Chicago in particular were surrounded by a vibrant civic culture. Various women's groups belonging to the Chicago chapter of the General Federation of Women's Clubs advocated for protection of women and children in the industrial workplace as well as for woman's suffrage. Club women imitated the WCTU framework by dividing their organization into departments to move toward the accomplishment of their goals more efficiently.

Initially, women reformers employed a moderate approach to community organization. As new issues continued to surface in the course of their community work, reformers initiated broader campaigns that required more comprehensive solutions. Settlement women skilled in the use of social science methods began to adopt more assertive tactics to accomplish their goals.

Reformers' activism effected real change in the real world. Although settlement workers were not exclusively female, talented women leaders with skills to organize across class boundaries became more visible. And as women began to realize their competence and gained such footholds, their political activism began to radiate from the settlement houses. Not surprisingly, Hull House became the focal point for Chicago's female reformers, women who came together to speak for the welfare of the entire society. Florence Kelley's biographer, Kathryn Sklar, maintains that "women's activism was crucial because it served as a surrogate for working-class social welfare activism." Politically active women realized that to achieve their goals of expanding social services, such as mother's pensions, protective labor legislation, public health programs, and juvenile justice systems, they would first need to establish their agency by building a public presence beyond their neighborhoods.

Women reformers pushed forward at an unrelenting pace. As they formed cross-class alliances, they drew upon one another's work to inform their methods. Eventually, they adopted a three-step approach: they investigated and documented conditions; next, they publicized the problems or abuses they had uncovered in books, articles, and speeches; and, finally, they employed persuasive tactics such as lobbying influential citizens and staging model projects. Their tactics often proved successful.

Jane Addams elevates settlement activism

Early in her career, Jane Addams realized that she had to become involved in Chicago's political arena as a natural course of action. Addams quickly became one of the most vital players in the Chicago storm of reform. Supported by clubwomen, she focused her settlement work on successfully lobbying for local reforms such as the creation of the nation's first juvenile court system, which Addams helped establish in 1899. Until this time, youthful offenders were treated and tried in the adult court system. If the young offenders were found guilty of crimes, they were housed with adult prisoners. John Altgeld, who later became governor of Illinois, publicized the plight of juvenile offenders in a book based on his investigation of Chicago's criminal court and House of Corrections. Altgeld and several fellow Progressive lawyers drafted legislation to restructure the Illinois judicial system. Altgeld's and Addams's efforts, coupled with the support of state legislators, resulted in the erection of a Cook County juvenile detention facility serving the Chicago metropolitan area. Chicago's juvenile justice system for youth under the age of sixteen emphasized rehabilitation rather than retention and became a model for similar systems across the country.

Hull House quickly established itself as a base for activism. Its residents also hosted labor union and woman suffrage meetings. Addams offered meeting space to the nascent Women's Bookbinders Union, the Shirt Makers' Union, and the Cab Drivers' Union. Her efforts gained momentum as a result of her involvement in the Pullman Strike. When Hull House patron and major donor Louise DeKoven Bowen heard Jane Addams speak at a meeting concerning the strike at the Pullman Palace Car Company in 1894, Bowen left much impressed by Addams's "sympathy for the working man, and the sense of justice which made her see Mr. Pullman's side," even if George Pullman failed to heed Addam's call to arbitrate during the strike.

Jane Addams, Hull House cofounder Ellen Gates Starr, Florence Kelley, and several other Hull House women continually came to the defense of unions. In Addams's mind, the labor movement was an indispensable part of what she viewed as a reorganization of society. She reasoned that once unions helped workers meet their basic needs, the workers would move toward demanding greater government responsibility for workers' welfare. To that end, Addams went on to serve as an arbitrator during the bitter 1905 Teamsters' strike when the 4,600 biracial union members struck against Montgomery Ward's efforts to reduce the Teamsters' power by levying corruption charges against union leaders and trying to exacerbate racial tensions. Addams also intervened in a number of early garment workers' strikes.

Addams and a number of other Hull House workers forged strong ties to the labor movement as the Progressive Era advanced. In addition to devoting space and funds to the cause of organized labor, Addams mentored many working-class women in an effort to teach them how to work with politicians and become leaders in their unions and the broader political arena.

The Chicago branch of the WTUL held regular meetings at Hull House. Young Russian Jewish labor leaders Bessie Abramowitz and Sidney Hillman conducted strike meetings at the settlement during the 1910 Chicago Garment Workers' Strike. To protest an arbitrary wage cut in their piece rates, Abramowitz and a small group of other young Jewish and Italian immigrant women walked out of Hart, Schaffner and Marx (HSM), Chicago's largest producer of men's suits on September 28, 1910. Within weeks, almost 40,000 garment workers went out on the streets, paralyzing the entire men's clothing industry.

Ellen Gates Starr and other Hull House women marched alongside the workers on the picket lines. Margaret Dreier Robins, president of the WTUL, Jane Addams, and John Fitzpatrick, president of the Chicago Federation of Labor, worked to negotiate an agreement to end the strike. By February 1911, the HSM workers returned to their jobs after winning the right to arbitrate with their employer. Workers in other shops were not so lucky, however, and many were fired as a result of their strike activities. After the strike, Addams mentored Abramowitz, who eventually became a leader of the Amalgamated Clothing Workers of

America, the largest organization of men's clothing workers in the country. Although the Socialists rallied to the garment workers' cause, using their presses in an attempt to generate sympathy for those on strike, most reformers shied away from the affiliating with them. They joined Jane Addams in their desire to preserve the American system of enterprise and tended to ally with the more conservative elements of the labor movement. Yet it would be the networks evident during the 1910 Chicago strike that settlement workers, labor leaders, politicians, government officials, academicians, and some businessmen built at the grass-roots level that established a model of cooperation that could be easily expanded to the state and national arena.

Addams supported woman suffrage as a logical step on the political continuum toward direct government action. Women workers in the club and settlement movements wanted to see reform legislation passed, but as a disenfranchised group, they were virtually powerless. By the turn of the century, Addams and other prominent women reformers agreed that they needed the vote. In 1890, the two leading suffrage associations in the country had merged into the National American Women's Suffrage Association (NAWSA) led by Harriet Stanton Blatch, the daughter of acclaimed suffragist Elizabeth Cady Stanton. The newly merged organization planned to secure individual state victories as they worked toward a federal amendment to enfranchise women. By the early 1910s, suffrage had become a mass movement, with middle-class women enlisting the support of women workers, many of whom had been involved in the garment strikes in New York City and Chicago. Working-class women, it seemed, were quick to see the correlation between woman suffrage rights and conditions in the workplace.

Workers on the Move

The massive influx of immigrants from Europe after 1880 did more to change the face of urban America and its workforce than any other single factor. By 1907, more than eighty percent of immigrants who had come to the United States came from Southern and Eastern Europe. Between 1880 and 1920, seventeen million of the twenty-three million immigrants who entered the United States disembarked in New York. By 1910, more than one million Eastern European Jews comprised twenty-five percent of New York's population, most of them clustered on the Lower East Side, making it the world's largest Jewish city. By 1920, New York had 800,000 Italians in it, more than any city in Italy. Jewish and Italian men and women crowded into the clothing factories and tenement sweatshops in New York and Chicago. Only Washington, D.C., Indianapolis, and Kansas City remained overwhelmingly native-born, as these cities tended to attract primarily migrants from rural America.

The massive ethnic influx altered the nation's religious composition, too. One million Catholics arrived each decade between 1880 and 1920, including large numbers of Italian, Slavic, and Hungarian Catholics who poured into the cities and coalfields of the Northeast. With so many recent immigrants taking up residence in Chicago, it became a haven for Polish Catholics, many of whom ended up in the stockyards. Wherever they settled, Catholics brought their religious traditions with them. Catholic churches with their affiliated parochial schools became vital centers in urban neighborhoods.

Cognizant of the prejudice and discrimination that they would continue to face even if they were able to find work, African American men found little economic incentive from employers to migrate to Northern cities. The majority of African Americans who made the journey north were women, most of whom readily found work as domestics, although it did not pay well. African American women also took jobs as servants or laundresses in Northern and Southern cities. Regardless of race, the movement of women to cities transformed their economic lives as they took what were often menial jobs, lived in crowded apartments, and worried over childcare.

In 1900, two million American workers, or one in fourteen, were union members. Almost one-half of the unionized workforce belonged to one of the skilled trade unions that comprised

the AFL. These male-dominated trade unions preferred to union-
ize native-born white men and keep immigrants, women, and
African American workers out of their organizations. Semiskilled
and unskilled workers were rarely organized. As a result of the
AFL's exclusionary practices, the majority of American workers
remained unprotected and outside the union fold.

Health and safety in the workplace

Health and safety issues in the workplace emerged as one of the
primary concerns for Progressive Era reformers. Massachusetts
led the way toward labor reform. State officials were among the
first to arouse public concern for worker health and safety when
they began to compile and publish data on occupational accidents
and deaths. Enforcing the new 1869 reporting law, Carroll Wright,
Massachusetts State Commissioner of Labor and later head of the
Federal Bureau of Labor Statistics, conducted much of this pio-
neering work. Prior to Wright's tenure, workers' deaths remained
undocumented unless they died in a company hospital. Many
workers, like miners who succumbed over time to black lung
disease or textile workers who contracted white lung disease,
died after they left their jobs. Incomplete accident reporting persisted well into the twentieth century.

Organized labor groups in the United States, especially the
Knights of Labor, pushed hard for factory regulation. In 1883,
Massachusetts became the first state to pass a Factory Inspection
Act for workplaces employing women and children. The legisla-
tion was followed by a general Factory Inspection Act in 1885.
By the early twentieth century, other industrial states followed
suit, passing health and safety laws requiring factory inspections.
Despite these efforts, however, one political scientist concluded
in a 1908 state report that the existing factory laws were "a mass
of unconnected attempts" to do something vague for workers.

In general, the first factory inspection laws stressed compliance
through cooperation rather than coercion. Astute employers recognized that enforcing factory safety laws meant reduced turno-
ver, increased employee morale, and higher productivity. Many

factory owners realized that high concentrations of dust, steam, and heat in the mills caused lung disease, so they complied voluntarily. These changes would eventually offset any additional costs for employers as they brought their plants into compliance. Lists of improvements that employers made in working conditions became a frequent theme in inspectors' reports.

Even before the passage of their state's inspection law in 1894, Rhode Island mill owners began to improve factory conditions by building higher ceilings to assure better ventilation and providing adequate sanitary facilities. Some also built fire escapes and took measures to prevent fires. A doctor in a New York textile town informed the state labor bureau that little girls who worked in the mills often suffered broken legs because they used their feet to shift the belts that connected their machines to power shafts mounted on the floor. Improved technology soon eliminated these types of injuries.

Despite the many instances of cooperation and voluntary reform, the mere notion of factory inspection remained controversial. Some factory owners refused to comply on principle, as they resented what they saw as government interference in the private industrial sector. Others resisted mandates that force them to make costly improvements to infrastructure or procedure. Employers did not trust the factory inspectors or found them altogether incompetent. In any case, most factory inspectors preferred to admonish rather than prosecute violators.

Railroads and mines ranked among the most dangerous industries for working men. The manual link-and-pin method coupler used to join two railcars was a major cause of worker injuries, with fingers or hands easily getting lodged in between parts and crushed by the heavy metal couplings. Innovations such as Eli Janney's knuckle coupler, a semiautomatic device that kept rail workers from getting in between cars, and George Westinghouse's invention of the airbrake revolutionized safety practices in the railroad industry.

In 1893, the federal Railroad Safety Appliance Act was signed into law, making it illegal for trains to operate without automatic couplers and air brakes. The same year that Congress passed the

Act, 2,727 railroad workers were killed on the job, and 31,279 were injured, figures that typified work-related deaths and injuries at the time. Railroad corporations termed most accidents "acts of God" or accused the injured workers of negligence. In 1903, President Theodore Roosevelt increased federal regulatory power when he created the Department of Labor and Commerce to regulate and investigate safety violations in firms involved in interstate commerce.

Coal was in such high demand after 1870, because of the spread of the railroads, that production of soft bituminous coal doubled between 1894 and 1912. Initially, the coal industry was comprised of highly competitive small operators in Pennsylvania, West Virginia, Kentucky, Illinois, and Ohio. After 1900, the industry mechanized to reduce production costs and to discourage unionization. Efforts to fix wages failed largely because of the Interstate Commerce Commission's regulations and antitrust suits brought against corporations for price fixing. Some owners tried to merge companies to stabilize prices, but overproduction caused a drop in the price of coal in the prewar years.

The whistle signaling coal miners to work blew before dawn in the mines of the coal regions. Even the most skilled miners toiled in filthy and dangerous conditions. They descended in the dark mines on gangways, lamps on their caps and tin lunch pails in hand. Separate crews carried in the tools needed for a day's work. The youngest boys drove mules or sorted coal after it had been brought out of the shaft. So-called breaker boys worked twelve to fourteen hours a day, breaking lumps of coal into smaller pieces and then picking out the impure ones. Some also went underground to haul the coal out in newly dug areas. When social documentarian Lewis Hine went to the mines to photograph children working, he found it virtually impossible to see through the coal dust. Work in the mines could always be found but at a tremendous cost. In the first decades of the twentieth century, one in every 282 anthracite miners lost their lives in the course of their work every year. Hundreds more succumbed to black lung disease.

The worst mining disaster in U.S. history occurred in a Monongah, West Virginia, coal mine on December 6, 1907. Despite traces of gas in the morning air, the miners began their shift in the mines. While the men were hard at work, an electrically sparked explosion, so powerful that it smashed the motors of the coal cars inside with them, ripped through the mine, killing 362 people. (One of the dead was an insurance agent who had gone into the mines to do business with the miners.) The accident prompted the U.S. government to create a Bureau of Mines in 1910 in an effort to prevent future tragedies.

The steel industry, in which a great many as well as some of the most violent workplace accidents occurred, came under intense scrutiny with the formation in 1901 of Carnegie's giant U.S. Steel Corporation, the largest business enterprise ever launched. With its rapidly mechanizing production processes that involved the hoisting, rolling, and dumping of molten ore in the production of rails, many workers were hurt, some fatally. The intense moist heat that prevailed in the steel plants also debilitated workmen's lungs and joints. Investigating conditions in 1907, the muckraking author of "Making Steel and Killing Men," William Hard, estimated that out of a workforce of approximately 10,000, each year 1,200 men were killed or injured on the job.

Workplace tragedies were not confined to the railroads, mines, or mills. On January 2, 1908, a blast rocked the Rochester Fireworks Company in Rochester, New York. One local paper described how the explosion "blew one of the company's buildings to pieces," claiming the lives of two women workers. An investigation by the city's coroner committee failed to determine the cause of the accident. Witnesses testified at the trial following the investigation that only six of the twelve women who worked in the room where the explosion occurred were on the job that day due to the New Year's holiday. According to one local paper, Sadie Ernst, who had been cutting fuses at the time of the accident, died instantly as a result of being trapped "in the midst of a great flame." Another young woman, Lillian O'Connor, succumbed to burns a few hours later at a local hospital. A third woman was slightly injured. The other three women workers were able to flee unharmed before a portion of the building collapsed. James Palmer, Jr., president of the company, conceded at the trial that followed the incident that his company had a permit to sell fireworks but had not been notified that it was necessary to obtain a separate permit for manufacture.

Only a few years later, fire and safety regulations were instituted across the state at the insistence of the New York State Factory Investigating Committee. Until then, Rochester manufacturers alone would continue to lose nearly one million dollars annually due to fires. At the time, Rochester represented a typical Progressive Era city, one that only recently had evolved from a hinterland town to an industrial center. Although the Rochester explosion resulted in deaths and injuries, it warranted only routine local newspaper coverage. The U.S. Bureau of Labor Statistics estimated that in 1908 alone, there were between 15,000 and 17,500 deaths due to accidents on the job. Industrial accidents, even those that resulted in death, were so commonplace that many Americans more or less accepted them as a necessary risk.

The limited coverage of the Rochester explosion did, however, reveal a few details about workers' experiences, especially those of working women. Like the women working at the fireworks company, most women who worked outside the home in factories at the turn of the century were from native-born farm families or ethnic groups like the German or Irish who had immigrated in the early to mid-nineteenth century. In Rochester and in other industrial cities, these female workers (and their male counterparts) were beginning to compete with the new wave of immigrants from Southern and Eastern Europe moving upstate from New York City in search of work. It would take the monstrous Triangle Waist Factory fire three years later to call national attention to safety conditions in the factories in which the vast majority of immigrants toiled.

By the late nineteenth century, health and safety issues in the workplace had become a paramount concern for reformers.

Frances Willard, national secretary of the WCTU, listed garment sweatshops, tobacco manufacturing plants, paint manufacturing plants, paper mills, and wool sorting shops under the category of "occupations that kill" in her 1897 book entitled *Occupations for Women*. Male and female workers in these industries experienced high death rates from diseases like tuberculosis. Girls in textile mills who breathed what one reformer called "fluff laden air" and worked bent over were especially susceptible to tuberculosis. In Mississippi, thirty-eight percent of girls, many of them under the age of sixteen, were afflicted with hookworm or related diseases. Hookworm and a condition called "cotton-mill anemia" – a malady that was a combination of hookworm and inhaling lint that caused severe anemia – prevailed especially among children laboring in Southern cotton mills.

Alice Hamilton, a former Hull House worker, the founder of the field of industrial medicine, and the first woman faculty member at Harvard Medical School, conducted some of the first systematic studies concerning workers' health issues, including the maternal health of women workers. In 1909, Hamilton became the chief researcher for the Illinois Occupational Disease Commission. She led twenty team members including scientists, physicians, federal officials from the Bureau of Labor, labor union leaders, and corporation managers in a systematic study of occupational hazards and maladies.

Hamilton became the country's leading expert on the dangers of lead, mercury, and arsenic poisoning. The most important section of the report Hamilton issued concerned lead poisoning. She found the potential for lead poisoning for industrial workers in smelting and refining, painting, printing, and the production of batteries. The first physician to combine modern laboratory investigation with fieldwork, she identified two forms of contamination: the first from the inhalation of airborne particles and the second from the ingestion of particles on hands or contained in food. Hamilton's toxicology work ultimately resulted in the passage of the Illinois Occupational Disease Act of 1911. The Act established the issue of industrial disease as a matter of public concern and stressed measures for more healthful workplaces.

Throughout her life, Hamilton advocated for Progressive welfare measures, including prohibition of child labor, protective legislation for women, workers' compensation, and compulsory health care.

The work of twenty-nine-year-old feminist and Greenwich Village lawyer Crystal Eastman, *Accidents and the Law* (1910), grew out of the Russell Sage Foundation's *Pittsburgh Survey*, which one Progressive had purported to be "the strongest single force in attracting and arousing public consciousness." Eastman's inquiry into industrial accidents in Pittsburgh revealed that more than a thousand of them had occurred in a single year. While employers almost always attributed accidents to workers' carelessness, Eastman found that only forty-four percent of such accidents could be partially blamed on the victim, while thirty percent of them were the sole fault of the employer. These reports, coupled with the explosive growth of labor unions at the time, intensified pressure to improve workplace safety.

By 1908, more than half of the states had factory inspection legislation in place, but industrial accidents continued to occur at alarmingly high rates throughout the next several decades. According to the 1915 Senate Report entitled *Report on the Condition of Woman and Child Wage-Earners*, which included a study of accidents in twenty-three industries, statistics "continued to be hampered by the failure of many establishments to keep accurate records." In hazardous industries like presswork, where workers relied heavily on machinery, the annual accident rate ran as high as twenty accidents for every one hundred employees.

Observers frequently commented on the absolutely haphazard and unstandardized character of industrial work. Since the decline of craftwork in the nineteenth century, working men and women in general entered the workforce without preliminary training, picking up what they needed to know as they went along. Whether they labored in clean, healthful, and comfortable surroundings or in buildings that were an outrage to health and decency depended largely on which employer they worked for.

In practically every industry, extremes existed: the number of hours and the frequency of overtime worked; the extent to which operators used machinery safely; the subdivision of work; and provisions for proper lighting, ventilation, and comfort. Investigations revealed wide variations, not only within a particular industry but also within establishments in the same industry located within the same state or city. Lack of standardization seemed most evident when it came to the question of earnings. Employers' attitudes toward their workers seemed to matter more than the worth of the workers' services. In addition, employees had to deal with management's ever-present efforts to control them. Progressive reformers took it upon themselves to help the employees fight back.

Florence Kelley and the Push for Protective Legislation

By the end of the nineteenth century, Florence Kelley had become one of the nation's leading advocates for workers and their families. Kelley, the daughter of Pennsylvania abolitionist Congressman William "Pig Iron" Kelley, learned the value of social action in part from her early education in Quaker schools. She graduated from Cornell University and while in graduate school at the University of Zurich, pursuing her interests in sociology and public policy, she met and married a Russian Jewish Socialist medical student, Lazare Wischnewetzky. Shortly after her marriage, Kelley joined the German Social Democratic Party and translated Frederick Engles's 1845 classic, *The Conditions of the English Working Class*, into English.

Several years after Kelley returned to the United States with her three children in tow, she took refuge from her abusive husband at Hull House in 1891. She quickly connected with Addams and assumed control of the settlement's new Labor Bureau. From the bastion of Hull House, Kelley championed protective legislation for working women and children. By fighting to improve the working conditions of wage-earning women, Kelley and other Progressive reformers provided what historians have referred to as an "entering wedge." In other words, the reformers reasoned that once the door of state responsibility for women's working conditions was forced open, in time, the same treatment would be extended to male workers.

Primarily as a result of Florence Kelley's efforts, the Illinois State Legislature passed an Illinois Factory Inspection Act in 1893. Crafted from Kelley's suggestions for labor reform, the Act restricted child labor, prevented women from working more than eight hours a day, and created the office of factory inspector at the state level. In 1895, much to Kelley's dismay, the Illinois Supreme Court struck down the eight-hour provision of the Act. However, the child labor and factory inspection provisions remained in place and enabled Kelley to serve under the Progressive and prolabor Governor John Altgeld as the state's first factory inspector from 1893 to 1897.

Florence Kelley's fight for women workers advanced to the national level. Kelley was one of many Progressive reformers who secured a position in an agency that eventually became vital to the New Deal. As the secretary of the National Consumers' League (NCL) from 1898 to her death in 1932, Kelley sought to enact industrial reform through labor regulation and consumer education. After first expanding its membership base, the NCL demanded protective labor legislation including a minimum-wage law and the restriction of hours for women and children. The NCL worked toward legislation that would improve the working conditions for women working as department store clerks and in the garment industry. The League's "white list," which published the names of manufacturing firms that treated their employees fairly and encouraged consumers to buy goods from them, became a popular coercive tool. The League also demanded consumer protection laws and concentrated on educating women, the active consumers in American families, by equipping them with the skills necessary to be responsible consumers.

In 1906, an Oregon laundry owner challenged the state's ten-hour statute for female employees after his company was fined when a supervisor asked a woman to work more than ten hours. At that time, some Progressives had suggested that if they could not restrict the number of hours in a workday for all workers, perhaps they could make a case in defense of limits for women. Florence Kelley convinced Boston lawyer Louis Brandeis to defend the law in front of the United States Supreme Court. Using sociological data and expert opinions, Kelley and Brandeis's sister-in-law, Josephine Goldmark, prepared a brief that ultimately convinced the United States Supreme Court that excessive hours damaged the health of mothers and future mothers. In the now famous decision, *Muller v. Oregon*, the Court upheld the Oregon law limiting the number of hours women could work. Hailed as a victory for the Progressives, the decision offered protection on one hand and official recognition of women's biological differences and motherhood as women's primary avocation on the other. Indeed, with the same *Muller* decision, the Supreme Court effectively blocked similar legislation for men.

Muller overturned the 1905 *Lochner v. New York* decision in which the Court had refused to limit the number of hours in a workday for bakers to ten. In essence, the landmark *Muller* decision resulted in workers having control of one aspect of the workplace for one of the first times in history. It also marked the first time sociological evidence such as reports from factory inspectors were used as part of legal reasoning. Working in conjunction with organized labor and settlement women, Kelley and her contemporaries helped to win protective legislation for women and children in state after state, forging close ties to the labor movement in the process. Men on the railroads and in the mines, where investigations revealed that overly long hours increased accident rates, had their work hours limited primarily at the state level between 1905 and 1908. In 1907, Congress passed a national hours law that applied to trains that traveled between states, which covered the majority of railway workers.

Child labor

In 1900, more than one-fifth of the children under the age of sixteen in the United States worked for wages in mines, mills, and factories. Girls and boys as young as seven-years-old worked on the streets selling newspapers, polishing shoes, and scavenging for rags and scraps of metal. Others followed behind wagons hauling coal or wood, scrounging pieces that fell on the streets to bring home for fuel. Children had little choice about where they worked. They tended to get work wherever they could, often where their friends or relatives did. Immigrants who settled in urban areas prioritized work over schooling expecting their children to work so that they could contribute their earnings to the family economy. Desperate parents even lied about their children's ages so that they could work for wages.

In the mid-nineteenth century, the Knights of Labor had begun to advocate publicly against child labor. By 1900, the movement to prohibit the practice was becoming, in the words of one reformer, "a force to be reckoned with." Knights leader and eventual cofounder of the Industrial Workers of the World (IWW) "Mother" Mary Jones traveled to Philadelphia in 1903 to assist involving more than 100,000 textile workers seeking a fifty-five-hour week and higher wages. Jones would later attest that as many as 10,000 of the strikers were the young children of miners forced to work because their fathers had been maimed or injured in the mines. Jones was moved by the condition of the working children she met. Many looked malnourished and some were missing fingers or even entire limbs. Some of the children were not yet twelve, but their mothers had been forced to lie about their age so that they could be sent into the mills to help their destitute families. (There were state laws in place that attempted to regulate minimum age, but they were poorly enforced so that parents who lied about their children's ages were rarely prosecuted.) With 120,000 children reported as officially working, but with twice that number missing from school and unaccounted for every day, Pennsylvania had one of the worst child labor problems in the nation. Jones knew that the children unaccounted for in school records were working dangerous jobs in mines and factories.

After she inquired about the lack of newspaper coverage concerning the textile strike and learned that the coverage was so slight because the employers of the children had stock in the local newspapers, the sixty-five-year-old Jones decided to lead her own march. With approximately 200 supporters, including some of the striking children, Jones traveled from Philadelphia to New York to raise funds for the striking workers. She stopped along the ninety-two-mile route to speak to crowds about the necessity of increasing adult wages so that children would not have to work. Newspaper coverage of the march highlighting the exploitation of child labor bolstered what quickly became a national campaign to abolish it.

Despite resistance from employers who disregarded state labor laws and from poor parents, for most reformers, children comprised the most numerous and foremost group in need of their help and entitled to social betterment. Reformers did not hesitate to tackle child labor head on. They subscribed to the evolving notion of the period, one advanced by the new social sciences, of a new kind of childhood, as a special time during which children needed protection from the evils of child labor and unsafe environments. In their push to do what they felt was right, social workers, educators, and Progressive activists concentrated on building municipal and school playgrounds and keeping children in school for longer school years and for more grade levels, often against parental wishes.

The creation of the National Child Labor Committee (NCLC) in 1904 by a group of concerned reformers built upon Kelley's anti-sweatshop campaign and the battle against child labor. Chartered by Congress in 1907, the NCLC initiated the formal crusade against child labor. It reduced the incidence of child labor through lobbying efforts that resulted in minimum-age working requirements at the state level. The adoption of minimum-wage and maximum-hour provisions worked toward ensuring fair wages and hours for child as well as adult workers. The legislation did not pass in all states, and where it did pass, it had many loopholes, especially in the Southern States. So despite the NCLC's initial successes between 1905 and 1907, "newsies" who worked the streets and child laborers in Southern textile mills remained unprotected. In 1908, the NCLC made a pivotal move by hiring

Lewis Wickes Hine, a tailor's son and budding anthropologist and photographer. Perhaps better than words could express, Hine's pictures captured the horrors of the workplace experienced by impoverished children and, in doing so, awakened the consciousness of the nation. Concluding that only a federal law would provide a workable and enforceable solution to the problem, reformers turned to Washington to remedy the weaknesses inherent in state legislation.

At a 1909 White House Conference on Children, reformers campaigned hard for a widow's pension and the establishment of a children's bureau, just as Henry Street Settlement founder Lillian Wald had suggested years earlier. Shocking some members of the Senate Committee by comparing the treatment of indigent children to that of pigs, Wald expressed the sentiments of her fellow reformers in declaring that children should be cared for in their homes, as opposed to the practice of removing them from poor single parents and placing them in an orphanage or asylum. Progressives made it clear that very poor children and their parents needed justice, not punishment.

Kelley, Wald, and a host of other reformers put child welfare on the national agenda. The NCLC accomplished one of its primary goals when the U.S. government established a Children's Bureau within the Department of Commerce 1912 in order to safeguard overall child welfare. The following year, the department was transferred to the Department of Labor, and Julia Lathrop, a leading Hull House resident, became its chief. Buoyed by the agency's investigative and reporting powers, Lathrop conducted one of the first studies on the causes and rates of maternal and infant mortality. Lathrop along with Florence Kelley and colleagues advocated the passage of the Sheppard–Towner Maternity and Infant Protection Act (1921), which allocated federal funds to nutrition programs administered by the Children's Bureau. Kelley also sought an early version of a national healthcare system, but it failed to garner government support.

While reformers pushed to regulate the hours and conditions of women and children in the workplace, women and children continued to perform so-called homework – working in their homes making small items in a piecemeal fashion such as artificial flowers, hats, bow ties, and gloves. Florence Kelley exposed the infamous "sweating system" in Chicago wherein manufacturers had cloth cut in their shops and then distributed it in marked bundles to contractors who hired immigrant women and children to finish garments by hand in their tenement apartments. By 1907, a large percentage of homeworkers were Italian women. The number of Italian immigrant women working in their homes (usually with help from their children) was highest in the nation's largest cities. Italian women made up ninety percent of homeworkers in Chicago and ninety-eight percent in New York. Italian men felt more comfortable with their wives working at home in the tenements of their ethnic enclaves, where they would be relatively sheltered from the many risks of the workplace, including sexual harassment. In *Home to Work* (1994), historian Eileen Boris recounts how unregulated homework endured until at least the 1930s.

Educational Reform

By the turn of the century, the Progressive reform spirit began to inform public education, first in urban areas and eventually in rural ones. More financial resources from property taxes meant that urban schools were much larger and better equipped than rural schools. Reformers, many of them affiliated with the settlement houses, pushed for changes in public education that included compulsory attendance laws and supported women's candidacies for school board membership, even though the introduction of school boards may have seemed like a hierarchal practice. They also successfully added physical education classes and kindergartens to the school curriculum, hired school nurses, created libraries, and hung artwork in school halls (Figure 3.1).

A 1910 *Outlook* magazine article praised the transfer of functions from families and religious institutions to the public schools declaring, "When the home and the church are unable for any reason to do their part, it is a tradition in America that the school shall try to fill the gap." Cooperation between the school and the

133

Figure 3.1 Children at a Washington, DC, school doing dumbbell exercises, 1899. Library of Congress, Prints & Photographs Division (LC-USZ62-14696).

settlements offered tremendous opportunities for social workers. At one Brooklyn settlement, the residents had all the children whose mothers were away at work come daily to the settlement house for lunch. Other settlement workers helped establish penny lunch programs that provided hot meals for students in the public schools. In 1912 alone, members of Boston's Women's Educational and Industrial Union, a Progressive women's group, served lunch to approximately 10,000 school children.

One of the most preeminent Progressive reform voices proved to be that of American philosopher John Dewey, author of *The School and Society* (1899), who proposed radical reforms in public school curriculums. Dewey envisioned schools in which students would learn through interactive, hands-on activities rather than by passive education focused on rote memorization. He stressed the importance of an atmosphere of freedom in the classroom, which entailed a trusting relationship between the teacher and the students. According to Dewey, education in a democracy could serve as a vital tool to encourage students to become active, responsible citizens who could and would engage as members of a social group in their neighborhoods and wider communities. He also supported the expansion of vocational education. In short, Dewey (who was such a close friend of Jane Addams that he named his daughter after her) worked in conjunction with settlement workers in an attempt to make the schools more like social settlements.

During the Progressive Era, more children than ever in American history attended school. By 1917, more than seventy-five percent of children under the age of eighteen had attended school at some point in their lives. High schools became increasingly popular as they moved away from the elitist male model of college preparatory courses to the more practical coeducational approach that included vocational education. By 1920, the United States had over 14,000 high schools, most of which were becoming an avenue for economic mobility among the working class. An increasing number of students also went onto college, but as late as 1920, ninety percent of the college students were still native-born.

By 1900, New York City schools held adult education classes for immigrants. Cities across the country like Boston, Philadelphia, Cleveland, and Cincinnati followed suit. New Jersey became the first state in the nation to allow school boards to hold evening schools for immigrants. Other organizations like the YMCA and the North American Civic League for Immigrants also offered cooperative educational services for immigrants.

Social Centers

Progressive Era cities grappled with innumerable problems by the late nineteenth century, but poet Walt Whitman, who had spent most of his life in and around New York City, optimistically wrote about cities and their institutions as democratic entities – places where every citizen could have a voice. In 1897, Columbia professor of modern languages and foreign literature Charles Sprague Smith established the People's Institute on Manhattan's Lower East Side so that workers and recent immigrants could be "uplifted" by hearing experts speak on the theories and practices of government and social philosophy. In 1902, John Dewey suggested that democracy might be enhanced by the use of evening school centers so that urban residents could come together and collectively discuss pertinent issues from race relations to public health. Dewey detailed his ideas in a 1902 article entitled "The School as Social Center." Schools proved the ideal venue for social centers, as they were readily available in every community and open in the evening at no cost. Dewey hoped to create the same sense of democracy that he had witnessed among immigrants at Hull House when they met to discuss neighborhood problems.

In 1907, five years after Dewey first described social centers, reformers in Rochester, New York, were the first in the nation to compel the city's Board of Education to open public schools in the evenings for community use. At its foundation, the Social Center movement called for the regeneration of participatory democracy in urban neighborhoods by providing all citizens with an opportunity to attend a weekly forum in the free and accessible setting of public schools. The movement's proponents also hoped that the social centers would begin to alleviate the challenges of overcrowded, chaotic neighborhoods by providing a semblance of order.

The Rochester Board of Education immediately hired Edward Ward, a disciple of both Jane Addams and John Dewey, to oversee the administrative details. Ward hoped to conduct experiments in participatory democracy by educating citizens to the point at which they could assume the responsibilities of self-government, so that they could gain the skills and knowledge necessary to exercise the franchise and to make their own efforts toward solving local problems. Rochester residents debated key contemporary issues such as local housing conditions, city planning, immigration, citizenship, and reforms in public education. Participants listened to all sides and often asked politicians to act as guest speakers. Social centers provided a venue for political candidates to deal with issues outside of the influence of special interests, creating an institutional basis for the Progressive Era challenge to political corruption.

The Rochester movement proved unique. A city caught up in the throes of industrialization and experiencing a major influx of new immigrants mostly from Italy and Poland, it was the first city in which the community rather than some local board created the social center's meeting agenda.

By 1909, Rochester reformers could point to seventeen social centers housed in city school buildings used to hold more than 300 meetings a year. A succession of various civic clubs and special classes met at the social centers. Debates were among the most popular activities held at the centers. Older people especially took the debates seriously and studied the topics ardently. A typical example of a social center meeting came in 1910, when a debate on the commission form of city government was held at School Number 9. Supporting the idea were a Polish washerwoman and the president of the local WCTU who were opposed by a day cleaner and a college professor. The judges were a prominent lecturer, the president of the local Consumers' League, and a high school "professor."

Nonetheless, some began to accuse the social centers of having anarchist ties. After University of Rochester Professor Kendrick Shedd spoke at a city social center on Socialism, such attacks intensified. Ultimately, due to lack of finances and the dominance of local politics by conservative elements, including Eastman Kodak founder George Eastman and his political ally, Mayor Hiram Edgerton, Rochester's social centers had disappeared by 1911, but they left a nationwide movement in their wake.

The Social Center movement to create spaces in communities where diverse individuals from all walks of life could meet each other in a social context caught on across the country. Even before the Rochester centers closed, Edward Ward was invited to Milwaukee to work as an "Adviser in Civic and Social Center Development" under the auspices of the Extension

Division at the University of Wisconsin. By 1912, there were over 160 social centers in cities like Boston, Chicago, New York, and Philadelphia.

The Chautauqua movement

In the last decades of the nineteenth century, many adults particularly in rural areas interested in furthering their own education attended schools sponsored by what came to be called the Chautauqua movement. In 1878, John Vincent, a Methodist minister in charge of coordinating the training of Sunday school teachers across the country, and Lewis Miller, an Ohio industrialist and inventor, founded a two-week experimental summer institute, the Chautauqua Lake Sunday School Assembly, for Sunday school teachers in the small town of Chautauqua in upstate New York.

Originally intended to provide both secular and religious education free of cost for beginning Sunday school teachers in a relaxed atmosphere, "Chautauqua" evolved into an all-inclusive summer program that was part college campus, part camp meeting, and part communitarian settlement that eventually attracted a broad middle-class audience of all ages. The offerings included operas, plays, and classes in art, music, ballet, and religion. As the Chautauqua camp grew into a community-based social and cultural movement, its leaders embraced the opportunity to provide democratic education. They also tried to convince attendees that idle pastimes like gambling, dancing, and theater-going posed a threat to moral health and should be replaced by cultural activities that promoted wholesome living. Chautauqua leaders called on prominent political speakers, including U.S. presidents, to lecture on contemporary issues. Theodore Roosevelt referred to the movement as "the most American thing about America." As the movement gained national momentum, other small communities began to create their own Chautauqua circles around literature and the arts or invite Chautauqua circuit programs to towns from Maine to Florida. By 1924, over one million Americans had attended Chautauqua programs.

Country Life Commission

With the economic prosperity that followed the Depression of 1893, rural property costs appreciated. Unable to afford to expand their holdings, many farmers and their families began to tire of the grueling days and unpredictable incomes offered by farm life. Many former farmers migrated to cities seeking steady employment, a weekly paycheck, and Sundays off. While employers welcomed the potential increase in the native-born workforce, what the potential end of the American family farm might mean to society began to worry some reformers. A group of professionals that included educators, businessmen, and journalists concerned with improving the quality of farm life and in part providing a type of rural leadership rallied around what became known as the Country Life movement. In 1908, New York City-born President Theodore Roosevelt had formed the Country Life Commission and charged it with studying the condition of rural Americans. Roosevelt hoped that an intense examination of the "rural problem" by the leading experts of the day would generate practical ways to increase the appeal of rural life and, in doing so, reduce the flight from the farms.

Liberty Hyde Bailey, the dean of the New York State Agricultural College at Cornell University, chaired the Commission and coordinated the six appointed commissioners. The commissioners conducted separate studies in their areas of expertise, held thirty regional hearings across the United States, sent over 500,000 questionnaires to rural residents, and solicited the results of a countrywide schoolhouse meeting held on December 5. President Theodore Roosevelt presented the findings of the Country Life Commission to Congress on February 9, 1909. The report suggested that one reason so many farmers had left the land was because they had failed to modernize, which had led to their victimization by land speculators. The Commission also found that farmers suffered from inadequate roads, seasonal labor shortages, and mismanaged natural resources. Their children lacked quality education and their wives suffered as well. While some farmers resented what they perceived as the government's intrusion in their lives and saw it as a threat to their autonomy, most had never heard of the Country Life Commission. By their very nature, the majority of farmers resisted the educational and scientific changes the Progressives championed. They refused to abide by compulsory school attendance laws for their children or be told how to grow their crops. Gradually, however, they began to take advantage of catalog shopping, free rural postal delivery, and improved roads.

Despite the contention the Commission's work generated among some farmers, several scholars considered the Commission's report the crowning moment of the Roosevelt administration. In reaffirming Progressive values, it proposed three substantive recommendations: a comprehensive government study and plan for all rural residents, nationalized extension work by state agricultural colleges, and a campaign for rural progress that moved the country forward toward rebuilding country life. The American Country Life Association grew in part out of the Commission's work. Formed in 1919, the Association revolved around forwarding the interests of those living the country life.

A number of nonprofit agencies and organizations also made overtures toward reviving rural life. The urban-based YMCA, which started in Boston in 1851 to provide a place to study the Bible and a refuge from life on the streets for young men, started rural outreach programs in Illinois in the 1870s to encourage rural Christian leadership and community building. By 1914, the YMCA's Rural Association operated in over 800 rural communities in twenty-four states touching the lives of roughly 25,000 young men and boys. With the passage of the Smith–Lever Act in 1914, a partnership between the United States Department of Agriculture and the agricultural colleges created the cooperative agricultural extension service. By sponsoring 4-H clubs for youth and various services for adults, the extension service tried to raise living standards and to encourage positive attitudes concerning agricultural life. The government supported land grant colleges like Cornell that trained agriculturalists and issued informational bulletins for farmers. Yet this combination of propaganda and reform did little to prevent the flight from farms.

Political Pathways to Reform

Mugwumps, machine politics, and municipal reform

The movement for political reform began in the same urban areas of the Northeast and Midwest manufacturing belt that advanced the industrial revolution in the United States. Progress toward good government officially began in the 1880s, when nonpartisan reformers who by the 1890s had become known as "mugwumps," a derivative of a Native American word meaning "great man" or "big chief," organized clubs in several American cities seeking to streamline government, clean up corruption, and convert municipalities into model corporations. Reformers' focused their efforts on curbing abuses of power within city governments where political power lay in the hands of professional politicians (bosses) and their party organizations (machines).

Political machinery drew support from a variety of sources. Machines placed bosses at the top and their representatives at every level of local government down to precincts of several thousand voters each. Machines derived their power from the masses who voted them into – and kept them in – office. For machines to be successful, party backing was also crucial. Since machines required the support of the majority of the voters, they catered to ethnic sensitivities.

Bosses granted political favors and dispensed "no-bid" contracts for city works and projects to contractors and others who hired large numbers of employees; it was understood that these contractors would pressure their many employees to toe the party line. In return for their constituents' votes, the bosses rewarded them with much needed jobs in the days and weeks following elections. As a result, on large-scale building projects such as subway systems, thousands of immigrant workers were hired. This format distinguished machines from the alternative political

141

groups that drew their strength from societal elites and the power players of the upper and middle classes. Outsiders, including many Progressive reformers, saw the boss-controlled machine system of city governance as the most vile form of politics, one driven by the ignorance of the easily exploitable masses.

Regardless of how some in society viewed them and their tactics, the machines worked in the eyes of the masses of the so-called immigrant residents. Not only did the bosses and their machines see that essential city services such as regular garbage collection and street paving went to the neighborhoods of "loyal" voters, but they also helped to coordinate the city's disparate elements into the same system. They provided entrepreneurs and corporations with lucrative franchises and contracts, criminals and vice merchants with protection from the law, and urban masses with material benefits as well as an accessible career ladder for promising individuals of some immigrant groups. Nonetheless, as the spending of city government and the accompanying property taxes escalated to meet growing demands to see that all parts of the machine were regularly "oiled," and as revelations of political corruption and corporate arrogance rose to unconscionable levels, affluent city residents began to clamor for Progressive reform.

Initially, historians assessed the turn-of-the-century boss system as a completely corrupt one, but in recent years, some scholars have modified their views of machine politics by pointing out that the bosses often provided the only viable assistance that immigrants received in making the transition to American life. Before the advent of settlement houses and ethnic mutual aid societies, bosses welded a particularly strong influence on Southern and Eastern European immigrants. They helped immigrants cope with the realities of city life by providing a sense of welcome and belonging. In Chicago, Irish-born saloon keeper and Democratic Alderman Johnny Powers sponsored neighborhood picnics and clambakes replete with entertainment. In return, urban ethnic groups demonstrated their appreciation at the ballot box. Nascent immigrant politicians, particularly young Jews and Italians, eventually broke away from the dominant political machines and tied their allegiance to whichever political party reacted against prohibitionists who wanted to outlaw liquor manufacturing and consumption and nativists who advocated restrictions on foreign immigration. Catholics in particular were afraid that if prohibition became the law of the land, then the wine used to symbolize the body of Christ during their masses would also be prohibited. Most Italians drank wine with meals and some liked to use it recreationally.

Many urban workers became entrenched in machine politics when they attempted to form their own labor unions or sought help finding jobs, housing, or financial assistance in hard times. Private charities tended to be suspicious of immigrant applicants and public assistance at the time was virtually nonexistent, so powerful bosses like Johnny Powers in Chicago and Charles Francis Murphy, chief of New York's Democratic Party headquartered at Tammany Hall for over twenty years, stepped in to serve the needy. Widows and others barely able to survive looked forward to receiving food baskets at holiday time, coal in winter, and even small loans in a crunch, all courtesy of the "boss."

The Good Government movement

The National Conference for Good City Government, or "goo goos," as the Good Government supporters came to be called, met for the first time in Philadelphia in 1894. Keynote speaker, the future President and Police Commissioner for New York City Theodore Roosevelt, preached the importance of morality and competency in city government. Political Progressives demanded that civic officials displace the bosses and assume responsibility by addressing social problems. Goo goos sometimes ran their own candidates who demonized bosses but were often defeated by machine candidates with wider appeal to the constituents.

The National Municipal League was established at the National Conference for Good City Government. It united various city reform groups from across the country. The founders included Theodore Roosevelt, attorney Louis Brandeis, landscape architect

Frederick Law Olmstead, and General Federation of Women's Clubs founder Mary Mumford. Participation in the League served as a good training ground for many Progressives. Dedicated to principles of good government, particularly efficiency in government, the League promoted administrative and structural reforms for city governments by encouraging the use of model city charters, especially for larger cities. League members wanted to destroy the bosses' political influence and block the ethnic-based politics of the ward system by putting politics in the hands of upstanding businessmen and professionals. Many cities set up bureaus of municipal research to run their municipality using a corporate-like model. In 1898, California, Indiana, Iowa, and Wisconsin formed statewide municipal leagues.

From its New York headquarters, in 1899, the National Municipal League published its own Municipal Program or, as it would later be known, Model City Charter. Encouraging "home rule" or local control of municipal government, the charter's structural reforms called for an expansion of mayors' power, the election of city councilmen from the voters of the city at large rather than those of individual wards, a reduction of state interference in city affairs, and the making of civil service appointments based on administrative rules and merit, as opposed to the patronage of the boss. The Charter also encouraged small- and medium-sized cities to adopt the manager form of government.

In 1908, Staunton, Virginia, became one of the first cities to introduce the City Manager Plan for municipal government. It provided a new structure to overcome the large unwieldy bicameral council and improve the city's infrastructure. By the second decade of the twentieth century, the City Manager Plan became a popular form of centralized, administrative decision making. The appointed manager, presumably an expert technician, engineer, or public administrator, was linked to a nonpartisan elected council. This format allowed the separation of policy from administration, thus removing the political element. The downside of the City Manager Plan was that the business community often stepped in to fill the political void. By 1920, reformers in over 130 cities had adopted the City Manager Plan.

As Galveston rebuilt after the horrendous hurricane of 1900 that decimated the city, civic reform leaders instituted another form of municipal governance, the City Commission Plan. The governor of Texas appointed a five-member commission to coordinate the rebuilding of the city after the disaster. It was so successful that it became permanent. By 1917, approximately 500 other small cities adopted the City Commission Plan, or "Galveston Plan," which often incorporated ideas of referendum, initiative, and recall. Under this structure, an elected commission had policy making and administrative powers. No one person was ultimately in charge, but five commissioners shared equal power.

Despite the support of the National Municipal League for the city manager structure, many large cities continued to favor the ward-based, partisan mayor–council form of government. These same cities also tended to favor city charters, which determined the political structure of the specific city. Larger cities wanted charters with discretionary financial and political power, allowing them to manage their own affairs without the involvement of the state legislature. Proponents of the ward system argued that incorporated cities stripped away the power of ordinary citizens.

Beautiful cities and urban planning: from aesthetics to efficiency

Belief in the city's potential as a means to the good life became a hallmark of the Progressive Era. The opportunity to methodically, even scientifically, plan the physical growth of cities offered another dimension to urban reform: that of aesthetics. American architects drew inspiration from chief architect Daniel Burnham's White City architectural composition at the 1893 World's Columbian Exposition. Burnham oversaw the placement of the adorned Baroque-style buildings grouped around boulevards and fountains replete with twinkling lights, presented grand vistas, and convinced many that cities could be more beautiful, more livable environments. Burnham wanted to sweep social ills away and to rectify urban decay by transforming the city in a way that would "complement the burgeoning reforms in other areas of society." Beautiful cities could become centers that inspired moral and civic virtue in its inhabitants. Notable architects Frederick Law Olmstead, designer of New York City's Central Park, the country's first professor of city planning, and the author of *The Improvement of Towns and Cities* (1901), and Charles Mulford Robinson dedicated their careers to spreading the principles of what became known as the City Beautiful movement. Most of the City Beautiful proponents were white upper class males who wanted to attract their contemporaries into cities to live, work, and spend their money there.

While the notion of urban planning comprising a broad set of ideas and techniques had been around since the inception of cities, historian Jon A. Peterson in *The Birth of City Planning in the United States* (2003), argues that Progressive Era architects and supporters of the City Beautiful movement developed their own, uniquely American version of city planning to make the city more efficient. While city planners and civil engineers concentrated on designing street patterns to provide grand boulevards, public plazas, and imposing civic centers in an appealing and efficient manner, they recognized the need to relieve the chaos, congestion, and sanitary issues already present in American cities.

In the wake of the 1907 financial panic, the City Beautiful movement evolved into a movement focused almost entirely on efficiency and economics rather than one that considered aesthetics. Creating a more functional city required a local planning commission for oversight. By 1909, the same year that the first city planning conference was held in Washington, D.C., Charles M. Robinson had produced a number of reports for individual city plans. Some critics felt these plans concentrated entirely too much beauty and pushed instead to institute strict zoning requirements to control urban growth and aid in constructing a comprehensive city plan. They encouraged illuminated streets, mass transit systems, public parks and gardens, and zoning legislation so that American urban spaces, like those in Europe, could be designated according to their intended uses as residential, commercial, or industrial. These so-called zoning laws allowed Progressive reformers to exert a degree of control over the development of their respective municipalities. In 1913, state legislatures in New York, Illinois, Wisconsin, and Minnesota passed laws authorizing municipalities to define residential zones from which businesses could be excluded. The notion of the city as a center for economic development clearly had triumphed over the ideal of a beautiful city.

While Robinson and Burnham did influence city planning in Washington, D.C., Chicago, and a number of other municipalities, by 1917, the vision of a comprehensive city plan was no longer a reality for most American cities. Two national organizations, the American Park and Outdoor Art Association and the National League of Improvement Associations (later renamed the American League for Civic Improvement), advanced the spirit of city beautification long after the City Beautiful movement faded from view.

As early as 1890, Jacob Riis in his aforementioned *How the Other Half Lives: Studies among the Tenements of New York* publicly exposed the wretchedness of tenement life in New York. Riis helped to draw a correlation between housing conditions and poor sanitation, which led to the creation of new housing legislation in the form of local ordinances. In 1901, New York became the first city in the country to pass an ordinance that addressed crowding and unsanitary conditions in the city's tenements. Other cities followed New York's lead; their laws were not, however, as strictly enforced. Indeed, the key to the effectiveness of New York's ordinance was rooted in its provisions for inspection and enforcement.

Much of the early Progressive effort in implementing good government went into identifying and addressing the practical defects of municipal governments, not the least of which was corruption. Through the work of the good government forces, city policies as well as the cities themselves would come to reflect progressive change. Charles Zueblin, former professor of sociology at the University of Chicago and later president of the American League for Civic Improvement, wanted to reorganize civic

147

life. According to Zueblin, problems stemming from triumphant industrialism and unrestrained commercialism included "smoke, noise, blatant advertising, congestion of population, disfigurement of nature, hideousness of home architecture and dearth of recreation." By 1916, he concluded in his book *Municipal Progress* that "the progressive satisfaction of the wants of all the people has ceased to be a utopian ideal; it is the only reasonable municipal program."

Ideally, the purposely planned and orderly growth of cities would complement the political and administrative structure of urban government. City planning, then, may be best understood as a multifaceted cultural movement that sought to give outward and visible expression to Progressive Era reform impulses to revitalize public life and instill civic awareness. The idea that the government should exact control over the physical development of the city, including its outdoor art and parks led to support for government regulation.

State Level Reform

LaFollette and the Wisconsin Idea

The impetus for reform at the state level seemed to move at a much slower pace than it did at the local level. In the Midwest, intense factionalism erupted inside the Republican Party. In the midst of these disputes, Robert LaFollette, the governor of Wisconsin from 1901 to 1906 and U.S. Senator from 1906 to 1925, emerged as a Progressive leader. A passionate orator who attracted both Democrats and Republicans, it was LaFollette who, perhaps better than anyone else, personified the Progressive principles that ultimately shaped the national political reform movement.

LaFollette's "Wisconsin Idea," as it would come to be known, encompassed a set of Progressive ideas developed while he served as governor of the state with advice from scientists and professors at the University of Wisconsin. Once elected to the Senate, LaFollette relied on the Wisconsin Idea to engineer Progressive legislation. During his six-year term as governor, Progressives gained control of the state's Republican Party, opening the door to push reform legislation forward. LaFollette successfully rallied dissident farmers and workers into a powerful coalition. Under his leadership, the Wisconsin Progressives mounted a campaign aimed at reducing the role that professional politicians played in elections and in government itself. The main fruits of this campaign were a direct primary law in 1903 and a civil service law in 1905. The direct primary law decreased the power of political parties in the state by calling for the direct nomination of all candidates by voters for county and state offices, rather than having them nominated by delegates to party conventions. The new civil service law did away with patronage appointment in the civil service by establishing a system by which all government employees were hired on the basis of the results of competitive civil service exams and created a commission to oversee the administration of the civil service system.

Wisconsin became a laboratory for democracy, a place where the support required for Progressive reforms escalated. Germans and organized labor who had not initially supported the Progressive movement became important players in Wisconsin. However, while LaFollette rallied diverse factions and interest groups to the Progressive cause, he never gained complete control over the Republican Party in Wisconsin. James Davidson, LaFollette's gubernatorial successor from 1906 to 1911, witnessed the enactment of a large number of LaFollette's reform measures. Other Progressive laws passed included provisions for state control over corporation stock issues, an extension of the power of the railroad commission to regulate transportation by setting fair freight rates, and stricter regulation of insurance companies. In 1911, the legislature established a state life insurance fund, protective legislation limiting working hours for women and children, and forest and waterpower conservation Acts. The state's tax system was transformed when in 1911 Wisconsin enacted the first workable state income tax in the United States. Perhaps most important, the legislature began construction of the state's modern social welfare system, by creating the Industrial Commission to investigate and regulate working conditions and by making

Wisconsin the first state in the nation to establish a workers' compensation system.

Beyond Wisconsin

LaFollette's version of Progressivism swept the country. By 1906, the platforms of both major political parties criticized the control of politics by big business interests. Reform candidates who called for Progressive reform measures won at the polls. What had once been seemingly sporadic movements in isolated states expanded into a nationwide reform crusade. Legislatures regulated lobbying, forbade campaign contributions by corporations, and prohibited railroads from issuing free passes to legislators and other state officials. Almost all states instituted direct primaries to wrestle selection of political candidates away from the influence of corrupt railroad bosses and corporations and place it in the hands of the voters. Most important, states expanded their regulation of utilities, railroads, and other corporations by creating scientific commissions to enforce new regulations. From 1905 to 1907, fifteen new state railroad commissions were established and the powers of many existing ones were expanded. These commissions had the authority to, among other things, set rates and supervise safety, service, and financial operations. Over the next few years, the powers of these commissions were expanded to street railways and gas, electric, telephone, and telegraph companies. An undeniably fundamental transformation occurred in state governments.

Battling Bob's (LaFollette) ideas spread as far west as California. Governor Hiram Johnson championed LaFollette's reforms when he attacked the domination of the state government by the Southern Pacific Railroad during his 1910 campaign. Once in office, Johnson limited the power of the railroads by establishing a state commission to set rates charged to consumers, forged an alliance with labor leaders who had not initially supported his candidacy, supported expansion of the state's workers' compensation legislation, and created commissions to investigate and regulate the conditions of working women and children. Johnson also enacted structural changes in the government including direct election of U.S. senators, the recall of public officials, and the ability to legislate by popular referendum.

Businessmen Left Behind

Businessmen rarely exhibited Progressive behavior. According to Robert Weibe, with few exceptions, businessmen did not try to improve the status of low-income Americans. Moreover, they opposed independent labor unions and protective labor legislation and often drove city politics to their own benefit. Nevertheless, the second aspect to consider when assessing businessmen's Progressive sentiments is the part they did play in reform. A few did institute private welfare capitalism, providing company-sponsored benefits for their employees, but since welfare capitalism was still in its infancy, it affected more middle-income workers than unskilled ones. The only real contribution businessmen made to the Progressive cause came as a by-product of their zeal for civic improvement. They joined chambers of commerce (which were often racist and protective, anti-union organizations) to form business communities at the local level and became aware of reform at the national level.

In a number of states, reformers helped to expose the extent to which businessmen bribed legislators, conspired with party chieftains, and bought nominations. In short, corporations received legislative protection in return for outright bribes and campaign contributions they showered on Republican candidates. In 1896, William McKinley was elected president with a $250,000 contribution from Standard Oil Trust after he ran on a platform favoring industry and Eastern manufacturers.

Worse yet were the insurance company scandals. Attacks on abuses by insurance companies began in New York in 1905 with the Armstrong investigations into fraudulent practices in the life insurance industry by a state legislative committee chaired by William H. Armstrong, a lawyer raised in Orleans, New York. The New York investigations were followed in 1906 by inquiries into the American Life (Insurance) Conference in Chicago. Both investigations revealed corruption in the form of political alliances between Republican Party officials and company executives. Politicians took bribes from company men in return for campaign funds and legislative protection. In the end, the investigations resulted in state regulation that demanded ethical practices.

The challenging economic climate in the aftermath of the panic of 1907 stripped the glamor away from reform and caused some businessmen to turn arrogant and rigid. Perceiving the new Republican President as more business-friendly than his "trust-busting" predecessor, Theodore Roosevelt, businessmen applied constant pressure during Taft's administration. They claimed victory with the passage of the Payne–Aldrich Act, which fulfilled their desire to raise import tariffs to protect their business interests. For politically astute Americans, however, the Act represented a conspicuous example of the influence of special interest groups on legislative policy.

The Radical Political Reaction

Socialists

Even in the face of the domination by the major political parties, beginning in the late nineteenth century, ethnic and religious groups searched to find a way around machine politics in the hope of influencing governmental policies. In cities like St. Louis and San Francisco, anti-corruption drives resulted in the working-class becoming more influential in local politics. Socialism, with its practical ideas such as public ownership of public utilities, began to appeal to an increasing number of workers.

In 1901, the Socialist Party of America formed, partially around the idea of befriending trade unions and encouraging them to pursue a political agenda. The Socialists recognized the importance of the AFL, but ironically, its immigrant president, Samuel Gompers, a man schooled in Marxism, chose to operate within the boundaries of the capitalistic system while Eugene Debs, son of the Midwestern free market system, emerged from his jail time (as a result of his leadership during the Pullman Strike in 1894) as a committed Socialist. In their heyday, the Socialists enjoyed support from a number of labor unions. The United Mine Workers, Boot and Shoe Workers, Machinists, Ladies Garment Workers, and Brewery Workers, all affiliated with the Socialists.

The Socialist Party won more than 400 public offices, including mayoral races, in twenty-eight cities between 1910 and 1911. The Socialists also presented a united front at the national level under the leadership of Eugene V. Debs in the election of 1912. In that contest, Debs earned six percent of the popular vote, close to one million votes. Other Socialist candidates made strong showings in 1912 as well. Two Socialists became members of the United States Congress, fifty-six became mayors, thirty-three won seats in seventeen state legislatures, and almost a thousand Socialist candidates won elections to town and city councils.

Industrial Workers of the World

Even more radical than the socialists were the Industrial Workers of the World (IWW), or "Wobblies" as they were commonly known. They held a founding convention in Chicago in 1905 where members converged around the goal of emancipating the working class "from the slave bondage of capitalism." IWW leaders believed that the impetus for change lay in union activism rather than through the machinations of a political party. Initially, the IWW appealed to members of Socialist organizations and even some unionists previously affiliated with the AFL. Like the Knights of Labor before them, the Wobblies wanted to organize all workers, regardless of skill level, particular craft, or ethnicity, into one big union. IWW leaders like the colorful, six-foot-tall William "Big Bill" Haywood of the Western Federation of Mine Workers shocked many Americans when he called for the overthrow of the capitalistic system. Stopping short of such notions, the Wobblies advanced a plan that would abolish the wage system and promote worker ownership of the nation's factories, mines, railroads, and other enterprises that employed industrial workers.

The IWW gained national attention when it supported a brutal strike over the intolerable conditions and wage cuts of 30,000 American Woolen Company textile workers in Lawrence, Massachusetts. In 1911, the Massachusetts State Legislature passed a law that went into effect on January 1, 1912, reducing the legal workweek from fifty-six to fifty-four hours. The mill owners cut the workers' pay by two hours and at the same time instigated speedups, which required workers to produce more with no extra compensation. Polish women were the first to shut down their looms and walk out of the factory. The strike quickly spread to all the mills in the city. Since the majority of the workers were immigrant women, rather than supporting the virtually leaderless strike, the AFL denounced it as revolutionary and anarchistic. IWW organizers including Elizabeth Gurley Flynn stepped in to coordinate the strike effort.

Women played a large part in the strike, walking on picket lines and carrying banners demanding "Bread and Roses too." This phrase would become a famous strike slogan, as it encapsulated the need for immediate financial remuneration like higher wages but also recognized that women strikers demanded the respect of the owners. Mill owners fought back with a militia, local police, and strikebreakers. In the strife, a woman striker was shot and a supposed dynamite plot was revealed. (The dynamite scheme was later proven to be the work of American Woolen Mill President William Wood.) As concerned citizens were in the process of moving the children of striking workers out of Lawrence to be clothed and fed in Philadelphia, the police attacked them, taking the children away from their parents and throwing thirty women and children in jail. Public sympathy mounted for the striking workers, mostly women, and public opinion turned against the employers. After more than two months, and largely due to public pressure, the owners settled the strike by granting pay raises, overtime pay, and promises of no discrimination against strikers. Earning massive national press coverage and an outpouring of support from the American public, the Lawrence

Strike marked the high point of the IWW. The circumstances surrounding the incident prompted the outgoing President Taft to create an Industrial Commission to investigate working conditions across the nation.

In 1913, the Paterson, New Jersey, silk workers struck, seeking an eleven-hour day and a six-day week. Wage cuts and speedups became an issue just as they had in Lawrence. Although the IWW tried to unite the silk workers in order to crystallize their demands, the skilled English-speaking workers prematurely settled with the mill owners and returned to work on a shop-by-shop basis, leaving the largely unskilled Italian and Jewish workers without the support necessary to win any concessions.

Too militant for most workers and wracked by internal divisions, the Wobblies did not win many battles, but by generating effective publicity in major newspapers and magazines, they did effectively convey the message that American workers were mistreated. While Progressives had already taken this message to heart, they increasingly agreed with the radicals that in order to rectify the conditions faced by the nation's industrial workforce, direct government intervention would be necessary to challenge and effectively redress the unregulated concentrations of wealth and power contained in the giant national corporations. In short, industrial capitalism had to be made to become more humane.

Labor Leans Political

Under Gompers's pure and simple doctrine, labor unions belonged in the private sector, where they would negotiate with employers for the immediate or "bread and butter" needs of their labor force: higher wages, fewer hours, and safer and more comfortable workplace conditions. Until the early 1900s, the courts virtually always sided with employers in cases regarding conflicts in the workplace. Gompers of the AFL firmly believed in voluntarism, the notion that workers should never seek at the hands of government what they could accomplish with their own activities. In keeping with the notion of voluntarism, Gompers also wanted to avoid involvement in partisan politics. But rather than strengthening the position of organized labor, Gompers's strictly nonpartisan policies contributed to organized labor's vulnerability.

Just two years into the twentieth century, labor suffered a series of hostile court decisions. One of the first attempts by employers to crush unions under the Sherman Antitrust Act came in 1902, when the D. H. Loewe Company in Danbury, Connecticut, refused to recognize the United Hatters' Union, an AFL affiliate. In response, the hatters called a boycott against the company and publicly asked people to refuse to buy the company's products. As a result of decreased sales, the following year, the company sued the union. By 1908, the case had advanced all the way up to the United States Supreme Court, which sided with the company, ruling that a boycott of the workplace restrained trade. The decision called the very legality of the union into question when the hatters, both as a union and as individual members, were held liable for $252,000 in damages. Samuel Gompers, president of AFL, helped to pay the fine, which amounted to more than $1,000 per member. The high court had clearly come down on side of employers, causing the entire labor movement to shudder in fear.

In 1906, a partially organized St. Louis Metal Polishers' strike for a nine-hour day resulted in the call for a similar boycott. After the union placed the company on the AFL's "Do Not Patronize" list, the owner of the Buck's Stove and Range Company, James Van Cleave, sued the AFL over lost revenue. Van Cleave, who also happened to be the president of the National Association of Manufacturers, won a sweeping injunction from the United States Court of Appeals against the union and its official newspaper, the *American Federationist*.

Labor's Bill of Grievances

The third in a series of incidents that finally pushed organized labor into politics concerned the Chicago Typographical Workers.

In 1906, workers from the oldest union in the city went on strike for an eight-hour day. Although they won their eight-hour day, Judge Holdom of the Illinois Supreme Court delivered an injunction that forbade picketing, prevented workers from informing scabs that there was a strike on, and prohibited workers from mentioning that a strike had ever occurred. During the course of the strike, the union president, Edwin R. Wright, was convicted with contempt of court for interfering in the operation of non-union printing establishments. Wright was jailed for thirty days. As a result, Gompers called a meeting with his executive board, which, in response, issued a declaration called Labor's Bill of Grievances, part of which demanded relief from the harsh injunction practices exacted against labor unions under the Sherman Antitrust Act, which continually defined unions as conspiracies capable of restraining trade.

The legislative and executive branches of government seemed more amenable to Progressive reform than the more conservative courts. The first efforts of the government to take a more active role in the economic arena came in the railroad industry in the wake of the 1894 Pullman Strike. In fact, the Erdman Act, passed by Congress in 1898 in response to the Pullman Strike, set the precedent for government intervention in the economy. For the first time, the federal government recognized the legitimacy of railroad unions and, with the establishment of a federal mediation board, provided a mechanism to settle disputes. It also outlawed the use of yellow-dog contracts, which forced workers to sign a written promise to their employers swearing that they would not join a union. The Erdman Act gave the Interstate Commerce Commission power to set rates and pointed to a federal role in the economy that moved in the direction of regulatory state.

Workers experienced a second wave of encouragement in 1902 when anthracite coal miners struck in northeastern Pennsylvania for a wage increase and an eight-hour day. The United Mine Workers' president, John Mitchell, appealed to the National Civic Federation, an advocate of collective bargaining, to help settle the strike, but this effort failed. As the strike attracted publicity, the public also called for intervention. President Theodore Roosevelt wanted to force the hand of the mine owners by threatening to seize the mines in the name of the federal government. As a result, a seven-man arbitration committee was formed and the strike was settled in March 1903 with a wage increase of ten percent, the employment of check weighmen (representatives elected by the coal miners to check the accuracy of the mines, wherein miners are paid by the weight of coal mined), and the prohibition of discriminatory hiring practices against union members. The new century seemed promising as the union gained a stronger foothold in the region and union membership in the AFL-affiliated United Mine Workers increased. In the resolution of the work stoppage, Roosevelt won a political victory and with his heightened image, his administration went on to win the Northern Securities case by 1904. Most important, the strike set a precedent for direct government intervention on the side of striking union workers.

Despite the victory in the mine fields, however, for the next few years, Samuel Gompers and his AFL continued to cling to an increasingly obsolete doctrine of voluntarism and frown upon direct governmental involvement in the economy. Instead, Gompers continued to encourage voluntary negotiations between labor and employers, even though such tactics had failed time and time again to protect the masses of workers.

Now labor, which apparently could wait no longer, reluctantly entered the political arena. Its first such foray into the world of formal politics came with its Bill of Grievances composed by AFL President Samuel Gompers and members of the Executive Board in March 1906. The bill pointed to changing industrial conditions and listed a number of issues that labor leaders felt needed immediate attention. Addressed to President Roosevelt, the Senate Pro Tempore, and the Speaker of the House of Representatives, the AFL letter demanded relief from ineffective antitrust laws and interstate commerce laws as well as legislation to enforce an eight-hour day for all work done on behalf of the government, including the building of the Panama Canal. Labor also encouraged the passage of laws that protected their workers from the competition of convict labor and restricted immigration. The Bill of Grievances also made reference to the hazards of the shipping industry, including the 1904 fire on the *General Slocum* in the East River. The more than 1,300 members of the East Village German Evangelical Lutheran St. Mark's Church aboard ship were headed for a Sunday picnic on Long Island. Within fifteen minutes of the fire breaking out, the ship sank, resulting in the death of over 1,000 of the passengers. The tragedy remained the greatest loss of life in New York City until the events of September 11, 2001. The Republicans rebuffed the bill.

In the presidential election of 1908, the Democrats, who tended to draw their strength from urban areas, addressed some of labor's demands. Several years later, as the election of 1912 approached, the candidates openly appealed to the labor vote. Indeed, the election of that year made labor history by marking the first time that the AFL formally endorsed a presidential candidate. Gompers gave a nod of approval to the Democrat Woodrow Wilson and encouraged AFL members to follow suit. It took the Clayton Antitrust Act in 1914 to ensure that unions were no longer to be regarded as conspiracies in restraint of trade. The Act established the legitimacy of unions.

In the opening decade of the new century, political realities – not the least of which were hostile anti-union court injunctions – compelled labor leaders to enter politics overtly. They needed to be able to effectively exercise solidarity and collective action. Historically, the government, especially the judicial branch, impinged on trade union security. Gradually, over the course of the early twentieth century, workers began to identify as citizens of a larger community.

For unskilled and unorganized workers, politics took on new meaning. They hoped that political activism would translate into effective labor organizations. Yet, the promise of collective action never fully came to fruition during the Progressive Era. The nature of working-class politics revealed that at state and local levels, labor was never a viable force. Workers suffered from internal conflicts and religious and ethnic divisions. Moreover, unskilled workers were disappointed that the AFL remained an exclusive aristocracy that organized only skilled white men while neglecting the masses of workers. It would not be until the 1930s that workers reaped the benefits of a more favorable political environment.

Workplace activism

While unions were struggling for political recognition, women workers were fighting merely to gain admittance into unions. Since male-dominated unions had failed women workers by refusing to organize them at all, Progressive women reformers based at the urban settlement houses stepped in to help. With the assistance of the National Women's Trade Union League (NWTUL), an organization founded in Boston in 1903 to organize working women into trade unions, women in the garment trades had begun to organize in order to barter collectively in the fight to force management to improve conditions in the workplace, which, in many cases, were sweatshops.

In their own way, working conditions in sweatshops in the garment trades rivaled those of the railroad and mining industries. Women comprised the majority of clothing workers in both the men's and women's garment shops. Sixty-hour weeks and half-penny piece rates were commonplace. In addition to putting in long monotonous hours for very little pay, workers were expected to bring bundles of work home to finish at rush periods and to stay at work during slack times even when there was nothing for them to do. They were fined for damaged goods and had to buy their own needles to hand sew with or rent the machines they operated. In addition, women workers routinely endured sexual harassment from their male supervisors.

To help improve working women's circumstances, NWTUL president Margaret Dreier Robbins extended the League's original goal of organizing women workers into trade unions to one that focused on activism in the political realm. By 1908, the League openly allied with the suffrage cause and lobbied for legislation that protected women and children. After the *Muller* decision, women reformers pushed past the courts to try to compel the federal government resolve the social, economic, and political problems that plagued the nation.

Drawing on a tradition of radicalism in their homelands and assisted by the NWTUL, Jewish and Italian women garment workers led strikes demanding union recognition in 1909 in New York and in 1910 in Chicago. In both instances, the workers achieved partial victories but in doing so were labeled by mainstream society as radicals. Fortunately, the assistance the women workers received from the middle-class women in the NWTUL, settlement workers, civic leaders, and even Socialists advanced the workers' cause. By virtue of the cross-class efforts of these Progressive reformers, the American public in general became aware of and more sympathetic to the plight of unprotected women.

Clothing workers congregated in the International Ladies Garment Workers' Union (ILGWU), which had established the Protocol of Peace, the brainchild of *Muller* attorney Louis Brandeis, whereby employers agreed to negotiate their differences with workers in the trade after women garment workers in New York struck for a second time in 1910. ILGWU leaders invited Sidney Hillman, a leader for the men's garment workers in Chicago, to administer the Protocol from the ILGWU headquarters in New York. Hillman's Progressive vision revolved around the idea of creating an industrial democracy replete with an expanded government whose purpose was to protect the workers. Rooted in the Russian Jewish tradition of *tsodeka* or obligatory giving, industrial unionism complemented the Progressives' concern for social justice.

Progressivism Takes Center Stage

Motivated by multiple factors, including the muckrakers' exposés of corruption and greed in business and urban politics, incidents of violence in the workplace, urban sprawl, the social settlement reform movement, progress at the state level, and perhaps even to a certain degree by the spirit of nationalism that followed the nation's dramatic victory in the Spanish American War (1898), Americans carried their activist causes to the national arena. Arthur Link convincingly argued that the reform impetus behind Progressivism at the city and state level transitioned to the national political stage as early as 1905, when it became apparent from the election results and from the exposure of scandals that only the federal government could provide effective solutions to the nation's problems. So the Progressives came to trust the government at the same moment ordinary Americans were beginning to ask what the government could do to help them.

Historians maintain that nonpartisanship became one of the hallmarks of the era. At almost every opportunity, the reformers united behind democratic rhetoric to attack political corruption and to inspire the passage of regulatory laws aimed at converting political parties from private to public entities. Nominating methods, campaign practices, and appointment powers had remained largely sporadic throughout the 1880s. By the dawn of the twentieth century, reforms, including direct primaries and elections and new civil service systems, became encased within the web of law.

Another long overdue transformation in American political life also began with the Progressives. Political parties lost some of their control over government at the same time the states and the nation stepped up their efforts to regulate the economy and ensure social welfare. These new tasks of government fell not to partisan legislators but to independent boards and nonpartisan commissions.

Progressive reformers strove to put government back into the hands of the people. They carried their demands from the local and state level into national affairs. New legislation enacted to address corrupt practices tore open the illicit relationships between greedy big businessmen and shrewd politicians. The direct primary was but one of many reforms designed to halt corruption, for it let voters at the polls rather than party machines at political conventions select candidates for important offices. The initiative made it possible for citizens' groups to propose legislation, while the referendum made it possible for the voters to propose and sometime pass state laws on specific issues. The Seventeenth Amendment to the U.S. Constitution stripped the power to appoint U.S. senators away from the state legislatures and required that Senators be directly elected by the people. New laws that regulated child labor and women's work and provided accident insurance, aid to the aged poor and dependent children, and mother's assistance also were passed. In some states, reformers were able to raise the age limits on compulsory school attendance laws.

As the strength of the major political parties waned, the power of public opinion began to grow. Special interest organizations like the NWTUL, the NCL, and the American Association for Labor Legislation numbered among the groups that expanded their agency. These groups, along with labor organizations, businessmen, and a plethora of others, appealed directly to the government to advance their respective agendas. Although it would be years before women achieved the vote at the national level, settlement women learned early on to ally with social scientists, clergy, civic leaders, politicians, and academics to accomplish their reform agenda. While civic-minded men sought access to the channels of government through party politics, empathetic women who wanted to affect policy directed their energies toward empowering themselves – so that they might empower other women – by assuming leadership positions inside the settlement houses. In retrospect, because they were excluded from the formal political world, virtually all leading women reformers in the United States were affiliated with the settlement movement during the Progressive Era.

In recent years, historians have suggested that during the Progressive Era, women, more often than men, were the catalysts for changes in the political status quo, for settlement leaders realized the importance of politics in accomplishing and expanding their goals. Historian Kathryn Kish Sklar contends, "In, but not of, the Social Gospel movement, the women at Hull House were a political boat on a religious stream, advancing political solutions to social problems that were fundamentally ethical or moral, such as the right of workers to a fair return for their labor or the right of children to schooling." Settlement women reached across class lines to empower early labor feminists like Bessie Abramowitz Hillman, cofounder of the Amalgamated Clothing Workers of America, and Rose Schneiderman, national organizer for the NWTUL and for the ILGWU, who fought to organize women in the workplace and as citizens. Their visions for industrial democracy included equal treatment within their unions and in American society at large. In advancing their version of social justice, they helped to visualize and create the social welfare state.

In short, virtually every Progressive reformer and organization called for government intervention in the private sector or private lives of Americans in an attempt to alleviate injustices or people's suffering. The activist, hands-on personality of President Theodore Roosevelt encouraged this direction. Herbert Croly's *Promise of American Life* (1909) articulated the demand for a government that promoted the welfare of all. A number of reformers coalesced around the idea of an activist and more democratic government. They held devout faith in statism, believing that the growing dimensions of the nation's problems meant that only the government could establish controls necessary to achieve social justice.

4

The Shape of Things to Come
Progressivism and the Transition to Modern Life, 1912–1917

The Rise of Consumerism

By 1900, American businesses had fully rebounded from the Depression of 1893. Agriculture, transportation, steel, and oil ranked among the nation's leading industries. Farms supplied the raw materials for cotton textiles, food, and other products for which rural and urban Americans were developing an insatiable hunger. Cotton remained the largest export: farmers actually grew more corn than cotton, but because animals and people consumed it, little corn reached the marketplace.

Following the example set by Rockefeller's Standard Oil, after the Depression of 1893, many large companies merged with their smaller competitors. By 1901, after a merger between Andrew Carnegie and J. P. Morgan's steel interests, U.S. Steel became the richest corporation in the world. Even more companies including Quaker Oats, Diamond Matches, Campbell's Soup, American Tobacco, Carnation, DuPont Chemicals, International Harvester, General Electric, and Goodyear Tire and Rubber, became household names. Many of these enterprises quickly surpassed railroads,

The Progressives: Activism and Reform in American Society, 1893–1917, First Edition.
Karen Pastorello.
© 2014 John Wiley & Sons, Inc. Published 2014 by John Wiley & Sons, Inc.

which throughout the nineteenth century had reigned as the largest companies in the nation, in size and complexity. However, since many American workers, particularly those in rural areas, blamed big businesses for having caused the depression in the first place, they did not necessarily approve of these giant corporations. But, with the return of prosperity, the middle class resigned itself to accept these companies, as they had prior to the depression, primarily because they welcomed the ready availability of the many products they could now afford to purchase.

As early as 1899, Thorstein Veblen, in his influential book *Theory of the Leisure Class*, criticized the lifestyles of affluent Americans, whom he believed spent too much of their time and money purchasing lavish goods for the sake of displaying their wealth. Veblen suggested that this "conspicuous consumption" by the upper classes paved the way for an increasingly materialistic world wherein those in the middle class also became obsessed with achieving status by emulating the buying patterns of those higher up in the social hierarchy. Working-class Americans soon followed the lead of the more affluent in becoming avid consumers. In the midst of rushing to purchase what became a vast array of manufactured items like packaged goods and foods, seemingly few Americans worried about the massive waste or exploitation of natural resources, the inevitable consequences of such rampant output.

The number and amount of goods available rose along with earnings. By 1910, the U.S. Patent Office had registered over one million patents, nine-tenths of them in the years after 1870. Inventions ranging from fishing reels to phonographs appeared in stores and catalogues. By 1915, women accounted for ninety percent of all consumer spending. From the remote country backwoods to cosmopolitan urban areas, marketers wooed shoppers especially women with highly inventive and "scientific" forms of advertising.

Manufacturers began to spend a great deal of money in the hiring of newly formed advertising agencies to stimulate consumer demand for their products. Targeting potential consumers' psychology, workers at the advertising agencies created catchy slogans and jingles to stimulate buying. Stores, magazines, and newspapers were filled with display advertisements that associated happiness, attractiveness, and well-being with products ranging from hair tonic to automobiles. One innovative dairy company built its success by advertising "milk from contented cows."

The widely read American political writer Walter Lippmann criticized manufacturers' attempts to inundate the public with advertising. According to Lippmann, the advertisements attempted to create an aura of an unreachable (and ultimately wasteful) consumer heaven in which "the eastern sky [was] ablaze with chewing gum, the northern with toothbrushes and underwear, the western with whiskey, and the southern with petticoats, the whole heavens brilliant with monstrously flirtatious women." Certain products including small appliances like radios or the kits to build them were so popular that they literally "sold themselves."

The science of advertising, coupled with the use of newly available "consumer credit" to purchase cars and trucks and other large-ticket manufactured items like sewing machines and home appliances, helped to create a thriving consumer economy in the early 1900s. By 1890, Americans' personal debt amounted to an estimated eleven million dollars. At this time, the first credit cards were issued by oil companies, hotels, and department stores. The type of limited use created by these single-issue cards encouraged customer loyalty. Americans' borrowing habits seemed to be divided along class lines. Urban workers turned to pawnbrokers, small-loan agencies, and marginal retailers to purchase clothing or furniture on the installment plan. Middle-class consumers patronized the more respectable building and loan associations for five-year mortgages for the construction of residential homes. As the cultural stigma against borrowing money (especially among some immigrant groups) decreased, Progressive Era reformers pushed to enact laws that would make credit more readily available regardless of social or economic class.

Impact of the automobile

After an initial failure to get his automobile business off the ground, Henry Ford, the son of a Michigan farmer, formed Ford Motor Company in 1903. In 1908, Ford's company, which originally manufactured the wooden-bodied Model A, began to turn out the metal-bodied Model T, which proved to be a smashing success. Ford sold 10,000 of his "Tin Lizzies" in the first year of production. Now the automobile industry, with its newly developed "assembly lines" and issuance of credit to those who wanted a car and were willing to do so through installment buying, revolutionized the national economy. Cars and buses made the rise of regional shopping in center city retail districts or "downtowns" possible. Americans began to flock to "retail stores" to buy ready-to-wear clothes, processed food products, small appliances, and big-ticket items. As the mass production of consumer goods rolled on and the average national income crept upward, Americans had to figure out how to live with the seemingly insatiable desire to have more.

The remarkable sales of Ford's Model T created a new world, one in which a corporation could profit handsomely from the ongoing production and wide distribution of a quality product offered at a relatively low price. Ford's first real competition came from William Durant, who took over the failing Buick Company and merged it with Cadillac and Olds to create General Motors, one big company that could produce and offer a variety of car models. Ford countered by borrowing the concept of the mass marketing of automobiles from Ransom Olds, considered by many to be the founder of the American automobile industry. He produced cars using the assembly line years before Henry Ford did so; Ford tends to get more credit than Olds, though, because once Ford adopted the idea of the assembly line, he used it more efficiently to produce massive numbers of automobiles. Ransom Olds, the Ohio-born son of a blacksmith, was more concerned with producing a high-quality product even if it meant producing a limited number of cars. Americans in general became so fixated with owning a car that some went as far as mortgaging their houses to buy one.

By 1914, Ford was producing a remarkable 250,000 Model T's annually. The same year, in order to ensure worker loyalty, Ford introduced the Five Dollar Day for his employees. Thousands of workers applied for work at Ford's plants. In 1916, Ford's Highland Park, Michigan, plant alone employed 16,000 workers. By paying higher wages than any of his competitors, Henry Ford not only encouraged worker loyalty but he made it possible for his employees to purchase the cars that they manufactured.

The rapidly growing automobile production boosted the manufacture of steel, petroleum, rubber, and glass as well-effected changes in the financial industry and society. By 1901, U.S. Steel chaired by the industrial genius Elbert H. Gary, controlled eighty percent of the country's steel production and went multinational to become a billion dollar business during World War I. Rockefeller's Standard Oil began to shift its focus from kerosene to concentrate on gasoline production. Travelers' Insurance Company issued the first automobile insurance policy in the United States in Dayton, Ohio, in 1898. Even state governments began to benefit from the fees charged to license drivers. Massachusetts, Vermont, and New Hampshire were among the first states to pass laws requiring drivers' licenses. The Ford Motor Company and the McCormick Steel Company soon came to resemble independent cities, replete with their own railroad terminals, water supplies, energy sources, telephone networks, fire departments, and security forces.

Regardless of which brand of cars families purchased, the advent of the automobile dramatically changed American life. It provided virtually all who owned a car with a sense of adventure and freedom. Sunday drives became a popular pastime for city dwellers, who after church, forgot their cares and explored the open spaces and small towns outside metropolitan boundaries. Driving schools sprang up. Tourism surged as travelers made the cross-country trek from New York City to San Francisco on the Lincoln Highway and stayed in motels (a combination of the words *motor* and *hotel*). Cars also made the practice of "commuting" to work possible. Many professionals and business owners who had previously maintained country houses outside urban areas could permanently move to those houses and still drive to their jobs in the city each workday morning.

The availability of electricity also changed American life. Stores, homes, and offices began to use incandescent lights. Streetlights brightened newly paved city streets after dark and illuminated basketball courts in public parks and dance halls. Industrial lighting meant that factories could operate around the clock, employing a second and then a third shift of workers. Thomas Edison's General Electric and George Westinghouse's companies became rivals in the lighting and high-speed generator businesses.

Corporate America Takes Control

For the self-made men running the country's largest companies, the bottom line was profit. Despite the absence of a monolithic business community, corporate leaders cooperatively maneuvered to increase their profits whenever possible. E. H. Harriman of the Union Pacific Railroad, James J. Hill of the Northern Pacific, and banking magnate J.P. Morgan created a huge trust, the Northern Securities Company, which combined virtually all the long-distance railroads west of Chicago. Farther east, Jay Gould built his own railroad empire, Andrew Carnegie's mergers created an unrivaled steel empire, and John D. Rockefeller created an oil trust. Gustavus Swift used an especially innovative method to build his meatpacking business. Rather than merging, he used horizontal integration to expand his company, revolutionizing the industry with his refrigerated railroad cars and network of warehouses.

Openly promoting the end of free competition, corporate magnates led by John D. Rockefeller argued that big business was the best hope of promoting the general welfare because of the greater efficiency of large units. By 1916, some corporate leaders, including those in charge at Standard Oil, U.S. Steel, and International Harvester, were doing all that they could, including creating propaganda bureaus to handle press relations and defend themselves against attacks by the social critics in the print medium known as muckrakers, who accused them of being unscrupulous and greedy.

Small businesses were much more volatile than big businesses and therefore came and went with far greater frequency. As time passed, small businesses became less important as employers in the national economy. By the early twentieth century, large plants, those who employed more than 100 workers, employed the majority of the nation's workforce.

Scientific management

The quest for industrial efficiency transformed the workplace. After 1900, businesses rushed to reorganize and adopt some form of administrative centralization. Manufacturers jumped at the chance to meet consumer demand but realized that they could do so only by elevating efficiency to new levels. To deal with the age-old "labor problem" of how to get the most out of workers, employers experimented with new tactics. The hand of management became visible as it employed a systematic and rational approach at every turn. Employing new midlevel managers to coordinate the workplace allowed employers to become more efficient.

In his study of managerial capitalism, *The Visible Hand* (1977), professor of business history Alfred Chandler first described how the invisible hand of the market and the visible hand of administrative coordination worked together to facilitate continued corporate growth. Chandler maintained that from the inception of large-scale railroad and telegraph companies, managers were essential in day-to-day operations. Corporations hired contingents of professional managers to coordinate and control the production and delivery of freight and communication services. Accountants kept detailed account books and devised intricate statistical controls.

After 1911, corporations began to subscribe to a form of scientific management pioneered by Frederick Winslow Taylor.

171

Born to an affluent Quaker family in Germantown, Pennsylvania, as a young man, Taylor displayed a rather obsessive personality. He channeled his energies into positive pursuits to complete an engineering degree while working full-time as an apprentice machinist. After graduation, he secured an engineering job at Midvale Steel Company in Nicetown, Pennsylvania, where he began to study employee productivity. Taylor believed in finding the right jobs for the right people and then paying them well based on their output.

Owners of large factories in particular were intrigued by Taylor's theories, which he meticulously detailed in *The Principles of Scientific Management* (1911). Industrial engineers used his findings to determine the most expedient way to manufacture specific products. Concerned with workplace efficiency, "Taylorism" used time-and-motion studies to break the production process into single, often monotonous, steps, timing workers with a stopwatch as they performed specialized tasks. In the quest for maximum efficiency, Taylor's system separated manual from mental labor and skilled from unskilled tasks. Whenever possible, machines completed the production sequence. Scientifically managed production plants, with their extremely proficient procedures, became the model for future corporations.

Once industrial managers introduced scientific management into the workplace, everything from how workers found jobs to how they were treated once they were hired changed. Job seekers, who had usually been hired through an informal network of friends or relatives, now found work through the daily newspaper "want ads" that instructed them to apply at company personnel offices. In *A Honeymoon Experiment* (1916), newlywed Margaret Chase recounted how she applied at "Eastman's Kodak Factory" in Rochester, New York, and had "a pleasant interview with a shrewd and capable businesswoman who engages hundreds of women employees every year in that gigantic, well-lighted plant." From the minute workers began their jobs, they were subjected to freshly minted rules and regulations. Hired in greater numbers than ever before, workers were often required to complete rigorous training sessions and punch a time clock to track precisely their arrival and departure.

Lacking generalized knowledge of the production process, however, workers lost control over the workplace and, along with it, their bargaining power. For workers, scientific management translated to diminished autonomy, close supervision, regimentation, piecework, and manager mandated "speedups." All of these made employees dispensable. While employers reaped higher profits and achieved new levels of domination over the workplace, for the workers, Taylor's management principles amounted to sheer exploitation.

Welfare capitalism

Many companies used welfare capitalism and/or Americanization programs in their efforts to control their workers. Welfare capitalism offered a plethora of benefits to workers. It often prevented them from joining labor unions as well as strengthened their loyalty to their employer. Large companies like Heinz, Sears and Roebuck, and Eastman Kodak provided worker incentives that included paid vacations, employee lunchrooms, showers, workers' savings clubs, gymnasiums, and company sports teams and picnics. Skilled and professional workers often took advantage of pension and profit sharing plans.

Some large companies refused to hire immigrants, while some that did encouraged Americanization in the workplace, meaning they offered immigrant workers free classes in English and U.S. citizenship in an attempt to help them assimilate into American society. Employers (and even some Progressive reformers) encouraged a break with old world customs and a complete embrace of the new. In the employers' eyes, the ideal worker became a true and loyal American, one striving to work as hard as he or she possibly could despite low wages, long hours, and dangerous conditions.

The Triangle Waist Factory Fire

While the countless disasters in the mines, on the railroads, and in the steel mills were all devastating, with the exception of the Monongah Mine explosion in West Virginia, which killed more than 300 people, virtually all of them escaped national attention. It took a tragedy of unimaginable proportions to raise workplace safety concerns to the national level and ultimately generate effective workplace safety legislation.

The wretched and dangerous conditions under which many urban immigrants worked were finally exposed to the entire nation on March 25, 1911, when a fire ripped through the Triangle Shirtwaist factory, a company sweatshop housed on the top three floors of the ten-story Asch Building in New York City. The fire broke out just before closing time on a Saturday and resulted in the deaths of 146 people, mostly young Jewish and Italian women workers, some in their teens, although several men also perished in the blaze. Frances Perkins, a thirty-one-year-old social worker who had been having tea with friends a few blocks away, was one of hundreds who stood helplessly by as women and men jumped to their deaths. The "horrid spectacle" Perkins witnessed changed her life. From that day forward, she dedicated her career to improving the situation of American workers.

At the trial that followed the tragedy, some who testified recalled that the doors had been locked that day on the orders of the owners to prevent workers from taking breaks or stealing pieces of fabric used to make shirtwaists, a popular women's high-neck blouse. Even though firefighters quickly responded to the scene of the fire, their ladders were too short to reach the upper floors of the blazing building and flimsy fire-escape ladders detached from the side of the building under the weight of the escaping workers.

Eraclio Montanaro witnessed the fire from the street with a friend. In an interview over forty years later, Montanaro vividly recalled: "We saw what was happening at the corner of Wash-

Figure 4.1 New York City firemen leading a commemorative trade union procession for the victims of the Triangle Waist Company fire, 1911. Library of Congress, Prints & Photographs Division (LC-USZ62-83858).

ington and Greene Streets. For a while we couldn't move. We watched in horror how bunches of women came hurtling down from the top stories of the building. The firemen were helpless. The nets were ripped from their hands. Many stooped and picked up the nets again with their hands bleeding. My friend collapsed and started to cry like a woman. All around us we saw people covered with blood. I got sick and could not look any more" (Figure 4.1).

More than a hundred years later, the exact circumstances of the tragedy remain uncertain, but one thing is clear – the factory owners, Isaac Harris and Max Blanck, were negligent in maintaining proper fire-escape routes. But despite the weight of the evidence against them presented at the trial, the court acquitted Harris and Blanck of all charges.

The legacy of Triangle

New York State had enacted its first factory inspection law in 1886, but it had focused almost entirely on accidents related to machinery. Immediately after the Triangle Fire, New York State Senate Majority Leader Robert Wagner and State Senator Alfred E. Smith introduced a bill that resulted in the creation of the Factory Investigating Commission (FIC). Legislators originally designed a one-year Commission but extended it for two more years to conduct the most comprehensive study of workers' health and safety to date. Supported by politicians, labor leaders, social scientists, and reformers, the Commission held fifty-nine public hearings across the state, heard from close to 500 witnesses, investigated 3,385 workplaces, conducted fifty plant visits, and produced over 7,000 pages of testimony covering industries ranging from bakeries to the chemical plants.

The Commission's study of the chemical industry was typical. Investigators visited 359 chemical plants and reported horrendous conditions. By 1912, the chemical industry accounted for twenty-eight percent of all U.S. industrial production and employed seventeen percent of the nation's wage earners. The report emphasized that "In no other industry are peril to the body and dangers to the health of the workers so many, so insidious and so deadly." Chemical workers routinely came in direct contact with lead, arsenic, phosphorus, mercury, injurious gases, irritating dusts, high temperatures, hot and corrosive liquids, and dangerous explosives. Yet, the commission observed, "There is no industry in which there is less protection to the health and interests of the workers." The most dangerous processes included the manufacture of dyestuffs, benzene, lacquer, coal tar, turpentine, and acids. Industry workers were largely unaware of the dangers of handling and breathing these toxic substances.

Labor historian Richard Greenwald, suggests that because the Commission's powers went beyond investigating to legislative action, by 1915, New York had the most Progressive legislative labor codes in the United States. In addition to providing the impetus for more than thirty protective laws strictly intended to regulate workers' safety and health, the Commission's work generated an increased public awareness of the extent of threatening workplace conditions. The Commission's success generated support from political parties including the Socialists and the Progressives. A number of men and women on the Commission, including Frances Perkins (who would become the Secretary of Labor under Franklin Roosevelt in the 1930s), had direct ties to the settlement movement. New York State reform legislation became the benchmark for the Progressive reformers. Many other industrial states soon followed its lead. Conditions in the South, however, remained precarious as Southern states rarely passed protective labor laws, or any laws that they feared might dissuade companies from opening new plants in the region.

Even in the North, not all factory owners complied with the requirements of the new safety regulations. Many refused to invest the money necessary to construct firewalls or to install fire alarms. In 1913, reminiscent of the Triangle Shirtwaist Factory Fire, a fire broke out at the Binghamton Clothing Company in Binghamton, New York, and spread quickly up staircases and air shafts killing thirty-three people, the majority of whom were young female workers. Two years later in the fall of 1915, the Diamond Building in the Williamsburg section of Brooklyn ignited, resulting in the death of twelve clothing workers. In short, owners and managers could not be counted on to safeguard the health and safety of their workers. As the twentieth century advanced, American workers seemed to have no choice but to turn to politics to achieve their demands.

Workers across the country held out new hope for laws mandating improvements in workplace conditions at the federal level with President Taft's creation of the United States Commission on Industrial Relations just before he left office in 1912. Social reformers affiliated with the *Survey* magazine had persuaded the president that something needed to be done. Formed in the wake of the 1910 dynamiting of the *Los Angeles Times* building by two labor union officials (angered by the newspaper owners' militant anti-union stance) that had resulted in the death of twenty people and the 1912 Lawrence Strike, in which two strikers were killed, Taft's new commission was composed of representatives of the public, employers, and employees charged with investigating union violence and workplace conflict. At first, business interests approved of the Industrial Relations Commission's mission, but most reversed their stance within a few years, after the various industrial hearings held across the country resulted in condemning open-shop campaigns, which held that employees were not required to join or financially support a union as a condition of employment.

Although Taft had chosen appointees to the Commission, he had waited too long to act, so it fell to Woodrow Wilson shortly after his election to forward a new set of largely reform-minded commissioners forward for Senate approval. Wilson's appointees ended up agreeing with union leaders that the lack of union recognition by businesses was detrimental to workers, but they did little to change workers' circumstances. Despite the genuine concern for workers demonstrated by the Commission on Industrial Relations, its efforts fell short when it came to enacting long-term meaningful changes. At the very least, workers sought what they considered their basic rights, including minimum-wage and maximum-hour legislation. Instead, the Commission's 1916 eleven-volume report merely recommended widows' pensions, compulsory school attendance, juvenile courts, and other Progressive measures that were not necessarily related to work conditions.

The Election of 1912

While some Americans put their faith in voluntary organizations and commissions, as the twentieth century progressed, many came to believe that urban and industrial problems, including labor and the trusts, should be addressed by government officials at the state and national levels. The elections of 1906–1907 demonstrated the need for reform at the latter. Most Progressive reformers did not start out trying to expand the powers of government, but they increasingly looked to the state to execute their demands. Within two years after Taft's election in 1908, the Democratic majority in Congress moved in the direction of Progressive reform. New legislation regulated mine and railroad safety by granting increased power to the Interstate Commerce Commission and initiated the passage of the Sixteenth Amendment to the U.S. Constitution, which created an income tax, and the Seventeenth Amendment, which authorized the direct election of U.S. senators. Congress also created the Children's Bureau in the Department of Labor and legislated an eight-hour day for federal workers. By 1910, the federal government clearly had begun to take action.

The presidential election of 1912 presented an extraordinary moment in American politics. Not only did the contest feature four viable candidates presenting a potential challenge to traditional two-party loyalties but, more important, it also marked the pinnacle of the Progressive reform sentiment at the national level. In addition to a Democratic (Woodrow Wilson) and Republican (William H. Taft) candidate, the election included a candidate from the Progressive Party (Theodore Roosevelt) and the Socialist Party (Eugene V. Debs). During the campaign, both Wilson and Roosevelt advanced their (parallel) visions of economic regulation and reform, the purposes and promises of governmental action, political leadership, and the changing nature of American society. Both candidates defended the less fortunate against the dehumanizing effects of industrialization and appeared to court responsible unionists, rejecting the absolute power of capital. Although Debs realized he had no chance of winning the election, his lively speeches advocating his future goal of "revolutionary industrial unionism" drew huge audiences. He hoped many of the 100,000 people who came to see him in Chicago's Riverside Park in June of 1912 would flock to the Socialist ranks. While Debs courted crowds, Taft avoided public appearances whenever he could. Robert Hillis, the chairman of the Republican National Committee, tried to compensate for Taft's lack of visibility by creating a print advertising campaign in the press and on billboards and on streetcars. When Taft finally decided to campaign actively in September 1912, his speeches consisted largely of bitter attacks on Wilson's and Roosevelt's plans for an inter-ventionist government. The presidential election seemed to indicate that the majority of Americans, like the majority of Progressives, supported a proactive federal government.

Theodore Roosevelt and the Progressive Party platform

Theodore Roosevelt, who during his presidency (1901–1909) had built a reputation as a "trust buster" with the promotion of antitrust regulation, was coaxed out of retirement to run the newly conceived Progressive Party, nicknamed the Bull Moose Party by his many admirers. By the time of his election to his first full term in 1904 (Roosevelt had become president upon the assassination of William McKinley in 1901), Roosevelt had used his executive office to promote major Progressive innovations. Despite his patrician family background, Roosevelt increasingly saw himself as a steward of the people charged with achieving a more equitable distribution of wealth. Reformers helped to create the Progressive Party platform, which grew directly out of the 1909 Conference of Charities and Corrections. Historian Allen Davis contends that reformers supported the Progressive Party's platform but not necessarily Roosevelt or the idea of the Progres-sive Party. New Nationalism amounted to a comprehensive package of reforms that embodied social and industrial justice. It demanded presidential primaries, conservation of natural resources, an end to child labor, workers' compensation, minimum-wage legislation, social security including unemployment insur-ance, a federal income tax, and a number of commissions to ensure all of these reform programs were carried out (Figure 4.2).

The Progressive Party platform insisted on women's suffrage. By the time of the presidential election, many politically active middle- and working-class women threw their support behind the candidate of the newly formed Progressive Party. The former Republican President Theodore Roosevelt promised citizenship rights including the right to vote and the right to hold office even at federal level. Addams herself worked as a delegate to the Progressive Party's national convention and served as a member

Figure 4.2   Theodore Roosevelt speaking to a crowd during the presidential election campaign, 1912. Courtesy of the Trustees of the Boston Public Library/Leslie Jones Collection.

of the platform committee. Disappointed by Roosevelt's loss in the election, women reformers regrouped. In 1913, with the help of massive efforts at the local levels across the country, NAWSA staged a momentous parade down Pennsylvania Avenue to the White House. Carrie Chapman Catt took charge of the suffrage campaign, devising her "Winning Plan" in 1916. Ultimately assisted by the more militant agitation of Alice Paul, a young sociologist who borrowed radical tactics from fellow British suffragist Emmeline Pankhurst, which included dramatic measures such as hunger strikes, American women saw the passage of the Nineteenth Amendment to the Constitution in 1920.

Perhaps what mattered most to the voters during the election of 1912 were the candidates' previous political records. Roosevelt's presidential track record included forty-four antitrust suits culminating with attacks on Standard Oil, Dupont Chemical Company, and the tobacco and meat trusts. During Roosevelt's tenure, the Department of Justice pursued over forty antitrust suits that challenged companies' competitive methods rather than the size of the company (since he believed bigness in business was inevitable). Roosevelt supported the Elkins Act of 1903,

181

which forbade rebates from railroads. He also created a Department of Commerce and Labor to investigate child labor practices and the conditions under which women and children worked. The Bureau of Corporations, created in 1903 under Roosevelt's watch as part of the Department of Commerce and Labor, continued to investigate corporate activities. Roosevelt effectively ended the era of merger for monopolistic goals with the notorious 1904 Northern Securities case. At Roosevelt's request, the Supreme Court invoked the Sherman Antitrust Act to dissolve the massive railroad combination. Secure in his second term as president, Theodore Roosevelt oversaw the passage of the Hepburn Act in 1906, which strengthened the Interstate Commerce Commission by adding more members, expanding its power over setting maximum shipping rates, requiring standard accounting practices for all carriers, and permitting governmental review of railroad finances.

Roosevelt's commitment to the conservation of natural resources and the preservation of the nation's natural beauty became evident when he backed the Newlands Act of 1902, which became the basis for irrigated farming and public works like major dam projects in the West during the Great Depression. Progressives viewed conservation (what would today be called the environmental or ecological movement) as a battle between the people and the "interests," which the reformers identified as the big mining, timber, and oil companies that exploited the country's resources. Roosevelt and other Progressives concerned with conservation sought to empower the federal government to act as a mechanism to administer the use and development of natural resources.

Roosevelt also supported Progressive measures such as the Meat Inspection Act and the Pure Food and Drug Act, both passed in 1906, which expanded government activity in the direction of regulation. Roosevelt biographer Kathleen Dalton has observed that Roosevelt firmly believed that the government had the power to and could act to solve human problems. He moved to the left during his second term in office, coming to support the idea of an activist federal government as a powerful force in initiating and maintaining the reform agenda.

Despite Roosevelt's rather belated support of women's suffrage, Progressive women reformers rushed to his side. Both Jane Addams and Lillian Wald served as stump speakers on his campaign trail. While these women and their settlement colleagues performed a variety of politically oriented activities, their inability to exercise suffrage rights meant their numbers were not counted at the polls.

While Roosevelt promoted mass appeals to male immigrant constituents, his record and his reception were mixed. In 1906, Roosevelt supported naturalization but, in doing so, expressed his opinion that first-wave immigrants (mostly from Northern Europe) were more suited to American life than were second-wave immigrants (primarily from Southern and Eastern Europe). Within a year, Roosevelt appointed the Dillingham Commission to examine the immigration situation, winning many skeptics over and enhancing his appeal to conservatives when the commission came out in support of immigration restriction. The majority of workers outside the AFL ranks tended to be more concerned with local politics and immediate issues like the eight-hour day than they were with presidential politics. In spite of Roosevelt's best efforts, he failed to unite the sometimes disparate Progressive forces.

Theodore Roosevelt helped to create the modern presidency and to define Progressivism. As the country's chief executive officer, he basked in his place as a media icon. Roosevelt craved media attention. And he got it. On October 14, 1912, an unstable John Schrank of New York City, who was vehemently against the idea of Roosevelt seeking a third term, shot him in the chest as Roosevelt waved to a cheering Milwaukee crowd from the car he was about to ride in. Although the fifty-page speech Roosevelt had in his breast pocket slowed the bullet's penetration, it did lodge deep in his chest wall. The wound did not deter Roosevelt, who went on, bloody shirt and all, to deliver an hour-long speech after declaring to a shocked audience that "it takes more than a bullet to kill a Bull Moose." Schooled in the art of cautious negotiation, Roosevelt skillfully maneuvered around a divisive Congress composed of business interests on one side and a strong Southern Democratic bloc on the other. After Roosevelt left office, some of the investigative material amassed during his administration was used in later antitrust proceedings. The Bureau of Corporations that Roosevelt endorsed expanded into today's Federal Trade Commission (FTC) in 1915.

The incumbent: William Howard Taft

When it came to progressivism, the record of the incumbent Taft could not compare to that of Roosevelt. Taft found it difficult to navigate the turbulent territory between Progressive demands and conservative resistance. He angered Progressives by supporting Richard Ballinger for Secretary of the Interior over Roosevelt friend and appointee Gifford Pinchot. In what became known as the Ballinger–Pinchot Controversy, Taft fired Pinchot, who accused Ballinger of aiding a coal mining syndicate that planned to plunder government coal reserves in Alaska. Progressives saw Taft's actions as a bow to corporate greed.

During the Taft administration (1908–1912), any Progressive impetus came from Congress, not the White House. In the end, Taft signed the Mann Elkins Act of 1910, which pleased the Progressives by strengthening the Interstate Commerce Commission and placing the burden of proof on the railroads to demonstrate that their rates were reasonable. On the other hand, the Progressives were disappointed by the passage of the Payne Aldrich Act, which did not lower tariffs but raised them at the request of big business. In his last year in office, President Taft ordered an antitrust suit against International Harvester after the McCormick and Deering Companies joined forces, but the suit remained stalled in the courts for many years after Taft left office. Despite the initial widespread support for Taft's Industrial Relations Commission, in the end, it generated mixed results. In trying to please big businessmen and Progressive reformers, Taft lost the support of both groups, rendering himself ineffective and unable to mobilize his power.

Eugene Debs and the Socialists

Eugene Victor Debs rode the popular tide that resulted from his leadership of the Pullman strike of 1894 (for which he served six months in jail). A staunch opponent of corporate capitalism, the fiery Debs dedicated his political career to attaining social justice for workers. Under the banner of Socialism, Debs ran for the presidency in 1900 and in four more subsequent elections, but his version of socialism, which proposed placing ownership of capitalist enterprises in the hands of the workers, proved too radical for most Americans, even for most workers, who found Progressive and Democratic candidates to be more appealing alternatives. Nevertheless, Debs's candidacy garnered almost a million votes in the election of 1912.

Debs's respectable showing brought workers' issues to the forefront of the political arena from an alternative perspective. The utopian society suggested in Edward Bellamy's 1898 bestseller *Looking Backward* also contributed to Socialism's zenith from 1900 to 1917, during which time some Socialists held office at local levels. But on the national front, the turbulent times fractured a potentially cohesive labor bloc and silenced Socialist ideology. The seminal question posed by German economist Werner Sombart in his 1906 pamphlet, "Why in the United States is there no Socialism?" remained unanswered.

Woodrow Wilson and the Democratic platform

At first glance, Woodrow Wilson's New Freedom platform, engineered by Progressive lawyer Louis Brandeis, seemed to echo Theodore Roosevelt's bold New Nationalism program. Possessing a Ph.D. in political science and well versed in the art of politics from his eight years as president of Princeton University and two-year term as governor of New Jersey, Wilson was able to convince voters that he was the true Progressive candidate.

Wilson reminded supporters that his plan for the future was one determined to effect a fairer and more-balanced economy without creating an overly big, powerful, and paternalistic federal government in the process. The son of a Presbyterian minister, Wilson's strong religious conviction aided his message. In the Jeffersonian tradition, Wilson respected states' rights and pressed for an alliance between the states and the federal powers to achieve reform. The New Freedom expounded three goals for a new political economy: restructuring the nation's banking system with the creation of the Federal Reserve System, strengthening federal regulations on corporations with the Antitrust Commission as a provision of the Clayton Antitrust Act, and preventing unfair competition in interstate commerce with the creation of the FTC Act.

As far as the labor vote was concerned, the Republicans ignored their pleas, the Progressives accepted their demands, and Wilson and the Democrats realized the value of courting the labor vote by actually writing their demands into their party's platform. The move paid off, as labor responded accordingly. For the first time in history, in 1912, Samuel Gompers and the AFL officially endorsed the Democratic presidential candidate. With the Republican Party irreparably split between those who favored the erstwhile Republican Roosevelt and the solidly Republican Taft, the Democrats stepped in to fill the void. Not only did Wilson sail to the presidency, but the Democrats also gained control of Congress.

Wilson in the White House

Wilson acted quickly to infuse the Progressive principles embodied in his New Freedom and reward his supporters. He set a new precedent by personally delivering his message to the special session of Congress he convened immediately after taking office in March 1913. Historians consider the passage of the Federal Reserve Act in 1913 (also known as the Owen–Glass Act) the most important measure of Wilson's administration. The Act transformed the nation's banking system by creating the Federal Reserve Board and granted it the power to adjust the rates of interest the nation's banks could charge one another and control over the nation's money supply. Although journalists and politicians alike hailed the Act as a public victory against the trusts, corporate leaders like J.P. Morgan and Wall Street interests who found ways to influence the Federal Reserve Board's centralized policies were the real winners. The Act's significance lay in the profound restructuring of the currency system to assure the money supply and the availability of credit needed to fuel a rapidly expanding economy.

The second major move Wilson made transformed trade regulations in two ways. He bowed to the same business interests that supported Theodore Roosevelt's proposal to establish an FTC to outlaw unfair competition. Hoping to generate an atmosphere of cooperation between business and government, the FTC established a procedure whereby the courts could issue "cease and desist" orders in cases in which unfair competition existed. In a separate reform measure also taken with his political interests at heart, Wilson signed the Underwood–Simmons Act reducing tariff rates on raw materials, especially those typically purchased by farmers and small consumers. The significance of this Act came with its public recognition that the United States had completed the transformation that had begun in the 1890s from being an importer of goods and capital to being a leading manufacturing nation with a surplus of goods and services that needed to be sold abroad. Any revenue lost due to tariff reduction could be recouped with the minimal personal income taxes contained in the Sixteenth Amendment enacted on the eve of Wilson's inauguration.

The third major change in the political landscape came with the long-sought passage of the Clayton Antitrust Act in 1914 as a measure designed to strengthen the 1890 Sherman Antitrust Act. The Clayton Act held executive officers of a corporation criminally liable for the actions of their companies and allowed companies claiming to have been injured by a trust in their same business to collect damages from those corporations against which the court had rendered a decision. Passed in conjunction with the FTC Act, the Act included provisions for monitoring unfair business practices by identifying and regulating them as they arose. Progressives envisioned using the Clayton Act to diminish the degree of control large corporations wielded in the marketplace.

In 1912, direct primaries put the nomination process in the hands of the people for the first time and helped win the passage of the Seventeenth Amendment in 1913, which allowed the direct popular election of U.S. senators. After he decided to run for reelection in 1916, Wilson signed many more pieces of legislation that the Progressives considered victories. The president signed the law Senator Robert LaFollette sponsored, known as the Seamen's Act of 1915, which regulated wages and working conditions for sailors. Businessmen, especially ship owners, disapproved of these measures, which largely prevented them from exploiting the labor of their workers. Although "Fighting Bob" LaFollette proved to be one of the strongest supporters of Progressive sentiment, the Seamen's Act was the only piece of legislation that LaFollette won passage of at the federal level.

Refusing to be distracted by the war raging in Europe, Wilson and the Sixty-Fourth Congress moved forward with New Freedom measures as he closed in on his second term in office. Legislation in the summer of 1916 resulted in both the Federal Farm Loan Act, which offered low-interest government-funded loans to farmers, and an Act hailed by conservationists that created the National Park Service. In September of 1916, President Wilson signed the Keating–Owen Child Labor Act and the Adamson Act into law.

The Keating–Owen Act came about largely as a result of the lobbying of the National Child Labor Committee and marked the first attempt at the federal level to regulate child labor by prohibiting interstate commerce of goods made by underage or exploited child workers. It banned the sale of products from any factory, shop, or cannery that employed children under the age of fourteen, from any mine that employed children under the age of sixteen, and from any facility that had children under the age of sixteen work at night or for more than eight hours during the day. Two years later, the United States Supreme Court declared the Keating–Owen Act unconstitutional on the grounds that it overstepped the government's powers to regulate interstate commerce. Effective child labor legislation at the national level, like minimum-wage and maximum-hour regulation, would have to wait until the passage of the Fair Labor Standards Act in 1938.

The Adamson Act, passed under pressure from Wilson, who wished to prevent a nationwide railroad strike of over 400,000 members of the four railroad brotherhoods, granted railroad workers the much needed eight-hour day after statistics proved that accident rates increased dramatically once workers put in more hours than that a day. A Workmen's Compensation Law for federal civil service employees injured on the job went on the books in 1916, as did the Revenue Act of 1916, which doubled the basic income-tax rate from one percent to two percent, designated a graduated inheritance tax, and, perhaps in anticipation of war profits, raised the tax rates on the richest Americans, those with incomes in excess of two million dollars and those reaping vast corporate profits.

The election of 1916

Wilson held fast to the democratic political conviction that the federal and state governments should work in tandem to protect the weakest and most disadvantaged Americans. With the exception of the winter of 1914, the national economy remained stable throughout the Wilson administration and therefore allowed him to overcome most opposition. The Democratic platform included a full range of compromises that appealed to middle-income groups including laws that protected federal workers, children, seamen, and railroad workers. Southern farmers, meanwhile, reaped the benefits of a variety of laws designed to assist agriculturalists. Previously neglected businessmen also shared in the general broadening of Progressivism that flourished under Wilson.

Lower tariffs helped distributors and agricultural brokers, and country bankers as well their suburban and urban counterparts benefitted from the auspices of the Federal Reserve Act and its oversight of the availability of credit. Small businessmen reaped the rewards of the Clayton Act's restrictions on finance capitalism and the oversight of the FTC. Finally, millers of grain, cotton merchants, and southern textile manufacturers, although disappointed by the Underwood Act, were aided by attempts to regulate agricultural exchanges.

In Wilson's 1916 bid to retain the White House in the election of 1916, several prominent big business leaders defected from the Republican Party, businessmen's traditional home, to join the Wilson camp. A group of Republican industrialists including Henry Ford, railroad executive F.C. Underwood, and shoe manufacturer H.B. Endicott ran a newspaper ad to support Wilson on the so-called peace issue, Wilson's oft-stated promise during the campaign to keep the United States out of the messy and brutal war that was consuming continental Europe and parts of Asia and Africa. Yet most businessmen still backed the Republican candidate and governor of New York, Charles Evans Hughes. Hughes, the son of a Welsh miner, had by 1910 managed to rise to become a Supreme Court justice. He gained a solid reputation for investigating unfair practices in the utility and insurance industries in the early 1900s, which had helped him win the governorship of New York in 1906. The honest but austere Hughes ran a formidable campaign, but in the end, Wilson's "He kept us out of war" slogan persuaded the voters to stick with the president. Although he won reelection, Wilson's record did not go unscathed. Trouble in the mining fields in Ludlow, Colorado, and Bisbee, Arizona, and in the mills of Paterson, New Jersey, in 1914 had ended in violence and a number of deaths, clouding the presidency in the prewar years. Astute corporate leaders also found ways to circumvent the Clayton Antitrust Act. One example was that of financier J.P. Morgan, who complied with the directive by resigning from the board of directors of twenty-seven different corporations but still managed to retain his membership on thirty-three other boards.

Progressivism in the National Consciousness

By the end of the Progressive Era in 1917, a profound political transformation had occurred. The identity of those who participated in the political process, the importance of public opinion, and citizens' expectations of government had all changed. Structure and policy at all levels of government, local, state, and federal, were affected. The political arena shifted from one centered on relatively simple rural bases to one that had to answer to complex, urban-centered, special interest groups. Politicians at all levels made formal attempts to respond to the demands of the electorate. Populism, progressivism, and machine politics all had been responses to the extremely rapid growth the nation experienced in the last decades of the nineteenth century and the first decades of the twentieth: industrial, economic, urban, and demographic, monumental changes comprised by the overall process of modernization taking place in American life.

Whether it was Jane Addams's experiences in the 1890s in attempting to found a juvenile court system in Chicago or the failure of the United States Commission on Industrial Relations to effect sustained protective labor legislation, the considerable efforts of the many Americans that today we look back to as Progressives demonstrated that reform at the local, state, and even national level efforts was necessary to ensure the regulation of business and the economy and provide sorely needed social services. As they moved toward political and educational reform, the Progressives and their fellow Americans of their day gained more confidence in government and, along the way, became more accepting of bureaucratic practices.

After the Triangle Waist Factory Fire, organized labor, which had been hesitant to enter politics, became an integral part of the Progressive coalition to push for legislation to counter the power of big business. Ordinary Americans, many of whom had previously rejected the idea of government visibility in their daily lives, became less resistant to governmental authority. After all, the only direct contact that they had with the federal government prior to the Progressive Era might have been through the U.S. Postal Service. Workers, particularly those who benefitted from new health and safety regulations in the workplace as well as from government intervention in the economic sector through the promotion of arbitration or the settling of strikes, also became tolerant of a more active government.

By advocating for a variety of reforms, the Progressives helped to expand the size and power of the federal government. In some instances, the state became more active as the power of the executive was expanded over that of the legislative branch. To promote new ideas, new administrative agencies were created. In the workplace and the educational arena, individual states often acted first in an effort to help Americans in need of assistance or protection. In 1917, in *Bunting v. Oregon*, a state court upheld the ten-hour law for working men and women. By 1920, the majority of states forbade the employment of children under the age of fourteen, set an eight-hour day for workers under sixteen, and mandated compulsory education. Although these laws were not always enforced, the number of children in school increased dramatically between 1900 and 1920. The number of high school graduates tripled between 1890 and 1920. With the passage of the Smith–Hughes Vocational Education Act in 1917, vocational education also became an option for American school children.

Reformers did what they could to change what they saw as the ills of society but soon discovered that they had to organize and formally enter politics in order to further and actually effect their goals. Progressive politicians encouraged the government to enter the domain of private enterprise and, when possible, give precedence to federal government control over states. By the early twentieth century, both the scope and the function of the political and governmental systems of the United States differed drastically from its nineteenth-century incarnation. Reformers had come to trust the government, even making it the government's responsibility to make decisions in the public's best interest.

Approximately a half a century ago, historian Robert Wiebe, in *Search for Order* (1967), explained that many turn-of-the-century Americans grew bewildered as the "island communities" of the nineteenth century, with their intimate personal relations and informal rules governing work schedules, dissolved with the rise of huge modern industrial corporations governed by impersonal, formal, managerial bureaucracies. Most people had little choice but to resign themselves to these changes and to accept increased governance both at work and in their private lives.

Using Muncie, Indiana, as a prototype for their now famous *Middletown: A Study in American Culture* (1929), sociologists Helen and Robert Lynd described how, prior to the turn of the twentieth century, Americans drove horses, worked on farms, pumped water, wore homemade clothes, and were lucky to finish the eighth grade. The Lynds observed that the changes that had occurred during the Progressive Era meant that by 1925, the residents of Middletown typified the majority of Americans, in whose homes one could expect to find furnaces, flush toilets, hot and cold running water, vacuum cleaners, toasters, washing machines, telephones, and refrigerators. In addition, a great many Americans lived in cities, drove cars, and worked for wages in offices and factories. In the three decades that elapsed between 1890 and 1920, the way in which ordinary Americans lived, worked, and thought had been transformed.

Conclusion
The Progressives' Progress

By the end of the nineteenth century, the United States was in the midst of a profound transition to modern life. Even for those in the farthest reaches of the land, change proved inevitable. Growth and bigness were everywhere, from new sources of energy such as electricity and oil to the total transformation of the physical landscape. The technological revolution encouraged by corporate growth resulted in new innovations in communication and transportation, which joined the list of new inventions like cafeterias, elevators, and gas furnaces.

In 1900, approximately two-thirds of all Americans lived in rural areas where small-town values informed their lives. By 1920 the U.S. population surpassed the 100 million mark and more than one-half of all Americans lived in cities. The average size of farms was increasing and the cities were expanding dramatically. The majority of Americans no longer had land on which to raise their own food.

Quantification of activities became a facet of everyday life for many Americans, occurring first in cities and then eventually spreading to the rural areas. An expanded middle class promoted

The Progressives: Activism and Reform in American Society, 1893–1917, First Edition.
Karen Pastorello.
© 2014 John Wiley & Sons, Inc. Published 2014 by John Wiley & Sons, Inc.

the rise and expansion of municipal hospitals, institutions of higher education, and life insurance companies. Historical holidays, official parks and monuments, and rituals like the recitation of the Pledge of Allegiance in public schools became features of daily life. World fairs staged in American cities occurred about once in every decade. During the Progressive Era, institutionalization and material culture grew to become accepted aspects of the American experience.

Immigration resulted in significant changes in urban composition. The migration of millions of European immigrants meant that, by 1910, a larger number of urban residents than ever before were immigrants or the children of immigrants. Despite the huge influx of a second wave of newcomers from Southern and Eastern Europe, the actual proportion of foreign-born Americans in urban areas remained virtually unchanged because of the migration of farm families to the cities and also due to natural reproduction.

Everyone from the upwardly affluent to unemployed vagrants seemed to be in motion. Migratory patterns proved extensive and unsettling. Migrants tapped every available form of transportation to reach their destinations. Large numbers of the native-born population moved from rural areas to cities, abandoning farm work for factory work. Americans moved from east to west, south to north, and from urban to suburban life. In cities, multiple-occupancy dwellings housed the majority of newcomers, while in suburbs, detached single-family residences complete with lawns were the dwellings of choice. Those who moved away from the city and out to the suburbs could now use the telephone to stay connected to family and friends they left behind.

Life acquired a more harried pace as Americans tried to earn enough to fund an increasingly materialistic lifestyle. Factories that turned out consumer goods employed the majority of the waged workers and occupied prime space in the centers of industrializing cities. Progressive Era Americans became caught up in the rush to acquire new products ranging from fishing reels to refrigerators. In 1906 alone, Americans registered more than 10,000 new trademarks. Consumerism had arrived.

Buying and selling took on an almost ritualistic cast, with advertisers appealing to the consumers' emotions to encourage them to buy, and then to buy more. The abundance of and assortment of newly available goods changed everything from eating habits to where and how Americans traveled. Those who had previously limited their diets to what they and their neighbors grew, stored, or processed, now purchased canned goods and precut meats from a variety of stores and butcher shops. In 1900, fewer than 10,000 Americans owned an automobile. Within two decades, there were more than eight million cars on the road. At first, anyone who could reach the pedals could drive. By the 1920s, most states had enacted driving regulations and insurance companies had begun to offer automobile insurance. Companies that catered to consumers grew immensely. Many went public and sold shares of stock on the open market.

In keeping with demographic patterns, the political landscape shifted away from relatively simple rural bases to more complex urban-centered groups. It became difficult for politicians at all levels – local, state, and federal – to think about politics separate from urbanization or industrialization. The job of most government officials became thinking of effective ways in which to cope with new problems. As a result of this transition, both sides of the political realm – both candidates and voters – changed.

Public opinion became a fundamental consideration for politicians and advertisers alike. To a greater extent than ever before, the nation's rising middle class shaped the country's political, social, and cultural agendas. Perhaps most important, what citizens expected and even demanded from their government fundamentally changed. Until the beginning of the Progressive Era in the early 1890s, for the majority of Americans, with the exception of mailing letters and parcels at the post office, federal authority had been invisible. Now, by the end of the Progressive Era, immigrants encountered the government's presence from their arrival at the induction center on Ellis Island to the citizenship tests required to become participatory citizens. This same government displayed a heightened presence for all Americans by stamping a seal of approval on meat offered for sale in butcher shops and stores, after the passage of the Meat Inspection Act in 1906, and, after 1913, required that its wealthiest citizens pay income taxes. As societal problems escalated, Progressive reformers pushed the government to begin to consider – and to do something to help improve – the well-being of its neediest citizens.

In urban areas across the country, Progressive reformers voiced their concerns and engineered solutions to the ills of their cities. Hailing primarily from the middle-class and occasionally enlisting the aid of the working class, Progressive settlement workers, politicians, academics, religious intellectuals, labor leaders, workers, and journalists called attention to overcrowding and health and safety issues inherent in urban life in the industrial age. Experts and professionals issued public pleas to address child labor, government corruption, and, in the South, the horror of lynching. Progressive reformers conveyed the urgent need for community services and safeguards that reached well beyond the capacity of local charities and which ultimately gave rise to a new conception of social welfare. Reformers also sought practical solutions to widespread socioeconomic problems, demanded housing and factory codes, public health and sanitation measures, unemployment, school reform, more equitable distribution of taxes, temperance, and an end to gambling and prostitution.

By the turn of the century, prominent groups of reformers seeking to better the conditions of the urban masses rose to political power in select cities. Historian Allen Davis observed that settlement workers helped to increase the number of voluntary agencies by assisting in the founding of the National Consumers' League, the National Women's Trade Union League, the Immigrant Protective League, the National Association for the Advancement of Colored People, the National Child Labor Committee, the Women's International League for Peace and Freedom, and the Progressive Service Committee. Settlement reformers were also involved in the National Conference on Charities and Corrections, the National Conference of Urban Planning, and the National Federation of Settlements and helped to establish the American Civil Liberties Union.

197

Between 1890 and 1920, increasingly powerful social reformers sought to use the political system to make America safer, more democratic, and more socially just for ordinary Americans. The coalitions that the reformers negotiated compensated at least in part for the decline of neighborliness that accompanied the cities' growth in size and daunting ethnic and racial diversity.

Progressive reformers found allies in liberal politicians like Detroit's Republican Mayor Hazen Pingree and Socialists in Milwaukee and New York who promoted radical ideas such as public ownership of utilities. Since social reformers had little interest in structural reforms such as the reorganization of city governments that were supported by business and professional elites, they drew their support from the immigrant workers they were trying to aid and through alliances with settlement workers.

Remarkably, Progressive Era reformers accomplished much of what they set out to do. At the local level, they suppressed red-light districts, expanded high school curricula, constructed playgrounds and public parks, helped to replace corrupt urban political machines with more efficient systems of municipal government, and heralded the call for social services to remedy the plight of the needy. In a few cities, they founded organizations to address the situation of African Americans coming up from the South and landing in the urban milieu of the North in search of a better life.

Progressives extended their efforts beyond their locales to the state and the national level. The Progressive scholar Arthur Link acknowledged that "political progressivism originated in the cities." What Link hailed as "a transformation of politics and government" began as a grassroots movement at the local level and eventually moved to the state and federal arenas. Progressive state governments enacted minimum-wage laws for women workers, instituted industrial accident insurance, restricted child labor, and improved factory regulation. On the national front, Congress passed laws establishing federal regulation of the meatpacking, drug, and railroad industries, and strengthened general antitrust laws. Congressional legislators also lowered tariffs, established federal control over the banking system, and began the long journey that would eventually culminate with federal legislation to improve working conditions.

While some saw progress as threatening to the status quo, the Progressives themselves saw promise in reform. Some reformers like the Social Gospelers encouraged church members to involve themselves in reform efforts limited to specific localities. An increasing number of Americans agreed, however, with the Progressives' demand for a more comprehensive reform strategy. As the era unfolded, Progressives moved from education to legislation, from analysis to activism. Ultimately, they hoped to transform the very essence of the state.

Not all Americans, however, felt comfortable with the reforms that the Progressives championed. Some, particularly those in rural areas, resisted change. Populists, Fundamentalists, and small businessmen often clung to the traditional morality and agrarian values of bygone centuries. They viewed the Progressive mindset as a dangerous one that was proposing too many changes too fast. They did not want to upset the nineteenth-century way of life or, worse yet, risk government intrusion into their private lives. The Progressives had, after all, proposed measures that regulated leisure time, restricted marriage and divorce laws, censored various forms of entertainment, and regulated sexual morality.

Insular in their outlook, many Americans feared radical politics, resented immigrants' patronage of urban bosses, and were uncomfortable with the rising status of women or African Americans. Some, like Billy Sunday, went so far as to promote "100 percent Americanism" as a reaction against immigrants and their religion. Andrew Carnegie and a number of other corporate leaders welcomed Spencer's application of Darwin's principles to humans in the school of thought known as Social Darwinism, which advocated a laissez-faire approach to problem solving. On the basis of this survival of the fittest mentality, they did not support the notion of helping the less fortunate, who often succumbed to the perils of urban life.

Despite the controversy that surrounded them, Progressive intellectuals dreamt boundlessly about what the government could accomplish if granted the opportunity. Herbert Croly in *Promise of American Life* (1909) and Walter Lippmann in *Drift and Mastery* (1914) proposed a political metamorphosis based on the possibility of resolving social problems through the expert application of tough critical analysis. Croly suggested that the government could exert a positive influence over human nature. Lippmann believed that the elite should use the state to foster economic equality. Both writers supported the idea of systematic government intervention in American life for the purpose of promoting the welfare of all.

Women like Jane Addams helped to lead the Progressive charge. Addams, the preeminent citizen of the era, championed better housing and sanitation, factory inspection, immigrants' rights, the construction of parks and playgrounds, child labor laws, and the rights of women and children. She offered her unwavering support to the causes of laborers' rights, civil rights, women's suffrage, and the peace of nations. In addition to cofounding settlement house movement, Addams played a vital part in numerous organizations. She was president of the National Conference on Charities and Corrections, cofounder of the Women's Peace Party, and long-time president of the Women's International League for Peace and Freedom. Along with William Walling, W.E.B. DuBois, Lillian Wald, and others, Addams helped found the NAACP and after World War I became a founding member of the American Civil Liberties Union. Addams became the first American woman to win the Nobel Peace Prize.

Political scientist Carol Nackenoff credits Addams with "embody[ing] political activism in an era of remarkable civic activity." In an effort to generate grassroots support, Addams cultivated friendships with local businessmen and civic leaders. She also possessed a remarkable penchant for compromise. Addams's civic engagement and her concern for social justice remain unparalleled. She worked fervently to enact public policies through organization and legislation while continuing to support her Near West Side neighborhood by encouraging cooperative activities.

When Chicago's Department of Public Health vaccinated over one million people during the smallpox epidemic of 1893–1894, Addams became convinced that the state could indeed embody the "commonality of compassion." This and a number of other experiences in Chicago helped her realize by 1910 that in addition to providing its citizens a public education, state and national efforts were necessary to increase government involvement in the regulation of economic life and the provision of social services. In the writing that set her apart from other reformers, Addams presented a strong case for government action in *Democracy and Social Ethics* (1902) and *Twenty Years at Hull House* (1910). In her mind, efforts taken to shape a more democratic society should not be solely the government's responsibility. Working toward achieving the ideal democracy through peaceful means, she espoused her version of social justice: "the complete participation of the working classes in the spiritual, intellectual, and material inheritance of the human race" in addressing corruption in municipal government, the labor movement, the classroom, and the household.

Even the most idealized version of Progressivism did, however, have its limits. African Americans did not experience the benefits of Progressive reform to the same extent that whites did. For one thing, in the last decades of the nineteenth century, blacks were not yet a visible presence in most Northern industrial cities and, of course, many Progressive reforms were designed to benefit an urban populace. As late as 1890, roughly ninety percent of all blacks lived in the South, where Jim Crow segregation laws dictated their lives. For another thing, even those African Americans who moved north at this time found that racist regulations largely kept them from joining trade unions, forcing them to take the most undesirable, unskilled, low-wage jobs, which only reduced any limited opportunities they had to secure an education or better housing. They were further marginalized when white Northerners refused to work alongside them in factories. Only in the closing years of the Progressive Era did substantial numbers of Southern blacks migrate to Northeastern industrial centers.

While white reformers generally deemed European immigrants capable of assimilation into middle-class American society, some of the same reformers tended to view African Americans as being incapable of entering mainstream American society. Even Jane Addams, failed to sustain her efforts to expose segregation and injustices against blacks beyond raising funds toward this cause. This type of prejudice ultimately led to segregation of black settlement houses from settlement houses geared toward European immigrants.

To meet the challenge, African American churches and middle-class black clubwomen took matters into their own hands and founded their own settlement houses to provide social services to newly arrived black migrants. In Chicago, for example, Reverend Reverdy Ransom started the African Methodist Episcopal Institutional Church to provide employment, education, and welfare services to black migrants. Whether affiliated with churches, nonproselytizing settlement houses, or black social service organizations, and despite their interactions with white reformers (even those involved in the founding of the NAACP), African American reformers were forced to pursue a parallel but separate path.

A few Progressive groups challenged discriminatory policies and called for equal justice. However, as news of race reform spread throughout the country, racists incited anti-black violence. Race riots broke out in New York, and lynching became a common tool in the South to control black agitators.

Issues surrounding race and gender also hindered advances in the public education system. Northern schools remained geographically segregated by virtue of neighborhood settlement patterns, and in the South (especially after the 1896 *Plessy v. Ferguson* decision declared separate but equal schools constitutional), segregation mandated by Jim Crow laws became the law of the land. Across the country, school administrators were almost exclusively male, while the teachers, particularly in the early grades, tended to be female. Even in the North, most public school teachers were native-born white men and women.

Several early Progressives advocated eugenics, or human engineering, to purge society's gene pool of undesirable traits. In *Looking Backward* (1898), socialist author Edward Bellamy pondered "race purification," a fantasy shared by other utopian novelists. In 1907, Indiana became the first state to codify the "negative eugenics" that Bellamy had suggested by legislating sterilization of those harboring undesirable genetic traits. More than two dozen states soon followed. Interestingly, the states did not consider the coupling of ideal mates, referred to as "positive eugenics," in such legislation.

Eugenics coincided with the Progressives' faith in science, the future, the regulatory potential of the state, and human perfectibility. Both the Rockefeller Foundation and the Carnegie Institution helped to fund organizations that advocated eugenics. Among the more notable Progressives to support the eugenics movement included communist Emma Goldman, NAACP founder W.E.B. Dubois, author H.G. Wells, political scientist Harold Laski, sex theorist Havelock Ellis, and Planned Parenthood founder Margaret Sanger.

Regardless of the work they performed, Progressive Era reformers demanded that the government act and, in doing so, helped to create a more expansive welfare system. During the Depression of 1893, a number of city governments established elaborate programs of emergency employment and relief. On the cusp of the new century, Hull House women helped establish the first juvenile justice system in the nation as well as the first mothers' pension law, which provided state support for widowed and/or deserted mothers so they could raise their children at home. Forty states passed similar laws. In 1910 in New York State, there was a move toward compulsory health insurance.

The creation of the New York Factory Investigating Commission in the wake of the Triangle Fire represented, according to commission member Frances Perkins, "a turning point" in American attitudes toward social responsibility. By 1912, thirty-eight states had passed child labor laws. Workers benefitted from the establishment of the Industrial Relations Committee, and by

1915, thirty-five states had passed workers' compensation laws. In 1915, Arizona became the first state to establish an old-age pension modeled after the German system.

Whereas Europeans safeguarded their citizens by regulating their industries and providing social welfare, Americans relied on privatism, volunteerism, and welfare capitalism. American workers had no safety nets and depended on charity or the kindness of their families in times of trouble. In the face of public outrage surrounding the Triangle Fire, the Progressive Party pledged to work for social and industrial justice. In the months leading up to the election of 1912, the Progressives presented what historians Arthur Link and Richard McCormick have characterized as a vision of "a collective democratic society presided over by a strong federal government to regulate and protect every interest."

Government intervention in the economic sector occurred first in the railroad industry. In 1893, the passage of the Federal Railroad Safety Appliance Act made it illegal for trains to operate without automatic couplers and air brakes, drastically reducing accident and injury rates. The state set a precedent for assuming a direct role in economic affairs with the Erdman Act passed by Congress in 1898; in the wake of the Pullman Palace Car Company strike by Eugene Debs's American Railway Union, the Act recognized the right of railroad workers to organize and provided for mediation of labor disputes by a government board. It also outlined provisions for the mediation of railroad strikes by the Interstate Commerce Commission's chairman and the Bureau of Labor's commissioner. In doing so, the Erdman Act established the model for government conciliation and mediation in railroad and other labor disputes. The New Deal's 1935 Wagner Act, for example, was based on this premise of labor's bargaining rights.

In 1913, the Erdman Act was amended by the Newlands Act, which created the first full-time board of mediation and conciliation; it was staffed by nine men appointed by a government committee composed of two federal justices and the Commissioner of Labor with equal power divided between management, labor, and the public. The authors of the Newlands Act emphasized the importance of mediation efforts. If they failed, arbitration would be used. In 1916, the Adamson Act established the eight-hour day and an enhanced overtime pay rate in the railroad industry. The individual states also began to regulate railroads, public utilities, insurance companies, oil producers, banks, lumber companies, and some types of farming operations.

Businessmen, too, began to place more trust in government after the alliances between civic and political leaders made during the World Columbian Exposition in 1893. More and more Progressive businessmen welcomed the regulation that the Progressives advanced. Some even came to rely on government for lucrative government contracts when the alliances grew especially strong with American involvement in World War I.

The one constant during the Progressive Era was the call to action. After the Triangle Waist Factory Fire in 1911, state and local governments immediately began to champion protective legislation in the workplace. The Triangle Fire and the presidential election of 1912 presented a national opportunity to address the problems that had consumed the Progressives for decades.

The federal government played a relatively minor role in social welfare during the Progressive Era, but reformers won the establishment of a federal Children's Bureau and, following the end of World War I, a federal program of infant and maternal nutrition in the Sheppard–Towner Infant Maternity Act. With its establishment in 1920, the Women's Bureau within the Department of Labor paved the way in the emphatic struggle to secure broad-based federal old-age, unemployment, and disability insurance. The American Association for Labor Legislation and settlement leaders also fought unsuccessfully for universal health care.

Progressives did make great strides in recognizing and analyzing the nation's problems. Due to their demands for resolutions to those problems, governments at various levels responded. Initiative, referendum, and recall laws passed easily in many municipalities. Protective labor laws limiting the number of hours in the workday, especially for women and children, and workers' compensation made headway, particularly at the state level. In addition to the creation of the Children's Bureau, legislative and reform victories at the federal level included the Meat Inspection Act (1906), the Pure Food and Drug Act (1906), the *Muller v. Oregon* (1908) decision, the creation of the NAACP (1909), the passage of the Clayton Antitrust Act (1914), and the Keating–Owen Act (1916). Four constitutional amendments also were ratified during the Progressive Era. The Sixteenth Amendment ratified in 1913 on the eve of World War I authorized a graduated federal income tax. The Seventeenth Amendment provided for the direct election of U.S. senators. Once the war ended, in 1919, the Volstead Act became the Eighteenth Amendment, which prohibited the manufacture and sale of alcoholic beverages. The Nineteenth Amendment ended the six-decade-long struggle to secure women's suffrage by extending the vote to women (Figure C.1).

Several Progressive victories were, however, only partial ones. For example, Progressives were more successful with garbage collection and sanitation campaigns then they were with monitoring air and water pollution. Other Progressive victories were only temporary. In 1912, Massachusetts became the first state to pass minimum-wage legislation. Fourteen other states followed. The legislation was struck down with the 1923 *Adkins v. Children's Hospital* ruling only to be resurrected again in 1938 contained within the Fair Labor Standards Act. Child labor regulations suffered a similar fate. The 1916, the Keating–Owen Act contained legislation to prohibit certain forms of child labor across the country, but the United States Supreme Court declared the Act unconstitutional only two years after its passage. Except for legislation targeting the railroad and mining industries, between the 1890s and the early 1900s, the federal government failed to establish national minimum-wage requirements, maximum-hour laws, and standard safety regulations across industries.

Indeed, despite attention from reformers, state bureaucrats, union leaders, muckrakers, and even presidential candidates, problems at the workplace persisted due to the lack of uniform standards at the federal level. In their 1916 book, *Principles of Labor Legislation*, John R. Commons, secretary of the American

Figure C.1 Jane Addams registering new immigrant voters, 1914. This image appeared on the March cover of *Life and Labor*, the Women's Trade Union League's official publication. Kheel Center, Cornell University.

Association for Labor Legislation, and John B. Andrews, professor of economics at the University of Wisconsin, remarked on four major problems inherent in state labor legislation: incomplete laws, absence of standards, absence of coordination and responsibility, and lack of responsiveness to change. Commons, Andrews, and other reformers felt that in many districts, there were simply not enough highly qualified factory inspectors. They also criticized the inspectors that were in place for spending too much time on paperwork and not enough time on actual fieldwork.

With their mantra of investigate, organize, educate, and legislate, reformers had a dramatic impact on problem solving and service delivery. They helped define social welfare and demanded social justice. In their quest for a more egalitarian society, Progressive reformers went beyond the right to hold a fair job to demands for social support for life outside of the workplace. Working women like cap maker Rose Schneiderman were among the first to propose the notion of "industrial citizenship," which she defined as decent wages, safe working conditions, and reasonable hours. She billed her cause as a necessary first victory in working women's battle to win their larger "right to citizenship." Schneiderman, Addams, and Wald envisioned citizenship as a complex entitlement that included "the right to be born well, the right to a carefree and happy childhood, the right to education, the right to mental, physical and spiritual growth and development." This form of citizenship, which embodies everything from educational opportunities for all children to old-age insurance for all Americans, became an integral part of the Progressive Party's social justice platform in 1912.

Slightly marred by labor unrest in the silk mills of New Jersey and in the mines of Arizona, and then interrupted by America's entry into World War I, the optimism that characterized Progressivism resumed as the United States rose to prominence among nations in the postwar decades. Virtually unscathed by the ravages of the total warfare that decimated major European powers, the nascent American military–industrial complex soared above the ruins. There was much to celebrate.

In the words of historian Kathryn Kish Sklar, "The Progressive Era formed a watershed in the history of state recognition of its responsibility for human welfare." Many of the Progressive goals became goals of the Democratic Party by the 1920s and were achieved in the 1930s in the New Deal legislation. Progressive reformer and secretary of labor in Franklin Roosevelt's administration Frances Perkins continued to push for national health-care legislation during the New Deal years. The Progressives' legacy set the stage for the 1935 Social Security Act and the 1938 Fair Labor Standards Act, both vital pieces of the American welfare state.

Although Progressivism is admittedly the gestation of the modern welfare state, work was left undone. Even in the twenty-first-century United States, there are glaring deficits in social policy. The United States remains the only industrialized nation in the world without universal health care or paid maternity leave. It also falls far behind other nations in terms of the care of its children. Quality day care is difficult to find and cost pro-hibitive for many working-class Americans, particularly for single mothers. The 1993 Family Medical Leave Act is weak. There is a need to broaden the basis of economic citizenship to include caring for families. Poverty, poor health, unemployment, and lack of access to health services still remain major concerns, especially among people of color a century after the formal Pro-gressive movement dissipated and a half century after the passage of the Civil Rights Act. A growing income gap has rendered inequality in the public education system a national disgrace. The cuts in the social welfare programs and the demands of "welfare reform" made during the George W. Bush administration impose unrealistic burdens on women and families in hard economic times. Currently, the Obama administration's good intentions are consistently blocked by House Republicans.

There are, however, points of promise. One of the first things President Barack Obama did upon assuming office in 2008 was to sign the Lilly Ledbetter Fair Pay Act into law, dictating that the 180-day statute of limitations to file a suit regarding pay inequity resets with every paycheck affected. It did not, however, address the problem of unequal wages. Women now earn approx-imately eighty cents for every dollar men make. Some argue that the gender wage gap is gradually closing, but almost all would agree it is not closing quickly enough. Legislation recently intro-duced in Congress is called the Fair Paycheck Act, which would close the loopholes in the 1963 Equal Pay Act, making equal wages for women and men a reality. Finally, the Affordable Care Act is intended to open the door for millions of American workers and their families to gain access to affordable health insurance beginning in 2014.

Perhaps the greatest legacy for the Progressives was their indelible spirit. Progressive reforms made it possible to attempt to reign in powerful monopolistic corporations. Progressives also made it easier to enact regulatory policies in general. One of the most recent examples reminiscent of the Progressive reform sentiment comes with the Occupy Wall Street movement that began in September of 2011, the supporters of which refuse to, in historian Steven Diner's words, "play by the rules of industrial capitalism." In the spirit of the Progressives, Americans are still seeking social justice. At least for now.

Bibliographical Essay

Introduction

Literature of the field

Some of the earliest historians of the Progressive period tackled the question of who the Progressives were. Progressives themselves, Herbert Croly, *Promise of American Life* (1909); Walter Weyl, *New Democracy* (1912); and Walter Lippmann, *Drift and Mastery* (1914), represented the variety of Progressivism expressed in Theodore Roosevelt's New Nationalism – vigorous centralized control of big business, for example. Benjamin Park DeWitt, *The Progressive Movement* (1915), was among the first to provide a coherent picture of the movement, which he favorably depicted as common people attempting to recapture power from corporate owners and party bosses who usurped it from farmers, workers, and small businessmen during the Gilded Age. Charles and Mary Beard, *Rise of Civilization* (1927), and Vernon Parrington, *Main Currents* (1927), saw Progressivism as the highest expression of the American liberal tradition of Jefferson, Jackson, the

The Progressives: Activism and Reform in American Society, 1893–1917, First Edition.
Karen Pastorello.
© 2014 John Wiley & Sons, Inc. Published 2014 by John Wiley & Sons, Inc.

Abolitionists, and the Populists. John Hicks, *Populist Revolt* (1931), noted that Progressivism fulfilled the objectives of the Populists, who had become frustrated before the turn of the century. Glenda Gilmore's *Who Were the Progressives?* revisited the question.

George Mowry's *The California Progressives* (1951) challenged early interpretations when he found Progressives to be educated middle-class men and women frustrated by the demise of nineteenth century individualism and the rise of huge labor unions and corporations. Building on this work, Richard Hofstadter in his now classic *The Age of Reform* (1955) argued that the Progressives were self-absorbed middle-class professionals stripped of their status by the rise of big business. According to Hofstadter, since Progressivism coincided with a prosperous period, the answer to who the Progressives were must be found in this psychologically based "status anxiety" rather than in economic woes.

Samuel Hays, *Response to Industrialism* (1957), and Robert Weibe, *Search for Order* (1967), contend that Progressives were not the backward-looking men and women described by Mowry and Hofstadter but a self-assured "new middle class" composed of professionals including doctors, businessmen, social workers, scientists, and engineers determined to import the systems of scientific management already so successful in the business world into all other aspects of American life. Their enemies were unregulated competition, haphazard use of natural resources, and machine governments in metropolitan areas.

Some historians like Gabriel Kolko, *The Triumph of Conservatism* (1963), and James Weinstein, *The Corporate Ideal in the Modern State* (1968), have argued that the staunchest advocates and beneficiaries of Progressivism were corporate giants that fought to preserve an exploitive capitalistic system by using federal regulatory measures to protect them from competition. These Progressives were certainly not interested in reforming the system in any meaningful way.

In spite of the 1970 effort by Peter Filene in his "Obituary to Progressivism," to deny the existence of the Progressive movement, the rise of social history in the 1970 and 1980s, encouraged historians to consider the place of new groups of reformers who were not white elites or middle class. One of the best examples of this historical revision was published in 1983 by Arthur Link and Richard McCormick, *Progressivism* (1983), which synthesized the vast scholarship on Progressivism and, in doing so, demonstrated that the era's reform spirit flowed from a core ideology that informed a plethora of political and social issues and causes. Although some found the claim that "Progressivism was the only reform movement ever experienced by the whole American nation" less than accurate, Link and McCormick's argument that the era was marked by a decline of political parties and the rise of special interest groups became a widely accepted ideology for understanding the relationship between Progressive reform and politics.

In 1995, Steven Diner, *A Very Different Age* (1998), analyzed much of the more recent work on Progressivism. Rather than divide his study into a specific political, social, or institutional approach, Diner's main concern was to document the ways in which "Americans sought to control their lives and their government" at a transformative time in American history. In Diner's estimation, individuals and groups were not victims of this very different age but proactive agents attempting to respond to a changing way of life.

Shortly after Diner identified individuals and groups with agency, other historians provided detailed studies on various groups. Daniel Rodgers, *Atlantic Crossings: Social Politics in a Progressive Age* (1998), painted the picture of Progressivism with broad strokes. Rodgers concentrates on the transatlantic exchange of "idea brokers," well-traveled reformers who were cognizant of and open to experimenting with both European solutions and government assistance as they worked toward their goal of peacefully mending a society shaped by the rapid rise of industrialism, urbanism, and democracy. For Rodgers, being a Progressive meant that you were simultaneously involved in multiple reform causes. It was clear to the Progressives that the United States had many of the same problems that Europe did but lacked a refined social consciousness. Reformers had to help Americans catch up with countries like Germany, where the state was already an active agency in the economy. Social politics centered around Progressive efforts to expand government involvement for the good of the people.

Alan Dawley, *Changing the World: American Progressives in War and Revolution* (2003), focuses on what he deems the new internationalism of global actors. Dawley explores the quests of reformers like Hull House's Jane Addams, Amalgamated Clothing Workers' president Sidney Hillman and Wisconsin senator Robert LaFollette who sought the grand goals of world peace and economic justice in a global context due to what Addams termed as "a growing world consciousness" on the part of reformers. In Dawley's assessment of the Progressives, they were altruistic actors who sincerely sought a politics of social justice and civic engagement over politics of patronage and power. Alan Dawley and Daniel Rodgers both agree that the New Deal marked the successful culmination of Progressive ideas.

Returning to a domestic account of the Progressives is Michael McGerr in *A Fierce Discontent: The Rise and Fall of the Progressive Movement in America, 1870–1920* (2003). McGerr concentrates on middle-class Progressives whose efforts to transform America into a kind of utopia involved restructuring cultural and societal values. McGerr argues that utopian ideals such as "Americanization" and "trust-busting" resulted in a convulsive upheaval and time of radicalism that reached far beyond the Revolution or anything since. McGerr views the Progressives fighting an uphill battle against virtually insurmountable odds. He sees middle-class radicals empowered by their status anxiety rather than crippled by it. They developed two paths for change: the state, for public issues, and associationalism, for private and social changes.

While reformers experienced at least some degree of success in helping the workers reshape their environment, they failed to alter the lifestyles of the elite. McGerr suggests that perhaps the most important failure of the reformers was their inability to curb the control that big business had in the marketplace, in politics, and on the people. McGerr leaves the reader with a sense of pessimism. According to McGerr, the Progressives lost their battle and with it, their movement and the expectations that the Progressives had raised ultimately collapsed.

Maureen A. Flanagan considers much of the work of the previous historians in offering a more hopeful account of how diverse groups of Americans participated in the Progressive reform movement. *America Reformed: Progressives and Progressivisms, 1890s–1920s* (2007) organizes Progressives along four thematic lines: economic, political, social justice, and foreign policy. Flanagan includes women, African Americans and other minorities in her account of a transforming relationship with the government. She explains how Progressives of many stripes organized to confront the problems they faced and, in the process, redefined the nature and the purpose of democracy.

In essence, the nature of Progressive reform becomes most evident with scholars' recognition of its enormous diversity. Historians' work begs the question of whether or not the Progressives accomplished their goals and what their legacy was.

Chapter 1: Setting the Stage: The Birth of the Progressive Impulse, 1893–1900

Urban life

Early treatments of urbanization include Progressives' own accounts of urban corruption. The best known is Lincoln Steffens's The *Shame of the Cities*. For a contrasting perspective, see Frederic Clemson Howe, *The City, the Hope of Democracy* (New York, 1905). Raymond A. Mohl, *The New City: Urban American in the Industrial Age, 1860–1920* (Wheeling, Illinois, 1985), traces the broad outlines of urban transformations and response to the industrial era. See also Alexander von Hoffman, *Local Attachments: The Making of an American Urban Neighborhood, 1850–1920* (Baltimore, 1994). Jon A. Peterson, *The Birth of City Planning in U.S. 1840–1917* (Baltimore, 2003), traces the birth of city planning prior to 1917 when Peterson argues planners abandoned the big picture out of necessity because they had never achieved the authority to implement it. They turned, instead, to piecemeal "opportunistic interventions" to widen streets or to establish zoning. See also Roy Lubove, *The Urban Community: Urban Planning in the Progressive Era* (Westport, Connecticut, 1981). Stanley K. Schultz, *Constructing Urban Culture: American Cities and City Planning, 1800–1920* (Philadelphia, 1989), argues that while most historians trace the birth of city planning to Chicago World's Fair, it needs to be seen in a more comprehensive manner and as a product of the entire nineteenth century. William H. Wilson, *The City Beautiful Movement* (Baltimore, 1989), traces the history of the men and women who focused on the aesthetics of urban environments. On urban transitions, see Robert Fairbanks, *Making Better Citizens: Housing Reform and the Community Development Strategy in Cincinnati, 1890–1960* (Urbana, Illinois, 1989), and Ann Durkin Keating, *Building Chicago: Suburban Developers and the Creation of a Divided Metropolis* (Columbus, 1989). Neil Larry Shumsky, ed., *Encyclopedia of Urban America: The Cities and the Suburbs* Vols. 1 and 2 (Denver, 1998), is a good reference source.

Corporate history

The ascendency of large corporations, and the men who led them, dominates the historiography surrounding the rise of big business from the turn of the century until the 1960s. The monopolistic trend known as the "merger movement" at the end of the nineteenth century heightened concerns about the future of the economy including the dominance of large corporations over individual opportunity. Early exposés of business came from a group of writers that Theodore Roosevelt deemed "muckrakers" – social critics with muck rakes. After Theodore Roosevelt used the term in a 1906 speech in reference to novelist David Graham Philips, who had exposed the insurance, finance, and political worlds in his articles and novels, it quickly became a familiar term.

Early corporate histories and biographies of corporate executives became part of the assault on big businesses. By the early twentieth century, with the establishment of monopolies by large private transportation and communications corporations, concern for the trust issue escalated. The simultaneous political sparring resulting from these economic developments provided a stimulus for a more scholarly business history. In the 1920s, Harvard business professor N. S. B. Gras used business case studies in his classes to explain how the firms started and their processes of operation. Whether criticized by muckrakers or analyzed by Gras, big businesses and the men who ran were them dominated American industrial development for the next century.

Robber barons

Historians turned to the debate over nature of the corporations. Were those in charge well-meaning captains of industry or "robber barons" out to profit at others' expense? The origin of the term robber baron is obscure, but E. L. Godkin, editor of *The Nation*, applied it in "The Vanderbilt Memorial," the *Nation* IX (November 18, 1869): 431–432, and Charles Francis Adams cited its use by the Grangers in *Railroads: Their Origin and Problems* (New York, 1893). The term implied greed, lawlessness, social irresponsibility, and immorality, which dominated the description of the origins of big business for a generation. The familiarity of mid-twentieth century Americans with the term dates from Matthew Josephson, *The Robber Barons: The Great American Capitalists, 1861–1901* (New York, 1934). The Great Depression renewed the muckrakers' attack on Wall Street and big business. Josephson portrays the clash of good and evil where the culprits of corruption were robber barons. Allan Nevins redeemed the barons with his majestic biographies of J. D. Rockefeller and Henry Ford, declaring them heroes.

To some, the robber baron debate seemed shallow. In the late 1950s, Alfred Chandler asked the more pertinent question of what happened rather than was it good or bad. He started with the centrality of technology to economic and societal change and went on to write about organizational innovation and the role of the manager. In this process, he compellingly argued for a reinterpretation of the role of the large corporation as a reflection of economic and technological forces in nineteenth century society. The Chandler school emphasized patterns of activity within and between firms rather than histories of individual firms.

It was not until the 1970s that historians Glenn Porter, Alfred Chandler, and Louis Galambos asserted that by concentrating the historical debate on the actions of businessmen and their influence on politics, scholars were ignoring other questions that would provide a more meaningful interpretation of the rise of big business as an institution in modern America. Factors such as the technology of production, the nature of distribution, and the kind of markets that the industrial enterprises served and the relationships between the function of an organization and its structure warranted consideration.

Most recently, historians have asked what changes in the economy, politics, and culture meant for corporate capitalists. They have expanded their studies to examine industrial and human relations policies including the creation of welfare capitalism. Community studies have also become an important part of business and labor history. Individual histories of businesses are often missing from this picture. With a few exceptions, individual businesses have not been willing to open their records to historians.

General business history

A starting point for general business history is Mansel Blackford, *A History of Small Business in America* (Chapel Hill, 2003, 2nd ed.), which provides a comprehensive account of the changing role of small businesses (including farms) in the nation's economic, political, and cultural development. Blackford shows how, by carving out niches in the market and developing new and often specialized products and after 1900, by enlisting government help, small businesses could sustain themselves. For details of social and economic developments in the industrial world of big business, see Walter Licht, *Industrializing America: The Nineteenth Century* (Baltimore, 1995); Glenn Porter, *The Rise of Big Business*

(Wheeling, Illinois, 1992, 2nd ed.); Daniel Nelson, "The History of Business in America," *Magazine of History* Vol. 11 (Fall 1996): 5–10; and Keith L. Bryant and Henry C. Dethloff, *A History of American Business* (Englewood Cliffs, New Jersey, 1983). Thomas K. McCraw's *American Business, 1920–2000: How it Worked* (Wheeling, Illinois, 2000) is an inclusive critique of American business history to the twenty-first century. Oliver Zunz, *Making America Corporate, 1870–1920* (Chicago, 1990), discusses changes from corporate capitalists' viewpoint. Scott Cummings, ed., *Self Help in Urban America: Patterns of Minority Business Enterprise* (Pt. Washington, 1980), examines the presence of minority-owned businesses in the marketplace and the presence of mutual aid societies serving ethnic groups. On the merger movement, see Naomi Lamoreaux, *The Great Merger Movement in American Business, 1895–1904* (New York, 1985). See also Herbert Hovenkamp, *Enterprise and American Law, 1836–1937* (Cambridge, Massachusetts, 1991), for how the anti-monopoly movement initiated mergers.

Biographies of business personalities

On businessmen, see Matthew Josephson, *The Robber Barons: The Great American Capitalists, 1861–1901* (New York, 1934), and Thomas Brewer, *The Robber Barons: Saints or Sinners* (New York, 1970). "American Problem Series" includes essays that present the creative and destructive aspects of robber barons. Recent biographies of businessmen include Ron Chernow, *The House of Morgan: An American Banking Dynasty and the Rise of Modern Finance* (New York, 1990); Ron Chernow, *Titan: The Life of John D. Rockefeller, Sr.* (New York, 1998); Harold C. Livesay, *Andrew Carnegie and the Rise of Big Business* (New York, 2000); Steven Watts, *The People's Tycoon: Henry Ford and the American Century* (New York, 2005); and Maury Klein, *The Life and Legend of Jay Gould* (Baltimore,1986). A'Lelia Perry Bundles, *On Her Own Ground: The Life and Times of Madam C.J. Walker* (New York, 2001), provides an account of one of America's first successful businesswomen.

For a classic study that examines the structure of the U. S. economy and the persistent individualism of businessmen, see

Samuel P. Hays, *Response to Industrialism, 1885–1914* (Chicago, 1995, 2nd ed.), and Samuel P. Hays, "Revising the Response to Industrialism," *Journal of the Gilded Age and Progressive Era*, Vol. 3, No. 1 (January 2004): 113–115. See also Louis Galambos, *The Public Image of Big Business in America, 1880–1940: A Quantitative Study in Social Change* (Baltimore, 1975), for the public's perception of business practices.

Technology

Technology and the effects of automated information on processing systems are detailed in David Hounshell, *From the American System to Mass Production, 1800–1932: The Development of Manufacturing Technology in the United States* (Baltimore, 1984); James R. Beniger, *The Control Revolution: Technological and Economic Origins of the Information Society* (Cambridge, Massachusetts, 1986); and Ruth Cowan, *A Social History of Technology* (New York, 1997).

Managerial revolution

The managerial revolution is brilliantly detailed in Alfred D. Chandler, *The Visible Hand: The Managerial Revolution in American Business* (Cambridge, Massachusetts, 1977). Chandler chronicles the transition from market economy to managerial capitalism including the transfer of company operations from one owner or partners to full-time, salaried managers. For the impact of Chandler's work, see Richard R. John, "Elaborations, Revisions, Dissents: Alfred D. Chandler, Jr.'s 'The Visible Hand' after Twenty Years," *Business History Review*, Vol. 71, No. 2 (Summer 1997): 151–200. Other related works include Daniel Nelson, *Frederick W. Taylor and Scientific Management* (Madison, 1980), and Alfred D. Chandler, *Scale and Scope: Dynamics of Industrial Capitalism* (Cambridge, Massachusetts, 1991). Daniel Nelson, *Managers and Workers: Origins of the New Factory System in the United States, 1880–1920* (Madison, 1975), analyzes management strategies.

Labor history

Serious study of labor history emerged in the second half of the twentieth century. Until such time, traditional historians studying labor history concentrated on organized labor movements and trade unions, working-class political parties, protest movements, and industrial conflicts. These dramatic developments seemed to lend themselves to scrutiny through the lens of economics much more so than the daily trials and tribulations of the working-class experience. Herbert Gutman, David Montgomery, and David Brody led the charge to examine the ordinary workers' experience and agency in the workplace. "New labor history," as it came to be called, resulted in the influence of social history on the study of workers and their cultures. Eventually, a rich body of scholarship centered on community studies emerged as a central facet of the new labor history. Historians expanded this realm of study to follow the culture of working-class politics and the effects of ethnicity and gender on worker policy and law.

Herbert Gutman, ed., *Work, Culture, and Society in Industrializing America* (New York, 1977); David Montgomery, *Workers' Control in America* (New York, 1979); and David Brody, *Workers in Industrial America* (New York, 1993, 2nd ed.), are considered premier labor history works. See also Patricia Murolo, *From the Folks Who Brought You the Weekend: A Short, Illustrated History of Labor* (New York, 2001); Melvyn Dubofsky, *Industrialism and the American Worker, 1865–1920* (Wheeling, Illinois, 1996, 3rd ed.); Randi Storch, *Working Hard for the American Dream: Workers and Their Unions, World War I to the Present* (Malden, Massachusetts, 2013); Nelson Lichtenstein, *State of the Union: A Century of American Labor* (Princeton, 2002); Kim Voss, *Hard Work: Remaking the American Labor Movement* (Berkeley, 2004); David Brody, *Workers in Industrial America* (New York, 1993, reprint); and James Green, *World of the Worker: Labor in Twentieth Century America* (New York, 1998). Jacqueline Jones, *American Work: Four Centuries of Black and White Labor* (New York, 1998), Ava Baron, ed., *Work Engendered: Toward a New History of American Labor* (Ithaca, New York, 1991), and Alice Kessler-Harris, *Gendering Labor History* (Urbana, Illinois, 2007), incorporate minority work experience into their accounts. David Montgomery, *The Fall of the House of Labor: The Workplace, the State, and American Labor Activism, 1865–1925* (New York, 1987), and Michael Goldfield, *The Decline of Organized Labor in the United States* (Chicago, 1987), both analyze labor's shortcomings.Reference works include Eric Arneson, ed., *Encyclopedia of United States Labor and Working-Class History* (New York, 2007), and Maurice F. Neufeld, Daniel J. Leab, and Dorothy Swanson, *American Working Class History: A Representative Bibliography* (New York, 1983).

Primary sources for labor history

Primary sources are also useful to help inform students about workers' lives. Turn-of-the-century periodicals like *Century Magazine, the Survey,* and *the Independent* published articles about workers' lives for their middle-class readers. *The Independent* ran a series of 75 stories about workers from boot blacks to sweatshop workers from 1902 to 1906, some of which were compiled in David Katzman and William M. Tuttle, Jr., *Plain Folk: Life Stories of Undistinguished Americans* (Urbana, 1982). See also Jonathan Rees and Jonathan Pollack, eds., *The Voice of the People: Primary Sources on the History of American Labor, Industrial Relations, and Working Class Culture* (Wheeling, Illinois, 2004).

Pressure from the Progressives resulted in valuable primary sources starting with the Aldrich Report (1893) prepared by Commissioner of Labor Carroll D. Wright, prepared report for the Senate Committee on Finance 52nd Congress, 2nd Session, March 3, 1893, chaired by Nelson Aldrich. The Aldrich Report examined wholesale prices, wages, and transportation. Some criticized the report's use of samples for not being representative enough and for problems with regional and industrial coverage. Other valuable sources include *Hull House Maps and Papers: A Presentation of Nationalities and Wages in a Congested District of Chicago* (New York, 1895); Jacob A. Riis, *How the Other Half Lives: Studies among the Tenements of New York* (New York, 1890); and Paul

Underwood Kellogg, ed., *The Russell Sage Foundation Reports: Findings in Six Volumes* (New York, 1909–1914) (includes the Pittsburgh Survey). Reports from authored by government commissions include the Francis Patrick Walsh, Basil M. Manly, and John Rogers Commons, *Final Report of the Commission on Industrial Relations* in 11 volumes (Chicago, 1915) provided a comprehensive inquiry into the condition of labor in the United States with recommendations. See also the U.S. Senate, 61st Congress, 2nd Session, *Report on Condition on Woman and Child Wage-Earners in the United States* in 19 volumes (Washington, D.C., 1910–1915). Josephine Goldmark, *Fatigue and Efficiency: A Study in Industry* (New York, 1912), prepared under the auspices of the Russell Sage Foundation, proved that excessive working hours hurt workers and impaired productivity.

Labor organizations

Trade unions tend to maintain their own archives. Labor economists and historians fascinated by this aspect of labor history employ an institutional approach when studying individual unions or workers' associations. David Brody, *Steelworkers in America* (Cambridge, Massachusetts, 1960) is first to break out of institutional structure of trade unions to place workers in the larger context of community, and Thomas Dublin's and Walter Licht's *The Face of Decline: The Pennsylvania Anthracite Region in the Twentieth Century* (Ithaca, New York, 2005) is one of the more recent examples. The labor movement and worker protest in the United States is detailed in Robert E. Weir, *Beyond Labor's Veil: The Culture of the Knights of Labor* (Pittsburgh, Pennsylvania, 1996); Michael Kazin, *Barons of Labor: The San Francisco Building Trades and Union Power in the Progressive Era* (Urbana, Illinois, 1989); Peter Cole, *Wobblies on the Waterfront: Interracial Unionism in Progressive Era Philadelphia* (Urbana, Illinois, 2007); Walter Licht, *Working for the Railroad: The Origin of Work in the Nineteenth Century* (Princeton, 1983); and Paul Michel Tailon, *Good Reliable Whitemen: Railroad Brotherhoods, 1877–1917* (Urbana, 2009). Shelton Stromquist, *A Generation of Boomers: The Pattern of Railroad Labor*

Conflict in Nineteenth Century America (Urbana, Illinois, 1987), and David Corbin, *Life, Work, and Rebellion in the Coal Fields: The Southern West Virginia Miners, 1880–1922* (Urbana, Illinois, 1990), detail unrest in a specific industry.

Labor conflicts

On strikes in the late nineteenth century, see Paul Avrich, *The Haymarket Tragedy* (Princeton, 1984); James R. Green, *Death in the Haymarket: A Story of Chicago, The First Labor Movement, and the Bombing that Divided Gilded Age America* (New York, 2006); Paul Krause, *The Battle for Homestead, 1880–1892* (Pittsburgh, 1992); and Susan Eleanor Hirsch, *A Century of Labor Struggle at Pullman* (Urbana, Illinois, 2003). For a general work on strikes, see PK Edwards, *Strikes in the United States, 1881–1974* (New York, 1981).

For women's participation in workplace protest, see Ileen A. DeVault, *United Apart: Gender and the Rise of Craft Unionism* (Ithaca, New York, 2004), which explores cross-gender strikes at transitional moments. See also Meredith Tax, *The Rising of the Women: Feminist Solidarity and Class Conflict, 1880–1917* (Urbana, Illinois, 1980); Joan M. Jensen and Sue Davidson, *A Needle, A Bobbin, A Strike: Women Needleworkers in America* (Philadelphia, 1991); Richard A. Greenwald, *The Triangle Fire, The Protocols of Peace and Industrial Democracy in Progressive Era New York* (Philadelphia, 2005); Nancy Schrom Dye, *As Equals, as Sisters: Feminism, Unionism, and the Women's Trade Union League of New York* (Columbia, Missouri, 1980); Ruth Milkman, ed., *Women, Work, and Protest: A Century of U.S. Women's Labor History* (New York, 1990); Stephen Norwood, *Labor's Flaming Youth: Telephone Operators and Worker Militancy, 1878–1923* (Urbana, Illinois, 1990); and Mary Blewett, *Men, Women, and Work: Class, Gender and Protest in the New England Shoe Industry, 1780–1910* (Urbana, Illinois, 1990).

Labor leaders

Biographies of labor leaders are contained in Melvyn Dubofsky and Warren Van Tine, eds., *Labor Leaders in America* (Urbana,

Illinois, 1987). Works on individual labor leaders include Robert Parmet, *Master of Seventh Avenue: David Dubinsky and the American Labor Movement* (New York, 2005); Steven Fraser, *Labor Will Rule: Sidney Hillman and the Rise of American Labor* (New York, 1991); Nick Salvatore, *Eugene V. Debs, Citizen and Socialist* (Urbana, Illinois, 2007, reprint); Elizabeth Anne Payne, *Reform, Labor, and Feminism: Margaret Dreier Robins and the Women's Trade Union League* (Urbana, Illinois, 1988); and Karen Pastorello, *A Power among Them: Bessie Abramowitz Hillman and the Making of the Amalgamated Clothing Workers of America* (Urbana, Illinois, 2007). On Samuel Gompers, see Nick Salvatore, ed., *Seventy Years of Life and Labor* (Ithaca, New York, 1984).

Male workers

For an exclusively male occupation, see Timothy Spears, *100 Years on the Road: The Traveling Salesman in American Culture* (New Haven, 1995). Patricia Cooper, *Once a Cigarmaker: Men, Women, and Work Culture in American Cigar Factories, 1900–1919* (Urbana, Illinois, 1992), conducts a cross-gender study in a single industry.

Women workers

For three classic works on working women, see Alice Kessler-Harris, *A Woman's Wage: Historical Meanings and Social Consequences* (Lexington, 1990); Alice Kessler-Harris, *Out to Work: A History of Wage-Earning Women* (New York, 1982); and Alice Kessler-Harris, *Women Have Always Worked: An Historical Overview* (New York, 1981). Annelise Orleck, *Common Sense and a Little Fire: Women and Working Class Politics in the United States* (Chapel Hill, 1995), and Lara Vapnek, *Breadwinners: Working Women and Economic Independence, 1865–1920* (Urbana, Illinois, 2009), detail working women's efforts to gain economic autonomy and political equality; Vapnek includes good on coverage of domestic workers. For more on specific topics regarding working women, see also Wendy Gamber, *The Female Economy: The Millinery and Dressmaking Trades, 1860–1930* (Urbana, Illinois, 1997), and Eileen Boris, *Home to Work: Motherhood and the Politics of Industrial Homework in the United States* (New York, 1994). Darlene Hine, *Black Women in America* (New York, 2005), offers a general account of black women's work.

On women immigrant workers, see Elizabeth Ewen, *Immigrant Women in the Land of Dollars: Life and Culture on the Lower East Side, 1890–1925* (New York, 1985), and Susan Glenn, *Daughters of the Shtetl: Life and Labor in the Immigrant Generation* (Ithaca, New York, 1990). On women in retail, see Susan Porter Benson, *Counter Cultures: Saleswomen, Managers, and Customers in American Department Stores, 1890–1940* (Urbana, Illinois, 1986).

African American workers

Historians of race have examined the Great Migration including James M. Gregory, *Southern Diaspora: How the Great Migrations for Black and White Southerners Transformed America* (Chapel Hill, 2005); James R. Grossman, *Land of Hope: Chicago, Black Southerners, and the Great Migration* (Chicago, 1989); and John Higham, *Strangers in the Land: Patterns of American Nativism, 1860–1925* (Rutgers, 2002, reprint ed.) remains a classic. Rick Halpern, *Down on the Killing Floor: Black and White Workers in Chicago's Packinghouses, 1904–1954* (Urbana, Illinois, 1997), looks at race in a single industry. Isabel Wilkerson, *The Warmth of Other Suns: The Epic Story of America's Great Migration, 1915–1970* (New York, 2010), chronicles the movement of six million African Americans from the rural South to cities in the North and Midwest.

Racism

For an early account of racism, see Ida B. Wells, *A Red Record: Tabulated Statistics and Alleged Causes of Lynchings in the United States 1892–1893–1894* (Chicago, 1895). Wells provided a compelling statistical account of lynching statistics of African Americans. Ray Stannard Baker examined the sad state of race relations in

America in *Following the Color Line: An Account of Negro Citizenship in an American Democracy* (New York, 1908).

Working-class life

For patterns of working-class life and culture, see Robert Asher and Charles Stephenson, eds., *Life and Labor: Dimensions of American Working-Class Life* (Albany, 1986); James Green, *The World of the Worker* (New York, 1980); and John Bodnar, *Workers' World: Kinship, Community, and Protest in an Industrial Society, 1900–1940* (Baltimore, 1982). See also Julie Husband and Jim O'Loughlin, *Daily Life in Industrial U.S., 1870–1900* (Westport, Connecticut, 2004).

Workers and Communities Scholars who place studies of workers in the larger context of their communities were initially influenced by classic European studies. In addition to the work of Herbert Gutman, David Brody, and David Montgomery (cited above), see John T. Cumbler, *Working-Class Community in America: Work, Leisure and Struggle in Two Industrial Cities, 1880–1930* (Westport, Connecticut, 1979), a comparison of Lynn and Fall River, Massachusetts, Frances Couvares, *The Remaking of Pittsburgh: Class and Culture in an Industrializing City, 1877–1919* (Albany, 1984); James Barrett, *Work and Community in the Jungle: Chicago's Packing House Workers, 1894–1922* (Urbana, Illinois, 1987); Ray Rosenzwieg, *Eight Hours for What We Will: Workers and Leisure in an Industrial City, 1870–1920* (New York, 1983); Donald L. Miller and Richard E. Sharpless, *The Kingdom of Coal: Work, Enterprise, and Ethnic Communities in the Mine Fields* (Easton, Pennsylvania, 1985); Ileen A. DeVault, *Sons and Daughters of Labor: Class and Clerical Work in Turn of the Century Pittsburgh* (Ithaca, New York, 1990); Richard Jules Oestreicher, *Solidarity and Fragmentation: Working People and Class Consciousness in Detroit, 1875–1900* (Urbana, Illinois, 1986); Young-soo Bae, *Labor in Retreat: Class and Community among Men's Clothing Workers of Chicago, 1871–1929* (Albany, 2001); and Oliver Zunz, *The Changing Face of Inequality: Urbanization, Industrial Development, and Immigrants in Detroit, 1880–1920* (Chicago, 1982).

Immigrant family life

For a description of the immigrant family economy, see John Bodnar, *The Transplanted: A History of Immigrants in Urban America* (Bloomington, 1985). A multitude of historians have studied various ethnic groups in a specific city; a small sampling includes Virginia Yans McLaughlin, *Family and Community: Italian Immigrants in Buffalo, 1880–1930* (Urbana, Illinois, 1981); Dominic Pacyga, *Polish Immigrants and Industrial Chicago: Workers on the South Side, 1880–1922* (Columbus, Ohio, 1991); and Judith E. Smith, *Family Connections: A History of Italian and Jewish Immigrant Lives in Providence, Rhode Island, 1900–1940* (Albany, 1985).

Worker autobiographies

A sample of previously neglected firsthand worker autobiographies includes Elizabeth Hasanovitz, *One of Them: Chapters from A Passionate Autobiography* (Boston, 1918); Rose Cohen, *Out of the Shadow* (New York, 1918); and Marcus E. Ravage, *An American in the Making: The Life Story on an Immigrant* (New York, 1917).

Leisure time and recreation

On leisure and amusement in Progressive America, see Steven M. Gelber, *Hobbies, Leisure, and the Culture of Work in America* (New York, 1999); Kathy Peiss, *Cheap Amusements: Working Women and Leisure in Turn-of the-Century New York* (Philadelphia, 1987); Judith A. Adams, *The American Amusement Park Industry: A History of Technology and Thrills* (New York, 1991); Lary May, *Screening Out the Past: The Birth of Mass Culture and the Motion Picture Industry* (Chicago, 1980); Lewis Erenberg, *Steppin' Out: New York Nightlife and the Transformation of American Culture, 1890–1930* (Westport, Connecticut, 1981); and Shane White and Graham White, *Stylin': African American Expressive Culture from the Beginnings to the Zoot Suit* (Ithaca, New York, 1998). See also Steven Reiss, *Sport in Industrial America, 1850–1920* (Wheeling, Illinois, 1995).

Chapter 2: Saving Society: Progressive Reformers Advance Their Causes

Muckraker exposés

Muckrakers' attacks on business included Henry Demarest Lloyd's chronicle of the rise of John D. Rockefeller and Standard Oil in *Wealth against Commonwealth* (New York, 1894), followed by Ida Tarbell's *McClure's* series detailing the business practices of Standard Oil, later published as *The History of the Standard Oil Company* (New York, 1904). Frank Norris, *The Octopus: A Story of California* (New York, 1901) provides a fictional account detailing the railroad monopoly in California, and Ray S. Baker added to the literature with his articles condemning the railroad practices in *McClure's*. Upton Sinclair, *The Jungle* (New York, 1906), built on the earlier work of A. M. Simmons. Both attacked the meat-packing industry and were largely responsible for federal legislation regulating food and drug practices. Samuel Hopkins Adams, *The Great American Fraud* (New York, 1906), became famous from his muckraking exposés of the patent medicine industry. Edwin Markham published an exposé of child labor in *Children in Bondage: A Complete and Careful Presentation of the Anxious Problem of Child Labor – Its Causes, Its Crimes and Its Cure* (New York, 1914). For a summary of muckrakers' work, see Louis Filler, *The Muckrakers* (Pennsylvania: University Park, 1976).

Social Gospel

For origins of the Social Gospel, see William H. Cooper, Jr., *The Great Revivalists in American Religion, 1740–1944* (Jefferson, North Carolina, 2010). Robert M. Crunden, *Ministers of Reform: The Progressive Achievement in American Civilization, 1889–1920* (New York, 1983), argues that a shared religious background provided the impetus for the Progressive social and political reform impulse. For writings of those involved in the Social Gospel movement, see Washington Gladden, *Social Salvation* (Boston, 1902), and Walter Rauschenbusch, *Christianity and the Social Crisis* (New York,

1907). See also Susan Curtis, *A Consuming Faith: The Social Gospel and American Culture* (Baltimore, 1991), and Ralph E. Luker, *The Social Gospel in Black and White: American Racial Reform, 1885–1912* (Chapel Hill, 1991), for the impact of the Social Gospel on culture.

For the life of fundamental evangelist Billy Sunday, see Robert Francis Martin, *Hero of the Heartland: Billy Sunday and the Transformation of American Society, 1862–1935* (Bloomington, 2002), and W. A. Firstenberger, *In Rare Form: A Pictorial History of Baseball Evangelist Billy Sunday* (Iowa City, 2005).

Settlement movement

For a primary source on the settlement movement, see Robert Woods and Albert Kennedy, *Handbook of Settlements* (New York, 1911). Allen F. Davis, *Spearheads for Reform: The Social Settlements and the Progressive Era, 1890–1914* (New York, 1967), remains the classic work on the settlement movement. See also John Higham, *Strangers in the Land: Patterns of American Nativism, 1860–1925* (Rutgers, New Jersey, 2002), who views settlement workers as exceptional individuals and sincere altruists who were cultural pluralists aiding both immigrants and blacks with their settlement work. Elisabeth Lasch Quinn, *Black Neighbors: Race and the Limits of Reform in the American Settlement House Movement, 1890–1945* (Chapel Hill, 1993), points to settlement workers who distinguished between immigrants and blacks and failed to redirect their energy from immigrants to blacks. Judith Ann Trolander, *Professionalism and Social Change: From the Settlement House Movement to Neighborhood Centers, 1886 to Present* (New York, 1987), describes the settlements' place in reform but only analyzes the race issue after 1945. Trolander also suggests that most settlement workers were not as open-minded as well-known leaders like Addams and Wald when it came to African Americans. Mina Carson, *Settlement Folk: Social Thought in the American Settlement Movement, 1885–1930* (Chicago, 1990), describes the part that settlements played in reform. On smaller settlement houses, see Ruth Hutchinson Crocker, *Social Work and Social Order: The Settlement Movement in Two Industrial Cities, 1889–1930* (Urbana, 1992), who studies "second tier" settlements; Howard Jacob Krager, *The Sentinels of Order: A Study of Social Control and the Minneapolis Settlement House Movement, 1915–1950* (Lanham, Maryland, 1987), contends that some workers shared the racist sentiments of the day and that early social workers used their influence as a mechanism to control blacks and immigrants. On Hull House, see Kathryn Kish Sklar, "Hull House as a Community of Women Reformers in the 1890s," *Signs* 10 (1985): 657–677; Rivka Shpak Lissak, *Pluralism and Progressives: Hull House and the New Immigrants, 1890–1919* (Chapel Hill, 1991); and Hilda Satt Polacheck, *I Came a Stranger: The Story of a Hull House Girl* (Urbana, Illinois, 1989), for the only existing [auto]biography of a working-class girl at the settlement.

Biographies of settlement leaders

Biographies of settlement leaders help students acquire insight into the efforts of the reformers. The life and thought of Hull House founder Jane Addams has attracted much attention in recent years. See Marilyn Fischer, Carol Nackenoff, and Wendy Chmielewski, eds., *Jane Addams and the Practice of Democracy: Multidisciplinary Perspectives on Theory and Practice* (Urbana, Illinois, 2009); Louise Knight, *Citizen: Jane Addams and the Struggle for Democracy* (Chicago, 2005); and Victoria Bissell Brown, *The Education of Jane Addams: Politics and Culture in Modern America* (Philadelphia, 2003). See also Allen F. Davis, *American Heroine: The Life and Legend of Jane Addams* (New York, 1973), and James Weber Linn, *Jane Addams: A Biography* (Chicago, 1935). Jane Addams was also a prolific writer. Two of her best-known works on her settlement years include Jane Addams, *Twenty Years at Hull House* (New York, 1912), and *Democracy and Social Ethics* (New York, 1902). For a reliable biographical account of Florence Kelley's impact on Progressive Era reform, see Kathryn Kish Sklar, *Florence Kelley and the Nation's Work: The Rise of Women's Political Culture, 1830–1900* (New Haven, 1995). Lillian Wald's life is chronicled in Marjorie N. Feld, *Lillian Wald: A Biography* (Chapel Hill, 2008), and Lillian Wald, *The House on Henry Street* (New York, 1915). For biographical sketches of the lives of Chicago settlement women, see Adele Hast and Rima Lunin Schultz, eds., *Women Building Chicago, 1790–1990: A Biographical Dictionary* (Bloomington, 2001).

Progressive thought

Two leading works on Progressive thought are Louis Menand's *The Metaphysical Club: A Story of Ideas in America* (New York, 2002), which examines the lives of four leading intellectuals to describe how pragmatism helped Americans cope with modern life, and Leon Fink's *Progressive Intellectuals and the Dilemmas of Democratic Commitment* (Cambridge, Massachusetts, 1997), in which Progressives believed in democracy but found it difficult to connect with the majority of Americans. For the influence of the Europeans on Progressive philosophy, see Mike Hawkins, *Social Darwinism in European and American Thought, 1860–1945* (Cambridge, 1997), and James T. Kloppenberg, *Uncertain Victory: Social Democracy and Progressivism in European and American Thought, 1870–1920* (New York, 1986). For earlier works on reform thought, see David Noble, *The Paradox of Progressive Thought* (Minneapolis, 1958); Charles Forcey, *The Crossroads of Liberalism: Croly, Weyl, Lippmann, and the Progressive Era, 1900–1925* (New York, 1961), and Jean B. Quant, *From the Small Town to the Great Community: The Social Thought of Progressive Intellectuals* (New Brunswick, New Jersey, 1970). See also Eric F. Goldman, *Rendezvous with Destiny: A History of Modern American Reform* (New York, 1952), who observes how intellectuals turn away from dominant conservatism.

Professionalization

Professionalization advanced during the era. No single survey of white-collar workers exists, but for the emergence of middle-class identity, see Stuart Blumin, *The Emergence of the Middle Class: Social Experience in the American City, 1760–1900* (New York, 1989), and Samuel Haber, *The Quest for Authority and Honor in the American Professions, 1750–1900* (Chicago, 1991), which reexamines the history of lawyers, the clergy, professors, engineers, and physicians. For an analysis of the professionalization of medicine, see Paul Starr, *The Social Transformation of American Medicine: The Rise of a Sovereign Profession and the Making of a Vast Industry* (New York, 1982). Documenting the development of hospitals is Charles E. Rosenberg, *The Care of Strangers: The Rise of America's Hospital System* (New York, 1987). The legal profession lacks a comprehensive survey, but Gerald W. Gawalt, ed., *The New High Priests: Lawyer in Post Civil War America* (Westport, Connecticut, 1984); Wayne K. Hobson, *The American Legal Profession and the Organization Society, 1890–1930* (New York, 1986); and Robert Stevens, *Law School: Legal Education from the 1850s to the 1980s* (Chapel Hill, 1983) show the dynamics and increasing educational requirements of the profession.

Women in the professions

On women in the professions in general, see Penina Migdal Glazer and Miriam Slater, *Unequal Colleagues: The Entrance of Women into the Professions, 1890–1940* (New Brunswick, 1987). See also Karen Berger Morello, *The Invisible Bar: The Woman Lawyer in America, 1638 to the Present* (New York, 1986), which provides an account of women attorneys' experiences. For a comprehensive treatment of the teaching profession, see Donald Warren, ed., *American Teachers: Histories of a Profession at Work* (New York, 1989). On nursing, see Susan Reverby, *Ordered to Care: The Dilemma of American Nursing, 1850–1945* (New York, 1987). On social work as a profession, see Roy Lubove, *The Professional Altruist: The Emergence of Social Work as a Career, 1880–1930* (New York, 1980), and Regina G. Kunzel, *Fallen Women, Problem Girls: Unmarried Mothers and the Professionalization of Social Work, 1890–1945* (New Haven, 1993). A useful biography includes Barbara Sicherman, *Alice Hamilton: A Life in Letters* (Cambridge, 1984). Barbara Miller Solomon, *In the Company of Educated Women: A History of Women and Higher Education in America* (New Haven, 1985), and Lynn D. Gordon, *Gender and Higher Education in the Progressive Era* (New Haven, 1990), detail educational opportunities for women.

Businessmen and reform

Robert Weibe's *Search for Order* (1967) remains the classic for determining what the role of businessmen was in reform. See also Judith Sealander, *Grand Plans: Business Progressivism and Social Change in Ohio's Miami Valley, 1890–1929* (Lexington, Kentucky, 1988). What was the role of governmental reform and state policy on business? Shelton Stromquist, *Reinventing "the People": The Progressive Movement, the Class Problem, and the Origins of Modern Liberalism* (Urbana, Illinois, 2000), attempts to tackle the question that historians such as Thomas McCraw have suggested is difficult to answer.

Politics

Traditional interpretations of Progressive Era politics emphasized the evils of the boss system and the ideals of Progressive reformers. This dichotomous view criticized by Jon C. Teaford, *The Unheralded Triumph: City Government in America, 1870–1900* (Baltimore, 1984), argues that bosses had less influence than engineers, landscape architects, and public health officials. The functional view between politics and (often illegal) business is examined in Robert Merton's *Social Theory and Social Structures* (New York, 1957), which observed that bosses garnered votes not from stealing elections through bribery, corruption, and fraud but from sincere support of working class and immigrants. Scholarship that portrays city bosses as decisive, centralizing figures able to overcome urban disorder and diffusion of municipal power includes Seymour J. Mandelbaum, *Boss Tweed's New York* (New York, 1965), and John M. Allswang, *Bosses, Machines, and Urban Voters* (Port Washington, New York, 1977), suggests that many city dwellers are dependent on the services of rapidly responding bosses.

By the late 1980s, historians began to investigate the problem of power in cities, which shifts with influx of population and new pressure groups. See Richard W. Judd, *Socialist Cities: Municipal Politics and the Grassroots of American Socialism* (Albany, 1989). For more on politics specific cities, see Dominic A. Pacyga, *Chicago: A Biography* (Chicago, 2009); Zane L. Miller, *Boss Cox's Cincinnati: Urban Politics in the Progressive Era* (New York, 1968); James J. Connolly, *The Triumph of Ethnic Progressivism: Urban Political Culture in Boston, 1900–1925* (Cambridge, 1998); Maureen Flanagan, *Charter Reform in Chicago* (Carbondale, 1987); and Shelton Stromquist, "The Crucible of Class: Cleveland Politics and the Origins of Municipal Reform in the Progressive Era," *Journal of Urban History* 23 (January 1997): 197–220. On Progressive politics at the state level, see Thomas R. Pegram, *Partisans and Progressives: Private Interest and Public Policy in Illinois, 1870–1922* (Urbana, Illinois, 1992), and David Thelen, *The New Citizenship: The Origins of Progressivism in Wisconsin, 1885–1900* (Columbia, Missouri, 1972). See also Richard L. McCormick, *From Realignment to Reform: Political Change in New York State, 1893–1910* (Ithaca, New York, 1981), for part of literature considered "new political history" that focuses on voting behavior. For national politics, see Paul Kleppner, *Continuity and Change in American Electoral Politics, 1893–1928* (New York, 1987), an important work that continues in the vein of McCormick. See also Robert D. Johnston, "Re-Democratizing the Progressive Era: The Politics of Progressive Era Political Historiography," *Journal of the Gilded Age and Progressive Era* 1 (2002): 68–92.

Biographies of progressive personalities

There are numerous biographies of Progressive Era personalities. On the presidents, see Edmund Morris, *The Rise of Theodore Roosevelt* (New York, 1979); Edmund Morris, *Theodore Rex* (New York, 2001); and Kathleen Dalton, *Theodore Roosevelt: A Strenuous Life* (New York, 2007). Johnathan Lurie, *William H. Taft: The Travails of a Progressive Conservative* (New York, 2011), and Donald F. Anderson, *William Howard Taft: A Conservative's Conception of the Presidency* (Ithaca, New York, 1973), study Taft's troubled presidency; Arthur S. Link, *Woodrow Wilson and the Progressive Era, 1910–1917* (New York, 1954); John Milton Cooper, Jr., *The Warrior and the Priest: Woodrow Wilson and Theodore Roosevelt* (Cambridge,

Massachusetts, 1983); and John Milton Cooper, Jr., *Woodrow Wilson: A Biography* (New York, 2010), provide insight into the Wilson years and place him in the context of his times.

Other biographies of Progressive Era personalities include Paula Eldot, *Governor Alfred E. Smith, the Politician as Reformer* (New York, 1983); Howard Zinn, *LaGuardia in Congress* (Ithaca, New York, 1959); Carl R. Burgehardt, *Robert M. La Follette, Sr.: The Voice of Conscience* (New York, 1992); Elisabeth Israels Perry, *Belle Moskowitz: Feminine Politics and the Exercise of Power in the Age of Alfred E. Smith* (Boston, 1992); Melvin G. Holli, *Reform in Detroit: Hazen S. Pingree and Urban Politics* (New York, 1969); and Nancy Unger, *Fighting Bob LaFollette: The Righteous Reformer* (Chapel Hill, 2000).

Chapter 3: "Constructing the World Anew:" Progressive Agency, 1900–1911

Women's activism

Accounts of Progressive Era women and their activities include Paula Baker, "Domestication of American Politics," *American Historical Review* 89 (1984): 620–647; Maureen Flanagan, *Seeing with their Hearts: Chicago Women and the Vision of the Good City, 1871–1933* (Princeton, 2002); Alice Kessler-Harris, *In Pursuit of Equity: Women, Men, and the Quest for Economic Citizenship in Twentieth Century America* (New York, 2001); Annelise Orleck, *Common Sense and a Little Fire: Women and Working Class Politics in the United States* (Chapel Hill, 1995); and Robyn Muncy, *Creating a Female Dominion in American Reform* (New York, 1994). See also Lelia Rupp, *Worlds of Women* (Princeton, 1997), which details international connections on the part of women; Mari Jo Buhle, *Women and American Socialism, 1870–1920* (Urbana, Illinois, 1983), and Estelle Freedman, "Separatism as a Strategy: Female Institution Building and American Feminism, 1870–1930," *Feminist Studies* 5 (1979): 512–529. Anne Firor Scott demonstrates how women's organizations laid the foundations for the social justice movement in *Natural Allies: Women's Associations in American History* (Urbana, 1992). Kathryn Kish Sklar breathed new life into this contention arguing that women were the lead actors in the political reform arena in the twentieth century. See also Kathryn Kish Sklar, "The Historical Foundations of Women's Power in the Creation of the American Welfare State, 1830–1930," in Seth Koven and Sonya Michel, eds., *Mothers of a New World: Maternalist Politics and the Origins of Welfare States* (New York: Routledge, 1993). For formal political activities of women, see Melanie Gustafson, *Women in the Republican Party, 1854–1924* (Urbana, Illinois, 2001); Paula Baker, *The Moral Frameworks of Public Life: Gender, Politics, and the State in Rural New York, 1870–1930* (New York, 1991), and Sara Hunter Graham, *Woman Suffrage and the New Democracy* (New Haven, 1996). [In Living the Revolution: Italian Women's Resistance and Radicalism in New York City, 1880–1945 (Chapel Hill, North Carolina, 2010), Jennifer Guglielmo documents the culturally based radical activism of urban working-class women.]

[For useful website, see Kathryn Kish Sklar and Thomas Dublin, Women and Social Movements, 1600–2000, SUNY Binghamton and Alexander Street Press.]

Women's suffrage

Highlights on the movement for women's suffrage during the Progressive Era include Anne F. Scott and Andrew M. Scott, *One Half of the People: The Fight for Women's Suffrage* (Philadelphia, 1975); Eleanor Flexnor, *Century of Struggle: The Woman's Rights Movement in the United States* (Cambridge, Massachusetts, 1975); and Aileen Kraditor, *The Ideas of the Woman Suffrage Movement, 1890–1920* (New York, 1965). Two valuable anthologies of writing including debates on the suffrage movement are Marjorie Spruill Wheeler, ed., *One Woman, One Vote: Rediscovering the Woman Suffrage Movement* (Troutdale, Oregon, 1995), and Jean H. Baker, ed., *Votes for Women: The Struggle for Suffrage Revisited* (New York, 2002).

Societal reform

On attempts to regulate society, see Morton Keller, *Regulating a New Society: Public Policy and Social Change in America, 1900–1933* (Cambridge, Massachusetts, 1994). See also Christine Stansell, *American Moderns: Bohemian New York and the Creation of a New Century* (New York, 2001), for a reaction to social control. Ruth Rosen, *The Lost Sisterhood: Prostitution in America, 1900–1918* (Baltimore, 1982), and Ruth Bordin, *Women and Temperance: The Quest for Liberty and Power, 1873–1900* (Philadelphia, 1981), cover specific aspects of women's activism. Kathryn Kish Sklar, "Two Political Cultures in the Progressive Era: The National Consumers' League and the American Association for Labor Legislation," in Linda Kerber, Alice Kessler-Harris, and Kathryn Kish Sklar, eds., *U.S. History as Women's History: New Feminist Essays*, 36–62 (Chapel Hill, 1997). Another essay collection of interest on women and political activism are found in Louise Tilly and Patricia Gurin, *Women, Politics, and Change* (New York, 1990).

Education and reform

Two of the best works on Progressive educational reform are Kevin Mattson, *Creating a Democratic Public: The Struggle for Urban Participatory Democracy During the Progressive Era* (Pittsburgh, 1998), which discusses the social center movement as being based on the politics of democratic initiative and participation, and William J. Reese, *Power and the Promise of School Reform: Grassroots Movements During the Progressive Era* (New York, 2002), which argues that the "new woman" is vital to school reform. Progressive efforts directed toward child welfare are found in Victoria Getis, *The Juvenile Court and the Progressives* (Urbana, Illinois, 2000).

Origins of progressivism

For the origins and general history of Progressivism, see Robert Cherney, *American Politics in the Gilded Age, 1868–1900* (Wheeling, Illinois, 1997), and Richard L. McCormick, "The Discovery that

Business Corrupts Politics: A Reappraisal of the Origins of Progressivism," *American Historical Review* 86 (1981): 247–274. On popular politics and public policy, see Alexander Keyssar, *The Right to Vote: The Contested History of Democracy in the United States* (New York, 2000). For insightful studies of political structures and institutions, see Richard L. McCormick, *The Party Period and Public Policy: American Politics from the Age of Jackson to the Progressive Era* (New York, 1986); and Michael McGerr, *The Decline of Popular Politics: The American North, 1865–1928* (New York, 1986). For the election of 1912 see James Chace, *1912: Wilson, Roosevelt, Taft and Debs – The Election that Changed the Country* (New York, 2004).

Business and politics

For specialized studies detailing business and politics and a good starting point for studies of regulation and reform policies, see Gabriel Kolko, *The Triumph of Conservatism: A Reinterpretation of American History, 1900–1916* (New York, 1963). Kolko argues that corporations were the main beneficiaries of government regulation and that corporate leaders used government for their benefit to eliminate unfair competition. See also Gabriel Kolko, *Railroads and Regulation, 1877–1916* (Princeton, 1965), which attempts to prove the theory that railroads controlled regulation for their own benefit, and James Weinstein, *The Corporate Ideal in the Liberal State, 1900–1918* (Boston, 1968), for a view that Progressive reform was a tool of the corporate elite. Robert H. Weibe, *Businessmen and Reform: A Study of the Progressive Movement* (Cambridge, Massachusetts, 1962), studies the relationship between businessmen and reform. Weibe's now classic study presents the middle class as organizers and counters prior interpretations that perceive businessmen as persistent individuals. Albro Martin, *Railroads Triumphant: The Growth, Rebirth, and Rejection of a Vital American Force* (New York, 1992), also disputes Kolko's theory. Martin maintains that the railroads did not benefit from regulation. Stephen Breyer, *Regulation and its Reform* (Cambridge, Massachusetts, 1982), asked whether or not the practices of business were corrupt? Thomas McCraw, *Prophets of Regulation: Charles*

Frances Adams, Louis D. Brandeis, James M. Landis, Alfred E. Kahn (Cambridge, Massachusetts, 1984), explains public attitudes and government actions with regard to business regulation. In "Regulation in America: A Review Article," *Business History Review* (1975), McCraw posits what is considered a pluralist interpretation of regulation contending that both the public and the corporations rather than one or the other benefitted from government intervention in the form of regulation in the economy.

Louis Galambos, *The Rise of the Corporate Commonwealth: U.S. Business and Public Policy in the Twentieth Century* (New York, 1988), and Martin Sklar, *The Corporate Reconstruction of American Capitalism, 1890–1916: The Market, the Law, and Politics* (New York, 1988), describe the battle between advocates of corporate liberalism (welfare capitalism) and Progressive liberalism (public state regulation). See also Earl Daniel Saros, *Labor, Industry, and Regulation during the Progressive Era* (New York, 2009), which argues that mergers formed in the wake of the Depression of 1893 resulted in less competition for businesses that survived the economic downturn. See also Douglas Steeples and David Whitten, *Democracy in Desperation: The Depression of 1893* (Westport, Connecticut, 1998). James Livingston, *Origins of the Federal Reserve System: Money, Class, and Corporate Capitalism, 1890–1913* (Ithaca, New York, 1986), helps explain the history of corporate capitalism.

Radical labor

Accounts of radical labor activities include Melvyn Dubofsky, *Hard Work: The Making of Labor History* (2000); Melvyn Dubofsky, *We Shall be All: A History of the Industrial Workers of the World* (Urbana, Illinois, 2000, reprint ed.); and Rosemay Feurer, *Radical Unions in the Midwest, 1900–1950* (Urbana, Illinois: University of Illinois Press, 2006). Northern Farmers and Populists are discussed in Cindy Hahamavitch, *The Fruits of Their Labor: Atlantic Coast Farmworkers and the Making of Migrant Poverty, 1870–1945* (Chapel Hill, 1997). For a detailed account of farmers' lives in general, see also Hal S. Barron, *Mixed Harvest: The Second Great Transformation in the Rural North, 1870–1930* (Chapel Hill, 1997).

See also Sarah Elbert, "Women and Farming: Changing Structures, Changing Roles," in Wava G. Haney and Jane B. Knowles, eds., *Women and Farming: Changing Roles, Changing Structures* (Boulder, Colorado, 1988).

Labor and politics

Accounts of labor's political participation in the Progressive Era include Roy Lichtenstein, *State of the Union: A Century of American Labor* (Princeton, 2003); Mark Karson, *American Labor Unions and Politics, 1900–1918* (Carbondale, Illinois, 1958); and Julie Greene, *Pure and Simple Politics: The AF of L, 1881–1915* (New York, 1997). See also Eric Arneson, Julie Greene, and Bruce Laurie, eds., *Labor Histories: Class, Politics, and the Working Class Experience* (Urbana, Illinois, 1988). Accounts of early labor activity in the political arena include Leon Fink, *Workingmen's Democracy: The Knights of Labor and American Politics* (Urbana, Illinois, 1983); Irvin Yellowitz, *Labor and the Progressive Movement in New York State, 1897–1916* (Ithaca, New York, 1965); and Leon Fink, *In Search of the Working Class: Essays in American Labor History and Political Culture* (Urbana, Illinois, 1994). See also Philip S. Foner, History of the Labor Movement in the United States, Vol. 3, *The Policies and Practices of the American Federation of Labor, 1900–1909* (New York, 1981, 4th ed.), and Vol. 5, *The American Federation of Labor in the Progressive Era*. For a specific study of labor and politics, see Melvyn Dubofsky, *When Workers Organize: New York City in the Progressive Era* (Amherst, Massachusetts, 1968).

Politics and reform

On the relationship between politics and reform, see David Southern, *The Progressive Era and Race: Reaction and Reform, 1900–1917* (Wheeling, Illinois, 2005); Kenneth Finegold, *Experts and Politicians: Reform Challenges to Machine Politics in New York, Cleveland, and Chicago* (Princeton, 1995); and Martin J. Schiesl, *The Politics of Efficiency: Municipal Administration and Reform in America, 1880–1920* (Berkeley, 1997). See also Thomas Goebel, *A*

Government by the People: The Initiative and Referendum in America, 1890–1940 (Chapel Hill, 2002).

Civic concerns and citizenship

On civic consciousness and Progressive citizenship, see J. Joseph Huthmacher, "Urban Liberalism in the Age of Reform," *Mississippi Valley Historical Review* 44 (1962): 231–241, which demonstrates how urban ethnic workers want to become involved in politics and in implementing reforms. John D. Buenker, *Urban Liberalism and Progressive Reform* (New York, 1973), expands this argument. On ethnicity and Progressive reform, see James J. Connolly, "Progressivism and Pluralism," in Michael Grossberg, Wendy Gamber, and Hendrik Hartog eds., *American Public Life and the Historical Imagination* (South Bend, 2003). At the same time, nativist and anti-immigration sentiments present the dark side of Progressivism including the Dillingham Commission, Americanization programs, and proposed literacy tests. See Robert F. Zeidel, *Immigrants, Exclusion, and Progressive Politics: The Dillingham Commission, 1900–1927* (DeKalb, 2004). For both sides, see Rogers M. Smith, *Civic Ideals: Conflicting Visions of Citizenship in U.S. History* (New Haven, 1997). See also Morton Keller, *Regulating a New Society: Public Policy and Social Change in America, 1900–1933* (Cambridge, Massachusetts, 1994), and Roger Daniels, *Guarding the Golden Door: American Immigration Policy and Immigration since 1882* (2004).

Chapter 4: The Shape of Things to Come: Progressivism and the Transition to Modern Life, 1912–1917

Consumerism

For an understanding of the making a consumer culture, see Lawrence B. Glickman, *A Living Wage: American Workers and the Making of a Consumer Society* (Ithaca, New York, 1997); Susan

Strasser, *Satisfaction Guaranteed: The Making of the American Mass Market* (New York, 1989); and Andrew Heinze, *Adapting to Abundance: Jewish Immigrants, Mass Consumption, and the Search for American Identity* (New York, 1990). On the roots of consumer protection and humanizing industries, see Landon Storrs, *Civilizing Capitalism: The National Consumers' League, Women's Activism, and Labor Standards in the New Deal* (Chapel Hill, 2000). See also Lendol Calder, *Financing the American Dream: A Cultural History of Consumer Credit* (Princeton, 1999).

Welfare capitalism

Welfare capitalism is discussed in Stuart Brandes, *American Welfare Capitalism, 1880–1940* (Chicago, 1984, 2nd ed.), and Sanford M. Jacoby, *Modern Manors: Welfare Capitalism since the New Deal* (Princeton, 1997). Jacoby analyzes welfare capitalism where an urban manufacturing economy separates workers from their traditional family and community support. See also Sanford M. Jacoby, *Employing Bureaucracy: Managers, Unions and the Transformation of American Work in American Industry, 1900–1945* (New York, 1985), and Stephen Meyer, *The Five Dollar Day: Labor Management and Social Control in the Ford Motor Company* (Albany, 1981).

Corporate policies and labor

For the impact of corporate labor policies on the workers including scientific management, technological change, company unionism, and welfare capitalism, see Sanford M. Jacoby, *Modern Manors Welfare Capitalism since the New Deal* (Princeton, 1998), which analyzes welfare capitalism when urban manufacturing economy separates workers from their traditional family and community support. Companies offer paternalistic benefits such as cafeterias, medical clinic, housing, and stock options so they could develop a stable and dependable labor force. See also Nikki Mandell, *Corporation as Family: Gendering of Corporate Welfare, 1890–1930* (Chapel Hill, 2002); Andrea Tone, *The Business of Benevolence* (Ithaca, New York, 1997); and Gerald Zahavi, *Workers, Managers, and Working Class: Shoeworkers and Tanners of Endicott Johnson, 1890–1950* (Urbana, Illinois, 1998). For a historical account of workplace safety, see Donald Rogers, *Marking Capitalism Safe: Worker Safety and Health Regulation in America, 1880–1940* (Urbana, Illinois, 2010).

Government policy and labor

A recent area of study for historians of labor includes the effects of state law and governmental policies on workers and their movements. See Bruno Ramirez, *When Workers Fight: The Politics of Industrial Relations in the Progressive Era, 1898–1916* (Westport, Connecticut, 1978). Joseph McCartin, *Labor's Great War: The Struggle for Industrial Democracy and the Origins of Modern Labor Relations, 1912–1921* (Chapel Hill, 1998), chronicles rising labor militancy during the decade of the Great War. See also Melvyn Dubofsky, *The State and Labor in Modern America* (Chapel Hill, 1994); Graham Adams, Jr., *Age of Industrial Violence, 1910–1915: The Activities and Findings of the United States Commission on Industrial Relations* (New York, 1966); and Christopher Tomlins, *The State and the Unions: Labor Relations, Law and the Organized Labor Movement in America, 1880–1960* (New York, 1985) cover various facets of law and policy. See also Earl David Saros, *Labor, Industry, and Regulation during the Progressive Era* (New York, 2009). Saros argues that small- and medium-sized businesses remained competitive even when challenged by large corporations.

Despite the wealth of labor history sources, Alice Kessler-Harris and J. Carrol Moody, eds., *Perspectives on American Labor History: The Problems of Synthesis* (DeKalb, Illinois, 1989), emphasize the persistent lack of a comprehensive synthesis in the field.

Country life

The Country Life movement made an effort to modernize institutions like schools and the church. See William Bowers, *The Country Life Movement in America, 1900–1920* (Port Washington, New York, 1974), and David Danbom, *The Resisted Revolution*

(Ames, Iowa, 1979). Hal S. Barron, *Mixed Harvest: The Second Great Transformation in the Rural North, 1870–1930* (Chapel Hill, 1997), points out that many rural northerners initially opposed the kind of centralized urban society with control of local institutions in the hands of the state as envisioned by reformers. Farmers (like many others) did not make a linear progression to modern life. Elizabeth Sanders, *Roots of Reform: Farmers, Workers, and the American State, 1877–1917* (Chicago, 1999), offers a favorable view of Progressivism and resolves the issue of sectionalism by arguing that agrarian identity became more important than formal party affiliation.

Conservation

For conservation issues during the Progressive Era, see Donald Pisani, *Water and American Government: The Reclamation Bureau, Nation Water Policy and the West, 1902–1935* (Berkeley, 2002); David Stradling, *Conservation in the Progressive Era* (Seattle, 2004); and David Stradling, *Smokestacks and Progressives: Environmentalists, Engineers, and Air Quality in America, 1881–1951* (Baltimore, 1991). Martin V. Melosi, *Effluent America: Cities, Industry, Energy, and the Environment* (Pittsburgh, 2001), contains 11 essays chronicling the relationship between industrialization and pollution as well as the rise of the early environmental reform movement. Maureen Flanagan, *Seeing with Their Hearts: Chicago Women and the Vision of the Good City, 1871–1933* (Princeton, 2002), discusses gender differences between conservation and ecological approaches to environmentalism.

Social welfare policy

On social welfare policy, see John H. Ehrenreich, *The Altruistic Imagination: A History of Social Work and Social Policy in the United States* (Ithaca, 1985). Theda Skocpol, *Protecting Soldiers and Mothers: The Political Origins of Social Policy in the United States* (Cambridge, 1992), provides an analysis of social policy in the United States as does Linda Gordon, *Pitied but Not Entitled: Single Mothers and the History of Welfare, 1890–1935* (New York, 1994), which places public assistance in historical perspective. See also Seth Koven and Sonya Michel, eds., *Mothers of a New World: Maternalist Politics and the Origins of Welfare States* (New York, 1993). For efforts to protect children, see Kriste Lindenmeyer, *"A Right to Childhood": The U.S. Children's Bureau and Child Welfare, 1912–1946* (Urbana, Illinois, 1997), and Molly Ladd Taylor, *Mother-Work: Women, Child Welfare, and the State, 1890–1930* (Urbana, Illinois, 1993). Maureen Flanagan, *Seeing with Their Hearts: Chicago Women and the Vision of the Good City, 1871–1933* (Princeton, 2002), explores women's political activism and policy influence in Chicago.

Index

The Progressives: Activism and Reform in American Society, 1893–1917, First Edition.
Karen Pastorello.
© 2014 John Wiley & Sons, Inc. Published 2014 by John Wiley & Sons, Inc.